A Different Kind of Weather

A Different Kind of Weather

A Memoir

WILLIAM WALDEGRAVE

Constable • London

It would be idle to imagine why Mr Razumov has left this record behind him. It is inconceivable that he should have wished any human eye to see it. A mysterious impulse of human nature comes into play here. Putting aside Samuel Pepys, who has forced this way the door of immortality, innumerable people, criminals, saints, philosophers, young girls, statesmen, and simple imbeciles, have kept self-revealing records from vanity no doubt, but also from other more inscrutable motives. There must be a wonderful soothing power in mere words since so many men have used them for self-communion. Being myself a quiet individual, I take it that what all men are really after is some form or perhaps only some formula of peace.

The Narrator, *Under Western Eyes* by Joseph Conrad

CONSTABLE

First published in Great Britain in 2015 by Constable
1 3 5 7 9 8 6 4 2

A CIP catalogue record for this book
is available from the British Library.

ISBN 978-1-47211-975-9 (Royal hardback)
ISBN: 978-1-47211-976-6 (ebook)

Typeset in Garamond by TW Typesetting, Plymouth, Devon
Printed and bound by CPI Group (UK) Ltd, Croydon, CR0 4YY

Constable
is an imprint of
Constable & Robinson Ltd
100 Victoria Embankment
London EC4Y 0DY

An Hachette UK Company
www.hachette.co.uk

www.constablerobinson.com

For Caroline, Katie, Liza, Jamie and Harriet.
With all my love.

Acknowledgements

Douglas Hurd encouraged me to get going on this book. Alan Petty and Stuart Proffitt were responsible for encouraging me further. They both read drafts and made many improvements, as did Victoria Rothschild Gray. So also did my daughters, Katie and Harriet. Christopher Sinclair-Stevenson, my agent, confounded my natural pessimism about the result by finding Andreas Campomar of Constable as a publisher. Andreas turned his skilful eye on a manuscript which gained further from such experienced attention, as it did also from the work of my editor, Philip Parr. If the result counts as a book, it is mostly because of all this help. No one would have been capable of suggesting any improvements had Carolyn Raeside not turned the original pile of incoherent manuscript pages, in my illegible handwriting, into typescript; and if my assistant Sue Cruickshank had not then shepherded the result on its way.

The practical love with which my wife Caroline has supported me during this project, and helped me to avoid at least some mistakes and misjudgements, is merely a small example of the way in which she has underpinned my life, and the life of our family, for the last thirty-seven years. Plato thought that beauty and goodness were inextricably inter-mingled. In Caroline's case, he was undoubtedly right.

Contents

Preface		*xiii*
Chapter 1:	Foundations	1
Chapter 2:	Heroes	20
Chapter 3:	Paths of Glory	47
Chapter 4:	Oxford	65
Chapter 5:	Harvard and the World	79
Chapter 6:	Heath and Rothschild	90
Chapter 7:	Think Tank	107
Chapter 8:	Defeat	116
Chapter 9:	Strange Times	126
Chapter 10:	Escape	145
Chapter 11:	Not Typecast as an Adviser	158
Chapter 12:	Encountering Greatness	174
Chapter 13:	Parliament and the Press	186
Chapter 14:	Thatcher and Other Explosives	200
Chapter 15:	The Poll Tax: All My Own Work	218
Chapter 16:	Arms to Iraq, Rounded to Zero	229

Chapter 17:   What Was Happening in the Rest of the World:

the Wall, Mandela, Palestine and Hostages   248

Chapter 18:   Over a Precipice   267

Chapter 19:   Epilogue   275

Index   *284*

Preface

I thought, 'This is where I want to be. Here in this cockpit, at the centre of this maelstrom. I would rather be here, with my future hanging on the decisions of Quentin Davies and Rupert Allason, on whether David Trimble is offered the bribe he wants by John Major, than be ordinary, unknown. I would rather be here, looking up at Caroline's brave, pale face in the gallery – every seat packed, standing room only for the press, their Lordships squeezed in tight.'

Looking back, I think that was probably a little bit mad. Does a heroin addict feel like that? Knowing everything he knows about what will follow?

The vote at the end of the debate on the Scott Inquiry was won by a majority of one. I think Mr Allason voted for me; Mr Davies did not; the prime minister offered no bribe to David Trimble and the Unionists voted against. My much secretly rehearsed personal statement of resignation was not delivered. I was anxious whether in the uproar the Speaker would have allowed me to deliver it then and there at 10.15 p.m. Probably not. Instead, we went, Caroline and I, to the celebration, to thank Alastair Goodlad and his people in the Whips' Office. There I saw how peripheral I was now to be: a saved minister rescued by his colleagues; but never again to be on an upswing.

Yet still the addiction. In a car, a ministerial car, going down Whitehall,

I thought, 'How can these people, walking on the pavement, live? How can they find anything of interest, since they do not do what I do? Their lives must be shadowy, dull, have nothing compared to this insider life of ministries, secrets, parliaments, flags, interpreters, crises, fear, fame (of a sort); of being *somebody*.'

Already, by then, I was on the downswing – lucky still to be in that car, owing survival to loyalty and friends stronger than myself. But still I thought like that.

This account is not meant to be a narrative memoir. It is not, as was perhaps my duty dishonourably to record, the stolen inside version of what Ted Heath was like from his former private secretary. Nor a vigorous defence of – nor even a *mea culpa* about – the poll tax. Nor really an examination of the arms to Iraq scandal and Sir Richard Scott's subsequent inquiry. Nor 'Finally – the True Story of the Fall of Thatcher'. It is not false modesty to think that an account of my career is not justified; or at least, that I do not want to write it if it is. I want to have a go at answering the question you sometimes hear the journalist ask, advancing microphone in hand on the disaster victim: 'What did it feel like?'

There is authority for this kind of enterprise from a former fellow of my college, G. M. Young. He wrote that historians like himself needed to know not only what happened, but 'what people felt about it when it was happening'. Or, as the great literary critic Frank Kermode wrote, the autobiographer must try to describe 'the weather . . . the private weather'.

Any account of the weather of my life must start with an account of what it was like to be brought up in the strange old way in which I was brought up; then it must go on to describe what it was like to be an ambitious young Conservative politician in the seventies and eighties; to witness the fall of Heath, and the triumph and fall of Thatcher; to arrive at the end of one kind of English culture and observe the high point and the beginning of the long decline of Anglo-American, Americo-Anglian hegemony. On the surface, my life might seem to represent an extraordinary cycle of continuity. I still live at Chewton Mendip, the village in the Mendip Hills where I was born. I still hear the self-same church bells as I did in my childhood. I preside over the school I myself attended, where the boys still wear the same old antique uniform, and I host good dinners for senior boys just as my predecessor, Sir Claude Aurelius Elliott (who seemed of immeasurable age), once did for me. In 2014 there is even an Etonian prime minister, just as there was fifty years ago, when I launched my ultimately doomed attempt to precede him. Everything seems the same; but in reality, everything is completely different. It is perhaps the particular skill of the British to do the opposite to a snake. A snake changes its skin but remains the same inside; we keep the skin, but the body changes.

Another excuse for this undertaking is that I seem to have inherited the knack my family has exhibited for eight centuries or so – we always seem to stand quite close to great events in English history without ever achieving greatness ourselves. According to President Mitterrand's foreign minister Roland Dumas (who did, admittedly, end up in jail), I am a member of the family that fought with Guillaume. We were Sheriffs of London in King John's time; we were at Agincourt and Towton Moor and the Field of the Cloth of Gold; one of us was third (not first) Speaker of the House and another was chancellor of the Duchy (not Lord Chancellor) under Queen Mary. We were close to James II (and married a Churchill daughter of his); but then closer to George II (and asked by him to form a government, but failed to do so). We were at Minden, Yorktown (where a young Waldegrave, as senior ADC, accompanied General O'Hara when he handed over Cornwallis's sword to the Americans), St Vincent and Waterloo (where the Waldegrave feared the presence on the edge of the battlefield of his irate mother, who was determined to stop her son marrying his mistress, more than he did the French). We were in the Sikh wars and at the Alma, and we had a small role in the 1910 constitutional crisis. We descend from James II and Robert Walpole and connect to Gladstone's wife. I have continued the family tradition by serving Heath,

Thatcher and Major; never, truth be told, a member of that journalistic genus the 'big beasts of the jungle', although around for quite a long time.

My pride is therefore like my family pride. It rests on longevity and survival, not on sending heroes to Valhalla, let alone on arriving in that alarming place myself. Nevertheless, I would like to have heard the gossip from some of those forebears. What was Sir Richard Waldegrave's friend Geoffrey Chaucer really like? What colour was the dragon, with crested head and teeth like a saw, against which his son, another Sir Richard, rode out in 1405 near Bures in Suffolk? And did it breathe fire like Mrs Thatcher? After meeting either, the younger Sir Richard's experience at Agincourt would have seemed tame. Were these Richards, father and son, really, as my mother suggested, the very parfit gentle knight and his son of the *Canterbury Tales*? Chaucer dresses the son in our family colours, and the father had fought with the Teutonic knights in Russia and at the taking of Alexandria in 1365, just as the elder Richard Waldegrave had done. One can dream.

I would like to know more about the rumours of disgraceful goings-on involving a Waldegrave in the house of the young Mary Tudor, and ask Henry Waldegrave why on earth his father-in-law, King James II, played his cards so stupidly. I would like to have known what it felt like to walk, like Johnny Waldegrave, at the head of an infantry regiment straight towards the French cavalry at Minden.

I am grateful when there is a flash of direct light from the past, some intimate picture in a letter or diary, and a whole landscape is illuminated for a moment in the imagination of we who read it later. Horace Walpole writes about James, 2nd Earl Waldegrave being a delightful man, but very dirty. No sooner was he awarded the Garter than its blue ribbon 'has got fifty spots'.

My great-great-grandfather – a half-pay admiral for many years before at last assuming command of a seventy-four-gun ship, HMS *Revenge*, at the siege of Acre in 1840 – writes about his anxiety over whether he will be brave under fire. He worries whether the causes he ardently supports – namely, the Pastoral Aid Society, the Church Missionary Society and the Sailors' Home – will suffer if he proves to be 'bold at the table of the Committee, but a coward in battle'. Fortunately, as it turns out, 'it is otherwise, God be praised'. In fact, he sat calmly in an armchair under an umbrella on his quarter deck while directing his ship. A Marine drummer boy standing near by, waiting for orders, was killed.

The old admiral's son, dying, writes after the Battle of the Alma, 'My dear father, I am on my back in the hospital at Scutari, with a compound fracture of my left thigh, and several other wounds, one of which is through the palm of my right hand, so that I am unable to hold a pen.' He was brave all right, bayoneted through the hand as he stooped to raise his regiment's fallen colour as the British advanced through the river that ran across the battlefield.

I am grateful for these intimacies. Perhaps others might be for mine, less heroic though they are. If I would like to have heard more from Sir Richard about Chaucer, or from Sir Edward about Mary Tudor, it seems lazy not to attempt sketches of those I have encountered. There are the politicians – Macmillan, Heath, Thatcher, Major. There are Berlin and Rothschild, Weinstock and Pinter, Gray and O'Brian. I shook hands with Mao Zedong and discussed the Emperor Vespasian's taxes with Nelson Mandela. I cannot describe the sensation of walking across a battlefield or of facing a dragon, but I can try to explain what it feels like to be consumed by political ambition, and describe how it shaped my life, both on the way up and on the way down.

There is also, of course, a more selfish reason for writing this book. As I get older, it seems that peace of mind may be most often found among contemporaries who have mastered a craft, and left examples of their craftsmanship. If there are rules and disciplines, and one has fulfilled them, perhaps one has achieved all that can be achieved. Happiness may not be something to pursue directly; perhaps it is a side-effect of working hard at something to the best of one's ability. Even then, the relationship between achievement and happiness is not automatic. The titans themselves often struggle on Gerard Manley Hopkins's precipices of the mind:

> Cliffs of fall,
> Frightful, sheer, no-man-fathomed.

The most titanic of them all, Winston Churchill, struggled to keep his 'black dog' at bay. At my junior level, I sometimes suffer from anxiety and gloom, just as my father did. (My children once gave me *Eeyore's Little Book of Gloom* for my birthday. Then, forgetful, they also gave it me for Christmas, thereby confirming that great philosopher's, and my own, view of things.)

So, putting these three things together – the possible value of an account of the weather of my part of my times; a respect for and envy of those who make things; and, finally, Conrad's hint of a formula for peace – I offer my justification for ignoring my favourite Old Testament character, the Preacher in the Book of Ecclesiastes. 'Of making many books there is no end,' he complains in Chapter 12. It is rash to ignore the Preacher's warning, but I have done so.

This is not, however, the book I planned to write. Let me tell you what you are missing. When I was aged about fifteen, a schoolmaster told us to write out our life's ambitions. Does everyone from that Eton division remember theirs as clearly as I remember mine?

- Foreign secretary in Iain Macleod's administration.
- Swept to power as prime minister after touring the country in a red, white and blue Rolls-Royce.
- A hero for reversing the plan to demolish Trafalgar Square and replace it with office blocks.
- And finally, after many years of triumph, a graceful retirement from politics to produce the definitive translation of Thucydides.

This is not the definitive translation of Thucydides.

Later, I decided I would write the English *Leopard*. How the ancient families and the social contract with their equally ancient people faded away like ghosts as the fat little representatives of the Thatcherite Risorgimento sent their ancient relics to Christie's and threw their moth-eaten dog pelts from high windows designed by Lord Rogers.

Alas, this is not the English *Leopard* either.

Sir Alec Douglas-Home's memoir, *The Way the Wind Blows*, described by Rab Butler as a book about fishing, and Rab's own slim book, *The Art of the Possible*, which was mostly written to mock Harold Macmillan's many self-regarding tomes, would be marks at which I would like to aim. But the one had great simplicity and the other extraordinary complexity, so that is a high ambition. Sir Jock Colville's beautiful sketches of Churchill and others, *Footprints in Time*, is an exemplar even more difficult to match. The nearest modern model might be Ferdinand Mount's elegant, self-deprecating memoir *Cold Cream*, although no amount of modesty on his part can disguise the importance of his account of how, in 1982, he wrote the central document of Thatcherism from which all subsequent British policy, including that of subsequent Labour administrations, has flowed. Arguably the most interesting and frankest modern political memoir is the oddest of the lot – Tony Blair's *A Journey*. But then, like all successful prime ministers, he is both odd and interesting, although he has not always been seen as frank.

The spirit I would really like to conjure to protect me on my way is not Alastair Campbell or Tony Benn, admirably and single-mindedly working to transmit themselves to a cowering posterity, but the gentlest and quirkiest spirit of English comedy, Laurence Sterne. Sterne's view is that most things happen – or do not happen – by mistake, and that the best way to deal with the inexplicable chaos of the world is to enjoy its absurdities when you can, while noticing that the people the world says are the most absurd are often, like Uncle Toby and Corporal Trim, the best and the happiest.

So, I would like to ask my wife's double-great-uncle, Montague Rhodes James – who knew how to slide a terrible, feather-light, sinewy fiend into the very same darkened College study in which I now sit – to conjure instead for me the amiable ghost of Laurence Sterne to peer over my shoulder and stand sentry against self-importance.

With all this, Madam – and what confounded every thing as much on the other hand, my uncle Toby had that unparalleled modesty of nature I once told you of, and which, by the bye, stood eternal sentry upon his feelings, that you might as soon— But where am I going? These reflections crowd in upon me ten pages at least too soon and take up that time which I ought to bestow upon facts.

I started this preface at the lowest point of all. There I was, at the centre of a completely foul national scandal, which left many sensible people pretty sure that I had tried to send innocent people to jail for arming Saddam Hussein, in accordance with secret government policy, and then disowned the agents of that policy when they were caught. And yet I was thinking (while Mr Davies and Mr Allason pondered my fate), 'There is nowhere I would rather be.' Pretty rum.

How did that narcotic get into my system? How could it get into anyone's system? Which narcotic was it? Who were the pushers? How might we ensure that our children do not buy from them, too?

Or, as the young local journalist would start, having established (more or less) the spelling of one's name: 'Why did you go into politics in the first place?'

CHAPTER ONE

Foundations

The central, fundamental festival of the year was Christmas. Christmas Day was also my mother's birthday: a double family festival of infinite power in a big family. (There was even a double day of build-up, as my sister Anne's birthday is Christmas Eve.) On the top floor, where my bedroom was, next to those of my brother and Anne, we would be woken by the shoot of coal into the vast Esse cooking range far below. The coal would have been brought in by Seward Heal or Reg Middle for Mrs Emmett, the cook (or, in later years, for Bessie Speed, her successor). Next there was a clatter as the milk churn was delivered from one of the farms to the back door. By then, all of the Waldegrave children would be in our parents' huge bedroom, clutching our stockings.

A breakfast of porridge and eggs was eaten in the dining room, decorated like the rest of the house with paper chains we had laboriously made ourselves. (Today, I make my family do the same.) In the drawing room stood a huge Christmas tree, with battered old cardboard Father Christmases around the base and precious coloured glass balls and candles – never electric lights – on the branches. After breakfast, Chewton Church and the magic of the extra last verse of 'O Come All Ye Faithful'

– reserved for Christmas Day only. The Reverend Kenneth Latter, who wore a watch-chain and had private means, took the service. My father, himself the son of a Church of England vicar and brought up in a parsonage, had inherited his estate sideways, from his invalid first cousin. He took the selection of vicars for the livings he controlled with the utmost seriousness; church music and the liturgy were central to him. It was no accident that Mr Latter was not given to long sermons.

The presents had all been laid out on chairs in the drawing room. Whose pile was the biggest? Some we opened before Church; most after. Then we paid a visit to the farm manager Tommy Thompson and his family at Manor Farm, at the bottom of the drive: sweet sherry in his old oak-panelled parlour.

Lunch would be a huge turkey followed by curtains drawn for the Christmas pudding, brought in by Bessie not much assisted by my father. The flames were never quite satisfactory, in spite of all the theories about how to light them ('heat the brandy first', 'put sugar in it'). Champagne, for the only time in the year, was allowed with the pudding. Bessie would return for the toasts before leaving to join her own family and repeat the whole meal for them. In the afternoon there would be a bonfire of such torn wrapping paper as my mother had not managed to salvage for next year, and a walk for everyone, including the schnauzer dog, up on high Mendip – All Eights or Nine Barrows on North Hill.

In the evening carol singers, or sometimes handbell ringers, with my father complicating matters by taking over the piano in the drawing room. The Christmas tree candles would be lit and the village (or that considerable part of it we employed) summoned for presents, distributed by my brother and me – socks for Reg and Seward. Then there was just time for one last present for each of us: always the *Eagle Annual* for me – almost the best present of all – with complete new Dan Dare, Luck of the Legion and Jeff Arnold stories.

It was a celebration of family, of community, of hierarchy, of the social contract. Good manners, perhaps, made the village go along with it; as well as loyalty to my parents. I believe my mother and father were genuinely respected as fair and concerned employers and landlords, although there must have been some resentment, jealousy and anti-Waldegrave sentiment. However, I never felt such resentment myself, or received anything other than kindness and courtesy.

I am – was – the youngest of seven children, by six years. When I was two, my brother went away to prep school and I became rather solitary. I did not go to primary school. I had a governess whom I loved, Val Ross. She was central to my life. She had been – the romance of it! – in the WRAF in the war. Her aunt was Mirabel Topham, who owned the Grand National course at Aintree; her brother was fighting communists in Malaya. Martin Howarth, son of the principal of the long-gone Wells Theological College, was her only other pupil. He lived in the Rib, a very ancient house built between the flying buttresses at the east end of Wells Cathedral. I lived in Chewton House. Chewton was my brother's name. Waldegrave was my name, and everyone else's name, and the name of the pubs in the three neighbouring villages. I did not know any children in the village, or any children at all during term time, except for Martin.

We were not great Whiggish aristocrats with tens of thousands of acres and property in London. We were proud of our old Ford V-8 Shooting Brake, our Standard Vanguards and later our Ford Zephyrs. But we were the top dogs of our little world: from Priddy to Litton and across to Ston Easton, then up to Green Ore and across high Mendip to where the line of Bronze Age barrows straddles North Hill. There were yellow printed luggage labels on our suitcases and school trunks which read 'Waldegrave' in large letters, and underneath 'Chewton Mendip'. That was enough for Pickfords, delivering from Bath Spa or from the freight station at Hallatrow, 'passenger luggage in advance'. We had a name and a place.

Chewton Mendip, with its magnificent church tower, was at its centre, the great majority of cottages painted in the estate colour of dark green, the farms tenanted by substantial farmers. There was a policeman, PC Casey, to whom I offered Rowntree's fruit gums when I met him; a district nurse in her bungalow; the St Johns in the post office and bakery, the source of incomparable mince pies and sweets from glass jars weighed into paper bags; a Co-op; Mrs Cornelius's shop, useful for buying bicycle tyre-repair kits; the pub, with our coat of arms swinging on the sign above the door; the school; and the filling station, which we owned for a time and where I worked during the school holidays to earn some extra pocket money. (Super was 4/9 a gallon, so I often got a 3d tip.) Dr Hughes visited in his Rover 90 and handed out Allen & Hanburys blackcurrant pastilles. Friars Balsam and a Sun-Ray lamp tackled colds. At Clark's shoe shop in Wells we examined the bones in our toes through the X-ray machine to see if our sandals fitted. We occupied the front two rows in St Mary Magdalene Church, Chewton Mendip – my parents and we two boys in front; our five sisters in the second row. We never set foot in the Waldegrave Arms, whether in Chewton, Harptree or Radstock.

In the school room, with its smoking fireplace, Val taught me until I went away to preparatory school, aged eight. (Even on that day – the worst day of her life, my mother later told me – there was still magic and family security. The Great Western steam engine that pulled the train was 5057 *The Earl Waldegrave*, Castle Class.) In the school room, or in my own room on the top floor, I would pore over books, often alone, counting the days to the return of my brother. At a concert in the village hall we sang Victorian songs: 'Boney Was a Warrior' and 'Stand by to reckon up your battleships: ten, twenty, thirty, there they go'. But there was dissonance. Why were they breaking up HMS *Vanguard*, Britain's last battleship? Why did the Comet crash?

The social hierarchy of an estate like ours was in three layers. Below my parents came the big tenant farmers: Speed, Duddon, Bishop, Oakes, Green, Bartlett and the others – all substantial businessmen themselves, with their own employees. There they sit, photographed for the tenants' lunch held in honour of my brother's twenty-first birthday in 1961, confident and formidable. Tommy Thompson, who managed the in-hand farms for us, was equally an independent and respected professional. Under him were cowmen, shepherds, farm labourers, and my favourite Tim Allen, farm mechanic, an expert welder who could mend a broken bike. Then came the separate estate staff, commanded by Mr Purnell, the master of works, who wore a waistcoat and a bowler hat, his foreman Edgar Salvidge and his staff, among them the beloved Charlie Ford and the youngster, Melv, who fifty years later, still works for my brother.

The estate yard was a treasure house of nails and screws and tools and wood from which we made huts. Joe Keen from Tyneside was the forester, with his own yard with its alluring but dangerous circular saw. In the Keeper's Cottage was Aubrey Eyles. Most important of all to me were those who worked in the house: Win Whitfield, Judy Ford, Eva Thomas, Mary Keen, and Mrs Emmett or Bessie in the kitchen. Meanwhile, Seward and Reg grew enormous quantities of vegetables in the kitchen garden: artichokes, asparagus and melons in the frame; strawberries, raspberries and gooseberries in the fruit cage, out of which I spent much time shepherding foolish thrushes. For a time, there were even orchids in hot houses behind the garages, which I wore in my buttonhole when I was in Pop at Eton. Elevenses, when I was a young child, were a ceremony: everyone working inside the house and in the garden would gather for tea in mugs, with me on a high stool, around the marble-topped kitchen table.

Aside from Christmas, the other central festival, at least so far as I was concerned, was my birthday, which fell in the middle of the summer holidays: 15 August. When, much later, we went on holiday to hot Catholic countries, I found that quite properly all the local inhabitants set off fireworks in celebration of my birthday. Everyone knew about it; everyone gave me presents. But Mediterranean holidays were in the future: Scotland was where we went in the early summers, every summer, when I was a child. Occasionally to my aunt Frances's family in Argyll, where my cousin, Robert Campbell Preston, sang a song in his Scots voice about the regiments of Scotland:

A Gordon for me, a Gordon for me
If you're nae a Gordon you're no use to me.
The Black Watch are braw, the Seaforth are maw,
But the cocky wee Gordons are the pride of them aw.

But above all, summer after summer, we took the sleeper to Fort William, then the local train to Acharacle, and then on to the *Curlew* launch commanded by John the boatman across the water to Margot Howard de Walden's Eilean Shona in Loch Moidart. Others would be there – Lindsays, Heathcoat Amorys, Davidoff-Orloffs, Seymours – but they were Other and I hid behind my tribe.

There was the ruined Castle Tioram on its island, and Shona Beag, and dangerous Ardnamurchan Point, where the fishermen drowned when their boat went down, and the great heavy horse which pulled the timber down to the puffer, which took it away. And there were frightening gobbling turkeys behind the house, and huge rhubarb plants (which were really gunnera), and always an immense wooden jigsaw puzzle from which I would steal a piece so that I had the honour of putting it in last, and no one minded as I was the youngest. Ivor Newton, quite famous as a concert pianist, played the grand piano in the drawing room. We played canasta and I timidly sailed my small boat which was called *Canasta* too, while my brother was allowed to play with the big German-made tin battleship which, if you put gunpowder in its guns, puffed white smoke. And lobster pots, and the day we (not really me – I was always too young) hauled up a conger eel. And John the boatman playing 'The Road to the Isles' on his pipes on the lawn outside the dining-room windows in the dusk of the last evening.

Similarly perfect islands have followed in sequence throughout my life. After Shona, Colonsay, home of my first and most glamorous brother-in-law, Euan Howard. His ancestor had built the Canadian Pacific Railway and then bought two beautiful islands – Colonsay, with its fine gardens and house, and Oronsay, with its incomparable early Celtic Christian remains. There were small lochs stocked with brown trout; a great flock of Canada geese winging in over the house in the evening; and a herd of very smelly goats that we firmly believed were descendants of survivors from the Spanish Armada. The last monoglot Gaelic speaker had died not many years before. Again there was a magical journey – a MacBrayne steamer with two funnels, the *Lochfyne*, from Greenock on the Clyde to Tarbert Loch Fyne; then a bus with wooden slats for seats; then by her sister ship with only one funnel, the *Lochiel*, from West Loch Tarbert to Port Askaig on Islay; an overnight stay, then across to Colonsay and the sometimes perilous disembarkation into one of Euan's boats – no pier then. His telephone number was Colonsay 1. Ginger cake and drop scones for tea; huge picnics at Kiloran Bay or Balnahard. It was not just the place-names that were poetry.

Next came the Greek islands, every bit as good in reality when I saw them for the first time as they had been in my dreams.

Part of the happiness of my childhood lay in the sheer beauty of the places where so much of it was spent.

There were pluses and minuses about the youngest-of-seven business. On the one hand, I was there: the only post-war child. One of the special places in my mother's love was reserved for me. On the other, when did I first hear someone suggest, 'You have guarded your king'? I was a fall-back position; a hedge, we would now say.

Conversation flowed over my head and left me always pretending that I too got the joke. In a taxi – I can locate it – passing by Buckingham Palace, my late-teenage sisters were discussing some suitor or other: 'What an idiot he was! He said it was *one* of Beethoven's *best* violin concertos!' I had no idea what was wrong with the poor sap's remark, but then and there I silently vowed never to allow myself to be in a situation where I could be humiliated like the poor young suitor. Head down over the years ahead, at three in the morning ploughing through Greek texts, or trying to understand the theory of relativity, or reading Nabokov or Sartre or Aristotle, I tried to equip myself to avoid humiliation.

Always straining to keep up makes you compete for attention, and it makes you work hard. I wrote a regular newspaper on my Imperial 'Good Companion' portable typewriter when I was four or five; it was full of energy, politics and stories (mostly science fiction). I strained at books with vocabulary far beyond my understanding. I thought there was nothing that could not be known. I was taken to the first great Picasso exhibition; sat in Malcolm Sargent's box at the Albert Hall with A. P. Herbert of the party while Sargent conducted Elgar's 2nd Symphony, and I had a waking vision of immortal heroes receding through the ages, the latest Peter Collins, killed at the Nürburgring just after I had seen him win at Silverstone in his Ferrari Dino 246. I had been at Farnborough six years earlier, a day before the beautiful DH.110 crashed. (Unperturbed, we still went every year.)

Everything was worth discovering. As far as I was concerned, there were none of the two cultures C. P. Snow described later: engines and Cubism and poetry and battles were all equally important in my mind. You had to be equipped not to be squashed by a sister in all sorts of unexpected fields. I knew in my heart of hearts that I could keep up; but I also knew that keeping up was hard work.

I was often alone, because all of my elder siblings were either away at school or grown up. Once morning lessons with Val and Martin were over, I would play by myself, perhaps bowling a cricket ball at a stump, collecting it, then bowling it again. I would hear waves of applause: 'Waldegrave has taken the tenth wicket! The crowd is on its feet.' I would say to myself, 'If I don't hit the centre stump in the next three balls, I will not be prime minister . . . Oh, all right, four balls.' Cheering crowds again: Prime Minister Waldegrave, cheers; General Waldegrave, cheers; the whole world cheering me. I see now that it was all a bit lonely; but I did not think so then.

Or I am playing with my Britains lead soldiers – Lancers, Horse

Artillery, Hussars, a set of First World War infantry in gas masks – or with the American wind-up tank with rubber tracks which puffed white chalk powder from its gun barrel. Or with my racing cars, Dinky, Solido, Corgi – Vanwalls always in pole position after the great Moss–Brooks victory at Aintree in 1957, but also beautiful Lancias with their outboard fuel tanks, Maseratis, Gordinis, Alfas, Ferraris, Mercedes, Talbot-Lagos, HWMs, the V16 BRM, and the Le Mans-winning Jaguar and Aston Martin sports cars. I have them still, rather battered.

My childhood had a recurring colour: red. The colour of the cover of the *Eagle Annual* under the Christmas tree; of my fire engine which pumped real water; of Muffin the Mule's saddle; of my collapsible canvas Canadian canoe and little *Canasta* up in Scotland; of the tunics of my Britains guardsmen; of my family's red and silver shield; of Alfa Romeos, Ferraris, Lancias and Maseratis; of the neat diamond birth-mark I have on my left wrist, which I convinced myself was a magical sign of Stuart blood.

If it was raining (as it often is on the Mendips), I would lie on the floor and read the usual Edwardian imperial stories (*Jock of the Bushveld*, G. A. Henty, Rider Haggard, *Susannah of the Mounties*) or pore over the beautiful Canadian epic, *Paddle to the Sea*. (My mother had brought it back from Quebec, where, much against her will, she had taken a crowd of children – hers and others – following the defeatist advice of her elder brothers in 1940. She had returned two years later, fearing Germans less than the Canadian winter, and ashamed of deserting Britain.) Other favourites were *Biggles*, of course, *Just William*, Arthur Ransome (especially *Great Northern*), Tintin (much better in even half-understood French than in the later, lamentable English translations), the American *Illustrated Classics* in strip-cartoon form (the best was Wells's *War of the Worlds*, even though the American artist could not draw British Army uniforms), *Puck of Pook's Hill*, and *The Jungle Book* – Kipling's original version, with the vicious mob of the Bandar-Log monkeys destroyed, in one of the most terrifying scenes in children's literature, by the ruthless hypnotic power of Kaa, the great python. (The sentimental Disney version is a travesty I will never entirely forgive.)

But I also read more precociously: Stevenson, Conan Doyle, especially the Professor Challenger stories (*When the World Screamed* gave me nightmares), Macaulay, E. Nesbit; Greek myths; beautiful Victorian and Edwardian illustrated books of insects and birds kept in the dark corridor outside my father's study; books of exploration; old, bound editions of *Punch* with their wonderful du Maurier and Partridge cartoons; war memoirs – anything I could find and even half understand.

Some things were absent. My mother banned Enid Blyton on stylistic grounds. More interestingly, she disliked C. S. Lewis's Narnia stories: she thought you should get Christianity straight, not dressed up with talking animals. She approved of *The Screwtape Letters*, *Out of the Silent Planet*, *Perelandra* and *That Hideous Strength* (another book which gave me nightmares), though. Later, I kicked up a storm about censorship. Someone had taken my copy of *Lolita* and I demanded my human rights. 'Have you looked behind your bedside table where your books usually fall?' my mother wondered. It was, annoyingly, there. Her advice on love and sex was delivered through books with themes more pertinent than Nabokov's. She did not preach, but asked me to consider the avoidance of hurt, the danger of the misuse of power in unequal relationships, the reality of love. *The Death of the Heart* by Elizabeth Bowen was one text; Margaret Kennedy's *The Constant Nymph* and Laurence Whistler's *The Initials in the Heart* were others.

I had a recurring nightmare: abstract, a representation of pure despair and impossibility, which continued intermittently until my early twenties and then disappeared. There is a gene that carries depression in my father's family and I am not immune to it. In him, gloom could become explosive anger, and that anger was often cruel; his skill with words could leave wounds that hurt for years. On the upswing, his charm and humour were entirely disarming; outsiders never saw the black side. Our mother, with equal intelligence and a far steadier discipline of mind, protected us from most of the damage and taught me that the black rages were more like an illness. I accepted this: when we sang the verse which begins 'Praise him for his grace and favour/To our fathers in distress' from Henry Lyte's great hymn 'Praise my Soul the King of Heaven', I would think of my father; and I still do.

He had a genius for seeing too many sides to any question, and an eloquence with which he drove himself to distraction over the simplest decisions. At the time of the Coronation, which my father and mother attended in their robes, my thirteen-year-old brother – who also participated, as a page – kept a rather brilliant short diary. It provides an account of the discussion at Chewton House about whether, on the drive to London, it would be wise to stop for a picnic. What if there was no suitable stopping point? What if it rained? Why not stop at a pub instead? And so on, back and forth. The many changes of plan imparted to Mrs Emmett led her to remark, 'His lordship will never hang himself,' which became a family saying. The outcome was that a picnic was taken, but Mrs Emmett, by then completely bemused, packed an uncooked chicken.

Conversations between my father and mother (who normally, quietly, made the decisions) were very like those between Tristram Shandy's parents. For example, on the matter of whether Tristram should be put into breeches:

We should begin to think, Mrs Shandy, of putting this boy into breeches.

We should so, said my mother.

We defer it, my dear, quoth my father, shamefully.

I think we do, Mr Shandy, said my mother.

Not but the child looks extremely well, said my father, in his vest and tunics.

He does look very well in them, replied my mother.

And for that reason it would be almost a sin, added my father, to take him out of 'em.

It would so, said my mother.

But indeed he is growing a very tall lad, rejoined my father.

And so on for the whole of glorious Chapter 18 in Volume VI.

There were many discussions like that at Chewton House, with my father's indecision often leading to explosions of frustrated rage which caused us all to flee to safe corners while my poor mother took the brunt and ensured that life quietly continued, as did their marriage, built on foundations stronger than could be damaged by such passing squalls, in the end for sixty-five years, until they both died within a few months of each other.

Among the stories my mother read to us (*The Unlucky Family* by Mrs Henry de la Pasture, a true neglected classic, was another favourite), she used the old English fairy story, *The Three Sillies*, as a warning against our father's excessive anxiety, although the story did not quite inoculate me against the same disease. A pretty girl, engaged to a fine young man, is asked by her mother to go to the cellar to draw beer for the family. She notices an old axe, stuck for years safely in a beam, and becomes paralysed with panic in case – if she should marry the young man, and they should have a son – the axe should one day fall on his head. 'I will not marry you,' says the young man, 'unless I can find three people sillier than you.' He then goes out into the world to look for them . . . and finds them, of course.

Loneliness and shyness also produced some good, clear thoughts. In my narrow first room, opposite my parents' huge bedroom where we all met on Christmas Morning, and where the ceiling once fell in (no one hurt), I used to pick the wallpaper off the wall with my nails, thoughtfully. I was ill there with measles, and the great paediatrician Beryl Corner visited me. (Twenty-five or so years later she reminded me of this when I, by now Conservative candidate for the Bristol, West, Constituency, canvassed her on her doorstep. I trotted out my spiel. 'The last time I saw you, you were five and had measles,' she said.)

When I was lying not very well in that bedroom, where the tremendous peal of Chewton Church's nine bells, very loud on that side of the house, filled me with inexplicable sadness, I found an odd thing. No one could know what my thoughts were. No one could know, if I chose to worship Poseidon, Zeus, or Athene, rather than another god. The sense of the discovery of freedom stays with me still.

Aged six, that first freedom swung me like a pebble from a sling towards Honour Moderations and Literae Humaniores at Oxford via my unwritten translation of Thucydides. It could, I guess, have been the *Song of Roland*, or nuclear physics, depending on what I had found on the shelves: my romanticism would have fled down any rich path. As it was, it was the glory that was Greece and the grandeur that was Rome: Leonidas in the pass and Horatius on the bridge. The ancient world was full of heroes: men whose fame derived not from their submission to the will of the implacable God of Abraham and Moses, but from the style in which they went to meet death, if necessary, out of pride and to seek glory. In Greece, I thought, Job would have fought God to protect his family and his honour and joined Prometheus as a defeated hero. To worship your torturer rather than fight him seemed all wrong. Not that the Greek gods were always kind: how could they be, when they were just ourselves writ large? But you had some idea how to keep in with them, and you could make them laugh. I pored over *The Greek Way* by Edith Hamilton, given me when I was ten by the author's fellow Bryn Mawr alumna, Rosemond Tuve, the fine American scholar of Spenser and George Herbert and a friend of my mother from Somerville, who was a regular visitor to Chewton. Now that I look again at Hamilton's book, much of it must have been above my head; but I remain certain that children who want to learn should be given books that they have to struggle to understand. If they cannot puzzle out everything, they imagine their own version. At least, I suspect I did that.

Something else was laid down as a useful deposit in my mind by this absorption, then and later, in the classical world. I am heterosexual, but if your myths are primarily the myths of classical Greece, you become used to the idea that Zeus, King of the Gods, falls for Ganymede as much as for Leda or Europa. This must help to inoculate you against homophobia better than an education grounded solely in all those comminatory books beloved by Christians, Jews and Muslims. It inoculated me, at any rate. It is odd to think of the passionate contradictions those Victorian churchmen must have felt, knowing every word of Plato's *Symposium* in the Greek, but going along with laws derived from the savagery of Leviticus, whose Aramaic they could read just as fluently.

The richness of my imaginary world was the product of benign solitude. I was surrounded by love, stability and security in a house full of books, with the epic myth of the Second World War all around me. In the foreground was an enormous, competitive and clamorous family, the great majority of them female. The youngest of the sisters, Sue, was more than seven years older than me; Sally, the eldest, was eight years older than Sue. I kept a league table of them and nominated a Sister of the Week. It was something of a precursor of John Major's Citizens' Charter. Unsurprisingly, teenage female concerns dominated my childhood. There were long periods sitting in the car outside the dressmaker in Bath; there were permanent waves and curling tongs as they tried to make their hair as curly as mine is naturally; there was the distant drama of the Season and presentation at Court (it went on until 1958); there were the mysteries of Queen Charlotte's Ball; there were boyfriends who sometimes fell, satisfyingly, into the mistake of imagining that half-a-crown or even a brown ten-shilling note might persuade me to champion their cause; plus marriages (two sisters married aged nineteen, as my mother had done) and uniforms for me as a pageboy. I have three daughters myself: they are strong women and close to each other, but their intimacy has been built on plenty of past arguments (though their brother joins in much more vigorously than I ever dared to do). My sisters were no less powerful, and there were five of them. The atmosphere was rarely contemplative.

It was perhaps natural that the youngest sibling – a boy in this female world, silent and shy – should begin to dream of ways of getting himself noticed. And what better way than by becoming the most famous person in the world, applauded by all? Then I would get a word in, surely? I would be general, prime minister, explorer, sporting hero, all rolled into one, universally popular, acclaimed even by my sisters. I kept that dream deeply secret, of course. I knew I had no skill with that cricket ball. In fact, I hardly dared open my mouth amid the crossfire of my sisters' arguments. But, as Disraeli (of course, another hero later) said in his much-ridiculed maiden speech, 'You will listen one day.' At least, that was the plan.

Another part of the culture of the time fed in some early, half understood but glamorous targets to aim for: the distant rumours of the great Victorian and Edwardian prizes. My consciousness of them derived from my mother's background, which was far different from my father's. There was no vicarage upbringing for her. Her father, Arthur Morton Grenfell, twice a millionaire, twice bankrupt, was a spectacular Edwardian and interwar entrepreneur. The rise and fall of his fortunes could be tracked by establishing where my mother and her siblings were born: some in Roehampton House, on the walls of which hung splendid pictures, including a Titian now in the Frick Collection in New York; others in cheaper places like St Leonards on Sea. His family – his brother the VC, his cousin the war poet, his kin the Grenfell of Morgan Grenfell – were imperial businessmen and public servants. His greatest pride was reserved for the fact that he had played at Lords in the Eton XI of 1892, and we went to the match every year, sitting on his coach inside which I disguised my boredom by pulling up and down the windows with the leather straps – just as it was my job to do when the train from Bath reached the Box Tunnel, to keep out the smuts.

Her mother was from even more spectacular stock: Hilda Lyttelton was related to half the intellectual and governmental elite of Victorian and Edwardian England. Sir Edward Grey was my mother's godfather, and she won a scholarship from the relatively new St Paul's Girls' School to Somerville, Oxford. She left before taking a degree to marry my father; she was perhaps an academic manqué and made herself a considerable amateur historian in later life.* In short, from all those Lytteltons and Grenfells came the fame of glittering prizes.

My uncle, Harry Grenfell, early on gave me lives to read and to emulate: F. E. Smith's by his son; Keynes's by Roy Harrod. I heard from that side of the family of distant glories: of firsts in Greats, of All Souls prize fellowships, of presidencies of the Oxford Union, of the Newcastle Prize at Eton, of brilliant repartee and public glory, of VCs and governorships, of triumphs in the House. F. E., Lord Randolph Churchill, Dizzy, Gladstone, Chatham, Pitt, Nelson, Churchill: these were the names, scarcely more real than the Homeric heroes, to emulate.

There was curiously little ideology attached to these glittering prizewinners. You did Greats because it carried most prestige, not because you wanted to be the next Wilamowitz. F. E.'s repartee was the best, and Lord Randolph's invective; it was not for their views on Ireland or fiscal reform that you loved them. It was a culture of competition, pure and simple – of winning, of life as sport, with a podium finish the only thing that mattered and the top spot all that could be admitted as a possibility.

I now think it is a poor model for life. The pious biographies by their sons did not tell us of F. E.'s alcoholism or Lord Randolph's syphilis. It was a poorer ethic, I now think, (though I did not then, nor for many years) than that provided by the gentle social conservatism of the Chewton Estate and my father's rectory upbringing. The tension between the two has remained with me all my life, and it was there from the very beginning: quiet continuity represented by the unchanging rituals of Chewton, and public service as duty, not for fame; or a life lived for the applause won by buccaneering heroes who bestride shattered worlds? Hence, perhaps, my recurrent later political schizophrenia: Heath or Thatcher? Enoch Powell or Quintin Hogg? Conservative or radical?

---

* I have often relied in this book on her meticulous unpublished family history.

* * *

There was rather little music at Chewton: *Music While You Work* on the Light Programme or the theme tune to *Mrs Dale's Diary*; my father playing hymns on the three-pedal Sohmer grand piano, or Gilbert and Sullivan, or *Salad Days*, or even strumming the ukulele he had brought back from America. But that was not my private music. I had three tunes and they had to be rationed, only thought about on special occasions, for example, when I had my lead soldiers out. One from a film, of course: *The Dam Busters*. One from Beethoven's Fifth: the obvious movement. And finally, *Tannhäuser*. Where did I get these? There was no record player in the house until my brother bought one and played *West Side Story*. 'Sounds like a car accident,' said my cultured and beautiful sister Elizabeth. 'Gee, Officer Krupke' became an anthem for my brother and myself nonetheless, alongside our other private theme tune: the 'Appassionata' Sonata by Beethoven, played by – and only by – Sviatoslav Richter.

My threshold of competence at music is very low. I think this is lucky. I am deeply moved by even poor performances: it is as if I have a pre-memory of what the composer intends, never mind how many wrong notes are played. When I first heard the choir at Pinewood, my preparatory school, sing a descant alongside our normal unison I thought for a second or two that angels had joined us. And it was not a particularly good choir. I am very easy to transport, and am therefore the despair of proper musical critics. So, the performances in my head then and now were and are anything but perfect, but they do the transportation job well enough for me.

The same is true of poetry. I have some block in my mind that prevents me recalling, word for word, more than a few lines from any poem that moves me, no matter how often I try to learn it by heart. During the Scott Inquiry I learned a poem a day from Field Marshal Wavell's anthology *Other Men's Flowers* in a bid to block out the pain – just as I had learned 'saying lessons' every week at school between the ages of eight and sixteen. I can recall none of them now, but I can move myself by taking myself in my imagination to a poem. I remember how it moved me, and why, even though I am unable to call to mind the actual words. Is this normal? It is certainly very annoying. I am not deprived of 'Frost at Midnight' or 'Felix Randal the Farrier' or 'The Whitsun Weddings' or the snow on Soracte, but I cannot write them down or recite them: not then, not now. Nonetheless, they are all in there, somewhere, as is the music I cannot play.

When I was eight, we took to skiing holidays in Champéry in the Valais, where there was a single téléphérique and two ski-lifts. Solitary again (my brother much faster), I sang 'Hang Down Your Head Tom Dooley' and 'The Rock Island Line' after (some way after) Lonnie Donegan, and – on the last day – 'Aux revoir Planachaux, au revoir Champéry' to the tune of 'I Know that my Redeemer Liveth'. What a cacophony it must have been.

Champéry was our other regular holiday destination, alongside Shona, imparting a wonderful steady rhythm to the year. We took a chalet, the Chalet des Frênes. A horse-drawn sleigh took us there from the station. There were cattle wintering under the farmers' houses. Skiing down the road from Planachaux, one would follow a farmer standing on the front of his huge wooden sleigh laden with the sweet-smelling hay he was bringing down from the snow-covered barns on the high pastures – our ski slopes – to feed his animals. We ate raclette and fondue, and I was allowed to drink white wine as my mother adhered to a benign doctrine that cooked cheese plus water led to disaster. There were more than twelve Swiss francs to the pound.

I had objected to the first visit to Champéry as it was abroad and I disapproved of change. (I refused, for quite some time, to sit on the new dining-room chairs at home, interposing a newspaper between my bottom and the alien fabric as a protest.) As soon as we got to Champéry I was found to have chickenpox, which I thought proved my point. My mother went to the chemist for medicine but made a mistake in her normally impeccable French (she spoke even better Austrian-accented German). Her child had *petite verole*, she said, rather than *petite verole volante*; an alarmed villager thought that Madame la Comtesse had brought small-pox to the Valais.

A couple of years later, fiddling with the chalet's ancient radio, we heard that Anthony Eden had resigned. Suez was inexplicable. A British defeat? An American betrayal? At Pinewood, there was a custom – a good custom – that one boy had to listen to the BBC news on the Home Service and summarise it for the morning assembly. Before the holiday, I had proudly reported the names of the RAF aircraft – Canberras and Hunters, intimately familiar from my Dinky and Airfix models – that were destroying the Egyptian Air Force. But now it was all muddle and confusion and retreat, not like 'The War', the real war, whose glorious shadow was the background to everything.

CHAPTER TWO

Heroes

Not far away in actual time, but immeasurably distant in my childhood time, was that real war. My sisters' boyfriends, and later their husbands, had flown in Halifaxes, commanded torpedo boats, and fought at Anzio; my uncles and cousins had been captured at Dunkirk, blown to pieces at Kohima, fought as Chindits in Burma, battled their way up Italy, gone down with HMS *Penelope*. Many years later, playing our regular game of bridge with my uncle Harry Grenfell and brother-in-law Dukey Hussey, my wife and I contributed four legs. Harry and Dukey had one between them.

I could recognise the imperial growl of a Merlin engine, but our world of de Havilland Vampires, Hawker Hunters and independent India, and we New Elizabethans who inhabited it, were as distant from the Battle of Britain as Telemachus was from Troy. In the woodlands, there were mysterious, bramble-covered, concrete structures left over like Cyclopean masonry from a heroic age that was already, only a decade later, infinitely remote. The great long railway shed at Swindon still had its zigzag camouflage. Abandoned pillboxes defended every coastal bay, every railway junction, and looked out westwards from the escarpment of the Mendips, in case the Germans decided to come the same way as William of Orange in 1688. Every metal object left by the tide on the shore at Burnham-on-Sea or Weston-Super-Mare might be a mine. High fences surrounded government mysteries which were not in those days centres of public suspicion, but places where, in red-brick utility buildings, heroes had built the secret machines that had destroyed Hitler. From similar places my television hero Professor Quatermass saved the planet from alien gunge (which was all the BBC special-effects department could manage), but he was the successor of the men who had invented radar and designed the Spitfire. Of course, we did not know yet about Bletchley Park. We knew that my brother's godfather, Admiral Somerville, had helped to sink the *Bismarck*; we did not know that his son, John, was the deputy director of something called GCHQ. We did, however, have a family friend who was a member of that brilliant and often eccentric cadre of inventors who demonstrated that a little intellectual anarchy was no bad thing when it came to lethal ingenuity: Colonel Stewart Blacker, he of the 1933 Westland bi-plane flight over Mount Everest, inventor of the Blacker Bombard, the Piat gun, and the deadly anti-submarine weapon Hedgehog, which played no small part in winning the Battle of the Atlantic. Visiting his house, with its twenty-five-pounder outside the door and trees scarred from his explosive experiments, was like visiting a very English version of Vulcan's forge, albeit with a host more welcoming to small, enthusiastic boys.

The silence the heroes – our uncles and brothers-in-law – maintained about the Second World War was quite un-Homeric. There was no boasting, in hexameters or otherwise. In all other respects, though, the previous generation was, to a solitary child surrounded by books but with siblings all at boarding school, mythic.

Occasionally, these mythological beings were present in the flesh: old Admiral Somerville in his beautiful house in the nearby village of Dinder; General Freyberg, VC, giving me tea as a twelve-year-old at Windsor Castle as did, a little later, Field Marshal Lord Slim, Britain's best Second World War commander. Lord Jellicoe, DSO, the famous irregular soldier, was a colleague of my father's in the House of Lords. And, much later still, there was Paddy Leigh Fermor.

Paddy Leigh Fermor, both the mythic version and the real, stands as the embodiment of the extraordinary intermingling in my mind of intense romantic commitment to the ancient world with an equally romantic dream of British imperial glory. A time slip forward in my life may illustrate what I mean.

One day in early 1990, when I was a minister in the Foreign Office, George Jellicoe rang me in my office to ask if I would go to Athens over a weekend in April to deliver the Onassis Lecture. Weekends at home were extremely precious. I said, "No." There was a pause of a few hours, then George rang back. Would I go to Athens over a weekend in April to deliver the Onassis Lecture and drive on to the Mani and stay with Paddy Leigh Fermor at Kardamyli? With Caroline? He might as well have asked, 'Would you like to go to Ithaca and meet Odysseus?' Of course I would.

As a boy, I had read *Ill Met by Moonlight* many times. I had seen the film, too; not as often as I'd seen *The Dam Busters*, but still often. Dirk Bogarde played Paddy. When I told my son bedtime stories I invented 'Paddy stories', once I had strung out the true one of the kidnapping of the German General Kreipe on Crete for as long as I could. A philhellene hero of the Cretan resistance – whom, I had been told when I was studying epic poetry at Oxford, the local mountaineers had woven into living oral epic, just as I had done for my son – Leigh Fermor was the author of several very fine travel books, a scholar soldier. He could not only complete the stanza, but recite the next five of Horace's Soracte Ode (1.9) which follow it when the captured German General Kreipe, whom he and his colleagues had kidnapped and taken high onto Mount Ida, watched the dawn rise and began: *'Vides ut alta stet nive candidum . . .'*

I have entirely forgotten what I said in the Onassis Lecture; I am sure the audience has, too. But I have not forgotten anything else about those few days. We arrived in Athens amid the firecrackers and horn-blowing of an election victory celebrated by the supporters of New Democracy, whose leader Konstantinos Mitsotakis had thankfully turned out of office their socialist rivals PASOK for a year or two. Jellicoe, hugely admired on the democratic right in Greece (and, like Paddy, equally hated and traduced by the Greek left – fellow travellers, many of them, of the Stalinist Greek Communists whom George had helped to keep out of power in 1944), was summoned to advise the prime minister-elect about the formation of his government. We left an excited Athens in a hired car that Caroline increasingly found herself driving the further we went, while George and I toasted the defeat of socialism at various stops along the way.

George, like most real heroes, spoke little and wrote less about his war. On that drive, however, he began to talk as we traced the route in reverse that the twenty-six-year-old acting Colonel Jellicoe had followed from the northern Peloponnese to Athens in 1944. He had driven out Germans, desperately tried to stop Greek ELAS partisans from massacring civilians (they had long been killing more non-Communist Greeks than Germans), and established order as he went, all with fewer than five hundred men. ELAS had already started a civil war aimed at delivering their country to the Soviet empire that Stalin was intent on constructing in Central and Southern Europe. (They did not know that Stalin, in a ruthless deal with Churchill, had sold them out in exchange for a freer hand further north.) And there were still Germans, whose behaviour throughout their occupation and now in defeat had been savage beyond belief, both towards the Greeks and now towards their erstwhile Italian allies.

Jellicoe's little force of the Special Boat Service (which he had helped to found) and others was reinforced by parachute drop to enable them to push on to Athens and take control before ELAS did. He made it, just, through a mixture of brilliant bluff, extraordinary diplomatic skill and military panache. He was, he told us, temporarily promoted to brigadier in a bid to add some dignity to the proceedings. 'No good!' he claimed. 'Brigadier means "corporal" in the Greek army!' Whether or not that joke was true (not true, I think), this most self-deprecating of heroes told us the story of that desperate but vital campaign as the places unfolded along our route.

He told us of what he said was the worst moment of his whole war. The reinforcing paratroops were dropped near Megara, which we were by then passing as we headed west. George said he had seen a young soldier being dragged by his collapsed parachute into a minefield and to almost certain death. He could have saved him by driving his Jeep across the parachute cords, but he could not take the risk. Only he knew what had to be done, and only he could do it. If he drove himself over a mine, the mission would be in chaos. He let the soldier die.

Not all of the tales he told us turned out to be entirely true, I later discovered. He told me how he had gone out to greet the cheering crowds from the balcony of the King George Hotel in Syntagma Square in Athens alongside the great Andy Lassen, the Danish SAS soldier who was later given a posthumous VC for his heroism in Italy. Lassen, George said, had already found himself a girl, but when he brought her on to the balcony there were boos and catcalls: she had been the mistress of a Gestapo officer. I repeated this story to Mary Carwardias, later the wife of Britain's ambassador to the UN and to Paris, Sir Nicholas Henderson. George's arrival in Athens meant that Mary and her mother were saved from a German death sentence after their own heroic resistance activity, and they had been in the crowd that day. She looked at me pityingly. 'George told you *Andy* picked up the girl?'

So we arrived at Kardamyli, George by now somnolent on the back seat. In the basement of Paddy and Joan's house were big barrels of local retsina. Over the next few days and far into the nights we drank them dry. George and Paddy talked and talked, while Joan looked on indulgently and I fed them lines to keep them going. Some afternoons, Caroline swam off the rocks below the house in a rather transparent white bathing suit which threatened early coronaries to two of England's greatest war heroes, George really the greater of the two.

If only I had fought off the daily hangovers and written all of it down, or secreted a tape-recorder. But I did neither. Nonetheless, those days were one of the high points of my life. My boyhood dreams of Homeric heroes not altogether clearly distinguished from the heroes of our own national epic of a generation earlier seemed to have become incarnate and were sitting before me on the terrace above the wine-dark sea, retsina in hand.

The strange thing for a child who lived in the shadow of such a heroic victory, won by such men, was that it soon became clear that this victory was not like those in the storybooks, where the victors claimed the spoils. All my atlases were pre-war: pink covered the globe. How awful it must have been to be French, with only that meagre expanse of light blue! But now what was happening to that empire? Lying on that school-room floor one day I raged at the famous American cartoon of empires sailing away as great ships towards a sunset horizon and oblivion: Rome's, Spain's, Britain's.

The American soldiers left Bath with a parade. My parents took me along in a big car with a motorcycle outrider to guide us. How I sneered at their chewing gum on parade, and turning left when it should have been right! Our soldiers had bearskins and red tunics again, the grouping of whose buttons had meaning which I understood. In the garden, Seward Heal trundled a two-wheeled cart called the 'bomb loader', services surplus, like the heavy, khaki-covered Bakelite field telephones we were given as playthings, or the wooden aircraft-recognition models we bought from the Services Surplus Store in Wells. I had a khaki battledress, with a Sam Browne. Our paddling pool had originally been an inflatable life-raft from an RAF bomber, with intriguing waterproof pockets and a Bowie-knife attached by a cord. My brother-in-law Euan Howard flew into the field opposite Chewton House in his triple-tailed, single-engined Miles Messenger, call sign George Able Jigger Fox Fox: army surplus at rather a grander level.

In retrospect, the heroism of my parents' generation lay not just in the way they behaved between 1939 and 1945. That heroism was indeed very great – voluntarily going to war against fascism before they were attacked, fully expecting the carnage of the First World War or worse; distributing gas masks to their children as protection against the chemical warfare they expected, and expending the long-accumulated wealth of the nation in the process. But there was a different kind of heroism in the myths they created after the war.

The first was of the unity with which the war was fought: all classes together in the great fight, a new social contract forged. Not quite so, in reality, sadly. The bitterness of the thirties was not so easily forgotten. Damaging strikes continued throughout the war. According to the great French fighter pilot Pierre Clostermann in *The Big Show* – the best book about the air war – the only Allied fighter as good as the best German aircraft in the winter of 1944 was the Hawker Tempest V, designed, like the Hurricane, by Sydney Camm. But while the Germans were at that time increasing production of their astonishingly advanced aircraft in spite of all the Allied strategic bombing, Hawker's factories were on strike. Dockers demanded special payments to unload the kit of troops returning from Dunkirk or embarking after D Day, and went on strike if they did not receive them. Alongside the heroism of so many in the air, at sea and in the army, some non-elite British regiments could not be trusted to stand against their German equivalents; and the quality of most of our military leadership was lamentable. A number of our leading poets and musicians found it convenient to continue their work in New York until the unpleasantness was over. Certainly there was stalwart courage during the Blitz; but there was also looting in bombed areas. When the historian Kenneth Rose went to mourn his brother officers killed when a V1 struck the Guards' Chapel in 1944, their bodies laid out like statues covered in white dust, he noticed that someone had stolen all their personal jewellery. If we had asked the people, in early 1941, whether to continue or not, who knows what the answer would have been. But there were leaders, the leaders led, and Britain's honour will never now be tarnished.

The second myth led on from the first. Britain, having won the war (with a little help from our allies), had freely chosen to dissolve its empire, and was now renewing itself, alone: Greece to America's Rome. We were the New Elizabethans, in power diminished, but lights to the world, as in Shakespeare's day. As a well-briefed young Elizabethan myself, I took to reckoning up not battleships but Britain's world leaders: Russell in philosophy; Moore in sculpture; Keynes in economics: Churchill in politics; Hillary on Mount Everest (New Zealanders counted); Bannister and the four-minute mile; Whittle and the jet engine; Logie Baird and television; Fleming and penicillin; Eliot (English by now) in poetry; Rutherford in physics; Peter Twiss and Neville Duke breaking world flying records; John Cobb, Old Etonian, capturing the land-speed record; Stanley Matthews and Tom Finney; Hutton and May; Britten, Walton and Sutherland; our police; Rolls-Royce; British farmers. There was only one problem: Fangio. I could not deny that he was better than Moss, let alone Hawthorn. But the Argentinians did not seem threatening.

For a shattered and near-bankrupt country, which in one long generation had gone from the world's greatest industrial and imperial power back into the pack of middle-sized European nations, it was a brave refoundation myth, and my parents were determined we should share it.

My own family refounded itself, too. A hundred years before, Frances, Lady Waldegrave, the brilliant Jewish wife of two ne'er-do-well young Waldegraves of the 1830s and '40s, had built Chewton Priory in an undistinguished Strawberry Hill Gothic for herself and her last husband, Chichester Fortescue, Lord Carlingford. At the end of that strange episode the house had reverted to our family in the shape of my great-uncle William Frederick, the 9th Earl. There he stands, photographed in the porch of the Priory, long-barrelled Gibbs shotgun over his arm, every inch the Conservative chief whip in the Lords during the constitutional crisis of 1910–11. His son, an invalid, was succeeded by his clergyman uncle, my grandfather, as 11th Earl. My father was number 12, nearly the last of a very attenuated, if ancient, line. He married my mother in 1930.

There are attractive pre-war pictures of the young couple, full of hope, parents by 1939 of five daughters, painted in pastel by Tom Van Oss, and in words by a visiting Tom Jones, the great civil servant, whose daughter Eirene White – a contemporary of my mother's at St Paul's and Oxford – left me some of her books. In a letter of November 1937, Jones described my mother as 'beautiful to look upon and mother of three charming little girls' and my father as a 'keen young farmer and active member of the County Council . . . drawn from the Liberal and Evangelical tradition of the Waldegraves and the Radstocks'.

Progressive in the management of their four-thousand-acre estate on the Mendips, they were deeply imbued with a sense of the duties that accompanied their relative wealth. My mother established a free mother and baby clinic in the estate office long before the National Health Service was founded; my father signed the Peace Pledge before he saw that war was inevitable and joined the Territorials. He believed, I think, in a sort of hierarchical Christian socialism that had more in common with Wilberforce and John Howard than with anything in the harsh politics of the time.

In 1945 Chewton Priory itself – in whose sunny drawing room Van Oss had painted them with their daughters and Rollo the schnauzer – was abandoned. It became a place of brambles, danger and mystery. Occupied in the war by the US Army, the GIs left it semi-derelict. They used their ordnance to blow open the locked strong-room door, ignoring the eighteenth-century silver and Strawberry Hill miniatures and stealing only the wine.

The abandonment of the Priory was a symbol of my parents' determination to welcome the new post-war world, something they shared with many others of their class. The pin-up frescoes the GIs left on the crumbling walls and the bullet-holes in the gilt weather cock (which later followed the family to the smaller Georgian house where I was born) added to the allure of the overgrown Priory gardens, with their huge weeping chestnuts whose branches reached the ground to make green caves, and the collapsed ice-house which gave birth to legends of underground tunnels. The Priory also had a tower, damaged by fire, and crenellations of the kind Frances Waldegrave had put on the state rooms she added to Horace Walpole's Strawberry Hill, which we had also owned during the nineteenth century. It was romantic, ruinous, dangerous and forbidden to us children; nothing could have represented the past more exactly. Finally, it was demolished. Only the stables survived, used first as the estate office and then to house the Cheddar cheese business my father started. I went there to get my 6d a week pocket money from Miss Mosely, in her tie and cloche hat, who was the book-keeper and lived with her sister Madge.

The new reign came at exactly the right moment. Driving down Wells Hill to the dentist with my mother, I was twiddling with the knobs on the car radio. It was all incomprehensible foreign stuff. Then, 'Go back to that,' said my mother. So it was we learned of the death of King George from a German news station. The beautiful young Queen Elizabeth could hardly have been a more potent symbol of renewal, just as Victoria had been in her day. Churchill, her first prime minister, and the nation as a whole did not miss the opportunity. We were to be the New Elizabethans. We were going to shed the past and look forward to the future.

The nation shed the empire while we shed our former grandeur. My mother's attitude to both was rather similar. The Priory, we were told, had miles of cold corridors and only two bathrooms; it had been ruined by the Americans; it was Victorian Gothic and therefore absurd; it was expensive and impractical. There was no sense in having servants living in as they only got in the way. We would move to a more up-to-date – that is to say, eighteenth-century – house with proper windows. And in any case they had lived quite simply at the Priory.

This latter was not quite true.

When I was in the public eye, a charming old lady of Austrian origin, Valerie Falge-Wahl, sent me her memoirs, *A Stranger in Gloucestershire*. She and her husband, both of them Austrian anti-Nazis, had managed to make their way to Britain after the Anschluss, partly thanks to my parents. This involved my father telling a lie to the immigration authorities that the husband (who was a senior executive at Shell) was a much-needed expert forester for the estate. During one visit, Mrs Falge-Wahl counted fourteen indoor servants at the Priory. 'What nonsense!' said my mother, but when my parents died in 1995, the records seemed to show that Mrs Falge-Wahl was right.

In her book, she gives an account of Christmas at the Priory. It was not so different from that of my childhood:

> In the Castle [as she calls it] it was like you read in Dickens . . . The length of the drawing room . . . And I'd never seen before in my life a fireplace for logs. A tiled stove stood in the corner of our rooms in Vienna . . . And the Christmas tree up to the ceiling, presents for everyone, and young fellows from the village with lanterns, singing carols, and Lord Waldegrave giving everyone a port.

My parents found jobs for both husband and wife, fixed all the permissions they required, and provided them with a furnished cottage. 'God bless them!' writes Mrs Falge-Wahl, 'These people were unique.'

But that was all in a pre-war world about which they did not speak. My mother believed in practical liberal optimism: the Priory was in the past, and the past was not something to sentimentalise. Though she made herself an expert in our family collection of Walpoliana, Gothic gloomth *à la* Walpole was not her thing. She was a rationalist, not given to whimsy. Still formidable on her deathbed in 1995, breaking up as the neural paths collapsed, she remained the same: 'I don't want any panting harts at my funeral, please.'

So, the house of my childhood – and indeed adulthood, as my parents lived there until they died, when my brother inherited it – symbolised practical progress and a new age. It was, of course, by no means small – it remains the biggest house in the village – but it was not a stately home.

As Anthony Powell, accurate as always in matters to do with the English class system, recorded in his diary after coming to tea, it might have been a good-sized rectory; it was not really the thing for an earl.

I was born there, and still live within half a mile of the spot. My children have roots there, too. Such continuity is no longer usual in Britain. When my son was four, I went to the little toy shop in Wells and picked up a potato gun. 'Oh no,' said the elderly lady when I went to pay, 'you always had *this kind* when you were a child,' handing me a better model. She had last served me forty years earlier.

My parents handled the new world with great skill. Yes, we were privileged – and I know exactly when I became conscious of that fact: passing that armorial pub sign in Chewton Mendip at the age of about five – but duties came with it. I did not have the intelligence to imagine what it felt like in a village where most people were our tenants, our employees, or both. Did the locals really enjoy that Christmas Day ritual? What did they think of calling me Mr William, and my sisters Lady Sally, Lady Jinny, and so on? On the other hand, it was an intricately interdependent community – what the great sociologist Peter Laslett called a 'face-to-face society' – with the implicit social contract conscientiously observed by my parents in terms of investment in the farms and support for anyone in trouble. My father boasted of how many local small businesses he had helped to start. But it was hierarchical, and the class separation was complete. I never played with a local child. When we mentioned 'our neighbours', we meant the Jolliffes at Ammerdown, eight miles away, or the Asquiths at Mells (both a little suspect, as they were Catholics), the Duckworths at Orchard Leigh, the Hobhouses at Hadspen, or the Bishop in his palace in Wells.

Yet there was undeniably a sense of social solidarity and of participation in the wider refoundation of Britain. It was a good thing, my parents thought, that Churchill lost the 1945 election. He might have led us to dictatorship or another war. If my father had had a vote then, I believe he would have voted Labour. Meanwhile, my mother helped Violet Bonham

Carter's Liberal campaign in Wells. We took the *News Chronicle* as well as *The Times*; and the Cadbury family's sell-out to the Conservative *Daily Mail* was a black day at Chewton House. The NHS was praised as a magnificent creation. The end of empire was right, although Elspeth Huxley (whom I was given to read) was right too. My Grenfell uncles, who had business in Rhodesia, told me that the Africans were a little like children who would need time. Of course, the empire itself, indeed the whole concept of imperialism, was nothing to be ashamed of: on the contrary, empires had advanced civilisation throughout history. Alexander was called 'the Great' for founding his; and we were the successors of the Romans who, according to Gibbon, had created at the end of the first century AD the golden age of the world. Had we not done even better? But time moves on, empires rise and empires fall, as Kipling had reminded us even at the height of our power in 'Recessional':

Lo, all our pomp of yesterday
Is one with Nineveh and Tyre.

It hurt that it was all over, and I often wished I had been born a hundred, or two hundred, years earlier. Then I could have been Chatham or Pitt! But at least the empire had ended in glory; or so I was taught and believed. We had introduced the concepts of law and self-determination to the people we ruled, so it was only natural that they should want to rule themselves – and they showed their gratitude by freely joining the British Commonwealth with our beautiful young Queen as its head. We were not like the French, fighting vicious, futile wars in Algeria and Indo-China. Their government changed every week or two, like the Italians'. They had none of our political wisdom. Even my beloved Tintin was a little lacking here: how could he travel all around the pre-war world and hardly encounter the British Empire at all?

Now, in the 1950s, deploying our famous political acumen, and our innate sense of moderation and fair play, we had two new tasks: to demonstrate civilised living to the rest of the world and to lead a transition to a fairer society at home, without violence and revolution, indeed without too much change at all. Of course, the hard left, still set on class conflict, was dreadful, and far too near to the Communists (there was no sentimentality about Uncle Joe Stalin in our household). My self-produced newspaper attacked the wicked Mr Bevan (about whom I must have heard some malign comment, in spite of the Health Service), but there was no corresponding hostility towards Mr Attlee. Indeed, the anti-Bevan sentiment may have derived as much from the trouble he caused his party leader as from his bitter attacks on Churchill and the Tories.

The Eagle, launched when I was three, was the inspiration for my newspaper and represented a good part of our New Elizabethan values. Its undoubted star was Dan Dare, a Spitfire pilot transported to a world space fleet under the command of the Dowding-like Sir Hubert and assisted by Hank the American, Pierre the Frenchman and Professor Peabody, the (female) scientist. The Germans were still – and why not? – in disgrace. They appeared only occasionally as villains in league with the Mekon. *The Eagle* was Christian (it usually featured the story of a saint on the back cover) and serious about science and engineering, with beautiful cut-away drawings of modern ships and aircraft on the centre pages, above Luck of the Legion.

It is hard to remember now how seriously Britain took its reinvention after the war. The 1960s created a false narrative that the preceding decade had been grey and wasted. Perhaps the transition from pre-war morality was a little sluggish, but even the social conservatism has been over-exaggerated. The years 1940–5 saw a revolution in social mores that was nicely encapsulated by my aunt Frances Campbell Preston in her memoir, *The Rich Spoils of Time*. When her husband Patrick – captured in the defence of Dunkirk in 1940 and incarcerated in Colditz and elsewhere for the next five years – finally returned home, they went to tea at Fortnum's. She had to rebuke him for the way he addressed the waitress. What had been normal in 1939 was simply unacceptable in 1945.

More fundamentally, Britain in the fifties, determined never to return to the terrible thirties, was serious about a much more centrally planned modernism than that represented by the miniskirts and freer contraception of the 1960s. C. P. Snow's novels, which I read when I was a teenager, may not be great literature, but they accurately describe the seriousness of the new men – meritocratic scientists and engineers – who in the 1950s built the prosperity off which those in the 1960s lived. Such men were much admired at Chewton. Enormous resources were devoted to science and engineering, with the government investing in civil nuclear power, aircraft design and power engineering projects of worldwide significance. Britain built the first jet airliner and commissioned the first civil nuclear plant, then attached it to the world's first integrated high-voltage national electricity grid. We watched all of this unfold on *Pathé*'s newsreels. The Laboratory of Molecular Biology at Cambridge, under the stewardship of Max Perutz, discovered the structure of DNA; Rover raced the world's first gas-turbine car; the Fairey Rotodyne vertical take-off aeroplane preceded Boeing's Osprey by thirty years. The sport my brother and I followed with passionate dedication was not football or cricket but the high-tech world of motor racing. *The Eagle*'s propaganda for engineering was in tune with the national mood. Robert Birley, headmaster of Eton when I arrived there in 1959, defined a civilised man as someone who might be the chairman of the Atomic Energy Authority and capable of following the second lesson at Evensong in the Greek. My brother went up to Cambridge to read Engineering, not Classics. Many fine new technical universities were founded. The culture most likely to replace the old classicism seemed certain to be technical: science was modernity.

But then the New Elizabethan dream faded, and even came to be seen as faintly ridiculous. The serious-minded national doctrines of planning and quasi-wartime discipline crumbled as prosperity continued to grow. It turned out that the new technologies delivered fame and fortune not primarily to those who had invented them, but to others. For the first and most spectacular product of the new technologies was the revolution in communications, and therefore in entertainment. Widescreen cinemas with stereophonic sound showed *Around the World in Eighty Days* (I saw it five times). Then came television, first one channel, then two, then three. Who would fill the vacuum for content and reap the rewards in fame and money? Not, as it turned out, civil engineers or ministry planners or the characters in C. P. Snow's novels. The principal beneficiaries were the (mostly) public school-educated products of humanities courses: the brilliant satirists of *Beyond the Fringe* and *Private Eye* were now the new men, replacing Professor Quatermass and the designers of the Spitfire.

In 1964, just at the moment when Harold Wilson deployed his vision of a new Britain forged in the white heat of technology, the nation began to turn back to an arts-based culture. However, this time it would not be based on Homer, Virgil and the Authorised Version, but rather on the newly expanded disciplines of literary criticism and the post-classical arts schools. The smartest, and best-paid, graduates rode the massive wave of expansion of the new content-hungry entertainment industries of television, film and radio that the previous generation's engineers and scientists had created.

My home was rooted in the 1950s renewal that the 1960s would eventually deride. Central planning by great men in Whitehall was the national equivalent of the tiny planned economy of the inherited estate. Capitalism got rather short shrift. One of my father's sayings was that people are paid roughly in inverse proportion to the worth of what they do. I am not quite sure he was wrong. His respect went to farmers, and to the technologists who were enabling them to feed the world cheaply in the first green revolution: to local ex-tractor drivers who started their own businesses, and to his friend Charles Hill in Bristol, who built ships.

He was a modern farmer himself, chairman of Research Stations and friend of the progressive agriculturalists of the day, one of whom was Anthony Hurd, father of my later mentor Douglas. We were never allowed to forget that it was Labour – with the 1947 Agricultural Act – that restored prosperity to British farming under their great minister, Tom Williams. I have a picture of him, in stick-up collar, with my father and the Secretary of the Somerset Agricultural Workers Union (who, by then long retired, sent it to me many years later when I was myself minister of agriculture). Thanks to Labour, money flowed back into estates like ours in the 1950s and 1960s. That picture of the tenants' lunch for my brother's twenty-first in 1961 shows substantial, profitable farmers on an estate with no debt and no reason to fear the future.

Even then, however, we were aware of the potential tensions that modern farming brought with it. Long before I learned to call what they did 'ecology', I respected the work of serious naturalists. One of my father's trustees was Max Nicholson, the father of British environmentalism, and Herbert Morrison's key civil servant when that great man was deputy prime minister. Nicholson was founder of both the Nature Conservancy and the World Wildlife Fund, as well as the godfather of the British town and country planning system. Much later, he turned down the knighthood I and others prevailed upon Margaret Thatcher to offer him. Ernest Neal, another family friend, founded the Somerset Trust for Nature Conservation and fought for badgers, which he took us to watch in the early morning in their great sett in the lovely steep field called Ant's Hay, beyond the church. Rachel Carson's book *Silent Spring*, which first raised the alarm about the damage man – and his chemicals – was doing to the natural world, was much applauded at Chewton House.

In the old-fashioned way, I, with little competence, collected moths and butterflies, killing them in jars of laurel leaves before pinning them in rows in a little cabinet. I blew birds' eggs ('never take more than one from a nest') and pored over Thorburn and Victorian books of birds and beetles. My sisters painted in the wild flowers as they found them in their Bentham & Hookers. Fox hunting was somewhat frowned upon (my father had the original view that it was unfair to chase a nocturnal animal in daylight), and I loved the story of Rory O'mory, the giant fox who put paid to hunting in Ireland and then England. There may have been an edge to this hostility to hunting, because my mother had broken her back when riding after the birth of her first daughter and had been told it would be unsafe to attempt to have another child, an instruction to which she paid signally little attention.

We approved of pheasant shooting, which my father reintroduced to the estate when I was a young teenager. My brother and I would go out after pigeons in the summer evenings, me with my .410. We would walk home from Buddles Wood or the High Beeches when the immense, swirling, argumentative clouds of rooks and jackdaws returning from the stubble told us that the pigeons had finally gone to roost. The first time I managed to shoot a pigeon was a very great day; far superior to bagging a rabbit. There was a contradiction here, because I always thought of pigeons, one of the most beautiful and fastest of all our native birds, as the Spitfires of the local avian population; but still I shot them down like a Messerschmitt. Nevertheless, I make no apology for a boy with his gun who brought home a pigeon or a rabbit for supper.

My father lived long enough to see much of the work he and all those others had done to feed Britain and the world reviled. Modern farming became the enemy of the new generation of conservationists, in rich countries at least. By the end of his life there were subsidies to encourage you to let the drainage systems which he had built to bring swathes of land into cultivation collapse again to let the bogs reappear; subsidies to replant hedges that had been removed to allow in combine harvesters. Feeding the nation from home resources, it was said again, as it had been in the 1930s, was a foolish notion when we could buy everything we needed cheaper abroad. Like the fallen heroes of modern architecture and civil nuclear power, any modern farmer who lived too long died with the knowledge that his life's work was now despised.

Class-consciousness was omnipresent in my childhood world; racism not. Looking back, I was extraordinarily innocent about it. I am not even sure I knew what it meant to say that someone was Jewish until I was a late teenager. There were ugly phrases on the fringes of my consciousness – in my Grenfell grandfather's language, 'Jews' Bentley' meant a Jaguar – but it never occurred to me to be interested in the fact that my hero of heroes, Stirling Moss, had a Jewish father.

However, racial prejudice about colour was an issue, and one that was addressed head on in a story my mother told against herself. Aged perhaps six or seven, I am riding my bicycle around the garden as my mother gardens, using a noisy and in retrospect very dangerous early version of a strimmer, called in our family the whirly whizzer – electric powered, with a cable. My father had an amiable habit of picking up stray people on aeroplanes. On his way back from Kenya, where my sister Sally was, he had befriended a young black Kenyan, who therefore came to stay. I crash my bicycle, and cry. My mother cannot hear me because of the electric strimmer. The young black man comes running up the lawn to rescue me. Her first thought, she tells us, in those days of the Mau Mau, as she sees him running towards her, is that my father has brought home a terrorist and she grasps the whirly whizzer, intending to sell her life dearly. But it is not so, as she sees the young man run past her, gather up her weeping younger son and deal with the blood on his knees. I think the fact that she turned this story into a family legend was evidence of my mother's clear-sightedness. In that society, only a liar claimed to have no colour prejudice. Rather than lie about it, it is better to confront it and defeat it.

There was luck, too, at, of all places, my prep school, Pinewood. The great Bishop Trevor Huddleston – author of *Naught for Your Comfort* and the white man who did more for South Africa than any other, according to Nelson Mandela – was a friend of one of the boys' parents, and he was invited to talk to us. So, the first time I ever heard the true story of modern South Africa, it came from the lips of one of the most powerful white voices raised against apartheid. Fifty years later, I was able to tell this to Mr Mandela himself.

One more family legend. It was said that when the US Army arrived in the village in 1943 – to prepare for Operation Overlord and meanwhile lay waste to the Priory – a group of villagers led by our beloved Bessie Speed, lifelong Labour stalwart and then a feisty youngster, prepared to hold a party for them in the village hall. Back then – and for many years thereafter – the US Army maintained its own strict apartheid, so Bessie was told that no black soldiers would be allowed to attend the party. 'Right,' she said, 'there'll be no party then.' And America crumbled. I have no way of knowing if this story is true, but I hope it is. I do know that it was told us as evidence of one of Bessie's many heroic attributes; and in the end it is the legends you believe that matter.

If racism barely registered in my childhood world, class certainly did. Although I was brought up to imagine a social contract of mutual obligation and duty between the classes, and to applaud meritocratic movement up – and down – between them, there was no question that class consciousness was a deeply rooted part of our family's culture. I know now, though I did not at the time, how shocked my parents were when my sister Sally chose as her husband from among the ADCs at Government House, Nairobi, not an upper-class young Guardsman but Ernie Wright, a colonial policeman, ex-RAF, a Geordie. The fact that he had flown in Halifaxes in the war and won a George Medal fighting Ethiopian bandits on Kenya's northern frontier simply made him another heroic brother-in-law as far as I was concerned; and I loved the aiguilette of the Kenya Police uniform I wore as the page at their wedding in Chewton Church. But I fear that his heroism – not to mention his good looks and charm – was little consolation to my parents at the time.

The world changed, and they changed with it. At least my parents' – and my own – snobbery was not about money; and they accepted the obligations that their moderate (at least in modern City terms) wealth laid upon them. They believed in hierarchy – open hierarchy, but hierarchy nonetheless. The results were sometimes odd. For instance, it did not occur to them that one of my brother's early, rather rackety, girl-friends might be more, not less, dangerous because she carried in her veins the blood of one of Charles II's more flamboyant mistresses. After all, our own peerage had emerged from the wrong side of the blanket covering Charles's less attractive brother, James II. They admired what they would have described as middle-class values – hard work, honesty, lack of ostentation – but they admired them more if they came with a reference in Debrett's.

I have to admit that my father did sometimes put on a show for the wealthy. There was talk of his taking a directorship of some great Australian agricultural enterprise, headed by the perfectly named Sir Ellerton Becker, who came to dinner. My parents had recently enlarged the house with a rather grand new dining room, and invested in the latest technology: a dishwasher of industrial proportions. To entertain Sir Ellerton, a butler was borrowed from the Merchant Venturers in Bristol to serve at dinner. 'We live very simply here,' my father explained to the great man, unfortunately in earshot of his disrespectful children, who made it a catchphrase. Meanwhile, no one had instructed Mrs Emmett not to put foaming detergent in the new washing-up contraption. In the middle of dinner, strange noises were heard from the pantry. My father, opening the connecting door to investigate, was met by a four-foot wall of foam.

Other grandees received special treatment, too. My father was Lord Warden of the Stannaries after he left the government, and chairman of the young Prince of Wales's Council. Consequently, the Prince came to stay. My father was anxious that, like Sir Ellerton, Prince Charles should see us at our best, so the drive was retarmacked. Unfortunately, it then melted in the unusually fierce September sunshine and was scraped off just in time. This was not, however, the only preparation for the royal visit. In autumn, flies hatched behind the shutters, so special chemicals were deployed to destroy them. And an extra electric booster was added to the hot-water system in the Prince's bathroom, which could not be trusted. When the Prince came down to dinner my father asked if all was in order. 'Well, Geoffrey, it was rather odd, since you ask. When I turned on the hot tap, nothing came out except dead flies, followed by a lot of steam.' The superheated flies did not prevent my father's Garter, but that became another source of anxiety to him, as he thought himself unworthy.

One other powerful background force in my childhood has to be noted: male primogeniture. There is a picture of me handing out Coronation mugs to the village. Mr Latter, in his waistcoat and wearing his watch-chain, is reading out the names, while Val, my governess, looks on together with my grandmother and aunt Re (short for Irene). Where was my brother when I was handing out the mugs? Such duties were usually his. He must have been in London, rehearsing for the great day: he was page to Lord Fortescue, hereditary bearer of the pall, or some such. He had a uniform and a sword, and was painted in all his finery by James Gunn. I was, after all, the guard, not the king. But at least I was not a sister. Although they were all much older, much loved, and glamorous, it was my brother and I who sat alongside our parents in that front pew in church.

From my earliest days, I understood that everything would go one day to my brother. I never resented it: that was how the world was, and he was a hero fit to be worshipped. Six years older than me, he was the stroke of the eight when I arrived at Eton (sent early, aged twelve, so I would overlap with him) and later stroked Cambridge. He was well supplied with beautiful girls; an undergraduate at the most famous college of all, Trinity, our father's college. When I was fourteen and he was twenty and drove his AC Bristol back from London or Cambridge, I used to wait for him, lying on my bed straining with all my concentration to hear the unmistakable Bristol whine as he took the smooth turns on Chewton Plain rather faster than is now allowed. How my heart jumped when I heard it.

But however much I loved him, here was another motive force for my ambition, alongside the fear of ridicule. If I was not going to have the family name, I had better make my own. Sisters could (and one perhaps should) stay at home; but not younger sons. Aunt Re had stayed at home. We were told that she had had a suitor when she was young, but he was considered too low, or too high – in church terms – so that was that. Instead, she was detailed to look after my grandmother after my grandfather – the vicar – had died in 1936. The old lady lived to be nearly a hundred, bedridden after a stroke for many years. Aunt Re loyally fulfilled her duty with the help of two other faithful spinster ladies, Helen and Patsy. Helen had a brother who was known to be a clerk of some kind in the Foreign Office. When I arrived there as minister of state in 1988 I found that Christopher Curwen was actually the chief of the Secret Intelligence Service, the famous 'C'. It was an example of the somewhat otherworldly, non-metropolitan culture of my parents' Chewton Mendip.

Perhaps one of my sisters would stay at home and look after her parents in their old age. But I would have to make my own way. The question was: which way? The glittering prizes might lead to elective politics, but I suspect that in my parents' minds the high civil service, perhaps overlapping with high academia, was thought to be a more proper ambition. After all, F. E. Smith and Disraeli were not quite respectable, no matter how brilliant they may have been. At home, my parents were more likely to talk with admiration about Oliver Franks, Professor of Moral Philosophy and the mandarins' mandarin; Max Nicholson; Isaiah Berlin (known to my father from wartime Washington); Sir Evelyn Baring, known to us as Uncle Bear, the Governor of Kenya; Roger Makins, permanent secretary and ambassador; or Roger Mynors, another Lyttelton connection, who was Professor of Latin at Oxford and whose brother was deputy governor of the Bank of England. The politicians who were my parents' friends were the not very partisan rising stars of the House of Lords, from both sides of the chamber: Lords Shackleton, Carrington and Jellicoe. The local Tory MP, a perfectly respectable person, was not a regular lunch guest.

Although my father joined Harold Macmillan's government in the

Agriculture Ministry in 1958 and served until he was sacked in the Night of the Long Knives in 1962, he was not really a party politician. He would have been alarmed by my secret dreams of political glory. Nonetheless, his service as a minister and his anecdotes about the prime minister and Alec Douglas-Home (who was married to yet another Lyttelton connection, Libby, the daughter of Cyril Allington, former headmaster of Eton) began to bring those dreams into sharper focus. But government for my father was public service, much like his long membership of the county council, not the advancement of ideology, let alone the pursuit of glittering prizes. *Noblesse oblige* is ridiculed now; but in the society we have created, which is even less equal than that of my childhood in terms of the distribution of wealth, no slogan exists to shame the rich into any semblance of solidarity with the poor. I am glad that my lust for prizes was tempered by my father's older and better doctrine.

Years later, when I was a minister, I became friendly with Macmillan, the distant prime minister of my childhood. As Howard Brenton argues rather brilliantly in his play *Never So Good*, I believe there was something rather unpleasant about the ridicule the sixties' satirists heaped on Macmillan: at the age when they were playing clever games at Cambridge, he was rescuing wounded soldiers from no man's land during the Battle of the Somme. In his fine biography, D. R. Thorpe writes that there was a saying in the Grenadiers – 'As brave as Macmillan'. He took on the hard and dangerous Tory right over the dissolution of the British Empire in Africa and beat them, thereby avoiding a British version of the French horror in Algeria. He was far ahead of his time, and indeed of the Labour Party, in his understanding of Keynes. And he was tough. In later years he would always greet me by saying, 'So sad about your father, such a good man.'

I would reply, 'But he is very well!'

'Good gracious! I thought he had died.'

Perhaps anyone he sacked became dead to him.

Caroline and I invited him to dinner at our beautiful house in Palace

Gardens Terrace, where we lived for thirty-three years. Caroline had taken special trouble with the food. I had taken trouble with the guests, who were all well known to Macmillan. But the first course went down too well: too much attention was paid to the asparagus and not enough to the old man. He bided his time. 'I was told to come here for high-minded conversation,' he announced, finally. 'But it is nothing but gluttony!' That silenced us. He turned to his neighbour, the meritocratic Sir Dick White, former head of MI5 and MI6. 'Such a pity they abolished the gold sovereign, you know,' he said. 'What does one tip one's loader?' Britain had come off the gold standard some time before; and Dick White was a very implausible participant in double-gun shoots. This sally wholly abolished all other conversation, as no doubt he had intended it to. Then the well-prepared anecdotes rolled out, and he held us spellbound.

His timing was always impeccable, though not always kind. In 1981 I attended the memorial service for Edward Boyle, the Old Etonian former education minister who had campaigned for the Conservatives to commit themselves to a policy of replacing grammar and secondary modern schools with comprehensives. Ted Heath gave a rather wooden address, in which he said that Boyle had no enemies. At the reception afterwards, Macmillan held court. 'Some people,' he began, 'say that Edward had no enemies. That is quite wrong, of course. The point was he had all the right enemies.' It was dangerous to try to compete with him.

One year, I was invited to address an anniversary celebration of the founding of the Oxford University Conservative Association. The other guest speaker was to be Macmillan, so I insisted on speaking first. In the middle of dinner he informed the appalled young president that he did not think he could manage a speech. 'But, Sir . . .'; 'Oh well then, I will do my best.' I knew what was coming and spoke very briefly. He got up and held some (probably irrelevant) sheets of paper very close to his eyes for perhaps a minute, until you could hear a pin drop and the president's nerves begin to jangle almost audibly. Then, off he went into a riff about the young men on the eve of the Somme, and how tonight's audience reminded him of them. Half an hour later, not a dry eye in the house, a standing ovation. Then up he got again and went on for another twenty minutes. It was magnificent. 'Doing his old man act' R. A. Butler used to call it. But he *was* old!

In the 1980s we used to lunch together in Boodles Club, at his expense. He would eat virtually nothing but a Brussels sprout, but we would have two Martinis each and share a bottle of claret followed by a brandy. All of this had no apparent effect on him at all; I would reel back to my disapproving ministerial office. On one occasion, when I was seriously late for some parliamentary business, I asked if he would mind if my car dropped me first in Old Palace Yard before taking him on to his next engagement. As we drove through the gates, he announced that it was the first time he had been within the precincts of the House of Commons since he had resigned as prime minister. Could that be true?

The last time I saw him was at Victoria Station. I was arriving very late back from some minor political engagement. There he was, proceeding in stately fashion across the concourse to catch the last train home, alone apart from the support of respectful Sikh railway staff. They knew who he was; the other late-night inhabitants of the station did not.

Harold Macmillan was a politician driven to very great achievements perhaps by some of the same demons that in lesser form drove my lesser talents. But in Chewton House that other form of public service – quiet mandarinate power – was also celebrated; and although I was driven by my ambition for front-line glory down the first path, some of the latter's appeal stayed with me. All my life I have retained a trust in – and an admiration for – the perhaps imaginary, quiet world of the meritocratic, wise and honest guardians of our civilisation; the decent and humane custodians – embodiments – of our institutions. The cabinet secretary; the regius professor; the master or warden; the chairman of trustees; the president of the academy; 'C'. These were the Sir Huberts who kept the Mekon at bay.

A childhood, then, which could not be repeated: a world we have lost.

All past worlds are lost, of course, but some do seem to be more lost than others. I arrived at the end of a culture and a social system that would not have been wholly unrecognisable in 1555, 1655, 1755, let alone 1855. Did it not feel strange to be living it in 1955? The Authorised Version and the Book of Common Prayer every Sunday in that front pew; the land, the estate staff, the servants. Was it not obvious that we were coming to the end of things – not just of imperial Britain, but of the old culture and its ruling class?

To a child, it seemed immeasurably secure. It did not feel like the penultimate chapter of *The Leopard*. But, of course, it was. Within twenty years, that world – Authorised Version, tenant farmers, hierarchy, deference, the Home Service, 5057 *The Earl Waldegrave*, classical tags from Virgil and Horace, Gilbert and Sullivan, *Jock of the Bushveld* and all – was gone. The old high culture that had underpinned Englishness for so long, whether you were Jude the Obscure or the Duke of Devonshire, suddenly collapsed. Only Shakespeare was left, dangerously exposed, like a monarch with no hereditary aristocracy.

CHAPTER THREE

Paths of Glory

So, we have a small boy, sometimes lonely in a silent house when all his siblings are away, afraid of ridicule, wanting above all to be part of the grown-up life which moves along just ahead of him, the grown-up life represented by half-understood things that others seem to understand much better than he does. His head is full of heroes who understand the magic of action and know the secrets: the heroes of ancient Greece and Rome and of the Second World War; and his own brother. Perhaps a lifelong tendency to seek out such heroes has already been established: surely, somewhere, there are people who know the truth, who deserve their prizes? It cannot be a rare story: a life's motivation derived from the desire to catch up with that patch of sunlight on the water just ahead which stands for understanding of the world's secrets.

I set about chasing the sunlight very systematically, albeit slowly, confining most of my efforts until about the age of thirteen to daydreaming and romance. A gentle and cultured English master at my prep school, Mr Vallon, encouraged me to read and write, even poetry with rather surprising rhymes. I was popular in the evening in my dormitory because I told good stories, and could make people laugh: Inspector Stanley, Sergeant

Matthews and Constable Hebblethwaite were my principal characters. We listened in the summer evenings, with the windows open and the bats flying in and out, to Miss Bishop playing Chopin's *Grande Valse Brillante* on the piano in the music room, part of her successful courtship, I believe, of the mathematics master.

My popularity was enhanced because my mother, with what now seems splendid insouciance about the rules, used to bring the family caravan up to Pinewood and camp in it for days at a time on the playing fields, brewing tea and sausages on a Primus stove for my friends. If her last child had to leave home, well, she would follow.

The sausages were welcome, because the other food was not so good: Spam fritters we smuggled out of the dining room in our pockets, and we poured the free school milk between the cracks in the art-room floor. One hot day there was a most magnificent stink.

I painted big, bold pictures with poster paint. Mr Walters, the classics master, reinforced my worship of the Olympians: he said the best prizes to win were always for classics. Clever boys did Greek as well as Latin. He confirmed what I already believed to be true – that the classical road was the high road, as it had been for centuries before Mr Walters and was no longer to be very shortly after I started down it. On Sundays we learned verses from the Authorised Version by heart; on Mondays we studied Virgil and Horace and Herodotus. It would not have been very different in 1859 or 1759.

Off I went, then, after the glittering prizes, although a good part of their glitter was extinguished at the moment of my arrival. I have sometimes thought that my effect on the old English *cursus honorum* was rather like that of Tyrone Slothrop in Thomas Pynchon's *Gravity's Rainbow*: wherever he makes love in wartime London a V2 arrives shortly afterwards. When I began to reel in the Edwardian prizes at Eton and Oxford they seemed to have reached their sell-by date just as I acquired them. Later, this became a recurring theme. I was the first Conservative MP to lose Bristol West since the Second Reform Bill. I was Margaret Thatcher's last cabinet appointment; she fell less than a month later. After my spell in the cabinet, the Tories enjoyed a prolonged period in opposition. GEC, which had once employed me, was Britain's largest private sector company. Now it does not exist. Later, Kleinwort Benson (foolishly) hired me: gone. UBS is still around . . . just. Are All Souls, where I remain a fellow, and Eton, where I am provost, safe? Five and a half centuries of survival may not be enough protection.

It is customary to write of one's schooling, especially if it was as traditional as mine, as if it were the cause of terrible unhappiness; to castigate the old English upper-class system for its bullying, sexual abuse and philistinism. It is almost a standard literary trope, like one of Cicero's rhetorical devices. But I cannot truthfully deploy it. Of course, between the ages of eight and eighteen I was intermittently plunged into despair, fury and gloom. Of course, I was homesick at first. (Although my mother had a cunning ploy to ease my pain, if not her own, by hiding a present in my suitcase – often a Frog rubber-band-powered aeroplane. This proved to be a particularly effective cure for a ten-year-old's sorrow.) But I am sorry to have to report that there was also plenty of happiness, friendship, fun, triumph and joy. Reading every year, as I do now as a judge of the Hawthornden Prize, some of the seemingly inexhaustible supply of miserabilist literature about every kind and class of childhood, I think the answer may be that in the years before and after puberty *everyone*'s life is quite troubled. But I cannot be a useful contributor to this genre. I was happy building huts with tin and wood in the beautiful grounds of Pinewood, although on one dreadful day I did manage to burn down the magnificent Prefects' Tree House, which I had no right to enter in the first place, by upsetting my home-made paraffin stove. The smell of paraffin still brings that terrifying incident back to me: a more robust form of Proust's madeleines. I was happy learning a little Latin and French and Greek, writing stories for Mr Vallon and reciting them for my friends. I was no good at cricket – my only appearance as a batsman in a competitive match was, happily for Pinewood, interrupted

by rain. I sang, embarrassed, in the chorus in *HMS Pinafore*. I stole cigarettes from the silver boxes at Chewton House and took them to school,
hidden in my shoes. On one occasion I was about to be beaten for smoking behind the pavilion but was reprieved by the intervention, in best
Victorian storybook style, of Polk – captain of the school. I could not
be beaten, he declared, because I had been sneaked on, not caught by a
master. This point of honour was readily accepted by Mr Walters and I
was not beaten, either then or subsequently. I led a gang with my friends
Harford and Costley-White. There was a rival gang too, but I cannot
remember what differentiated us from them. I raced my model Vanwalls
and Ferraris down ramps. I failed to breed stick insects, but my small
garden was more of a success, particularly with dianthuses and nastur-
tiums, the latter of which were particularly welcome as they were edible.
There was a tuck shop (my sixpence-a-week pocket money could buy
two tubes of Fruit Gums or a Mars bar and a stick of liquorice) and best
of all, once a year, a fair pitched in a field at the end of the drive and we
were allowed on the dodgems. On St Peter's Day and Ascension Day we
would take a charabanc to the White Horse, down which we rolled, like
small versions of Dr Johnson. All things considered, Pinewood really
was not remotely miserable.

I arrived at Eton in January 1959. Macmillan was now the Supermac
of the cartoonists: his electoral triumph came later in the same year. My
brother stroked the Eton eight, won the school sculling, and went up to
Cambridge, where he stroked the Cambridge boat too, in a glow of hero
worship from me and from the rest of the family. It was perhaps the high
summer of success for my childhood world: my father in the ministry;
my brother a rowing star; three of my sisters married to men who had
served in the RAF, the Guards and the Royal Navy during the war; and
I an Oppidan Scholar at Eton.

Early school at seven-thirty; chapel every day (and twice on Sundays);
coal fires in our rooms; smoke mingling with Thames mist at dusk;
hand-carts delivering our suits from Welsh & Jefferies; a beating from

the captain of the house if, as a new boy, you failed to show that you could recognise all the many school colours and caps (I did not sail) after a fortnight in the school; fagging; boy-calls. It was an unreformed Eton; anarchic for all its sometimes savage discipline; confident; all absorbing.

It was quite a tough place, at least in my house. Our house master, John Marsden, had won the Wingfield Sculls and beaten the world champion Russians at Henley in the double sculls. He had been a commando and an intelligence officer in the war, taking part in the famous raid on the Lofoten Islands in 1941 – the mission that brought back rotors from an Enigma machine that proved crucially valuable to Bletchley. He looked and acted the part. When I was thirteen, I told the dame in my house, the matron, that I could not sleep. Marsden heard of this. 'Next time you cannot sleep, boy, come through to the private side,' he said. (The private side was where he and his family lived.) Terrified, a few nights later, at perhaps eleven-thirty, I did so. 'Right, boy, we are going to run to Bray.' It was winter, and Bray is several miles from Eton. We ran there and back. I slept better.

James Fox, another boy in my house, and a stroke of the Eton eight some years after my brother, became a fine journalist and author. He wrote in *The Times* after Marsden died that he had 'made rowing subversive': that is, we always felt we were the underdogs, against the Establishment, and found strategies – based on harder work and tougher competitive will – to win. Always, when I was in a hard corner later, I would think of Marsden, and try to find courage. It worked until almost the very end of my career.

He knew his limitations, however. He had made my brother into an international-level rower, and me, with much less talent, into not a bad oar in a pair, at least when my more skilful friend, Hugh Williams, was in the bow seat. But Marsden concluded I needed more culture than he could provide, so he sent me to a young aesthete, Nigel Foxell, whom Robert Birley, the headmaster, had hired from Tübingen University.

I went timidly to his rooms. 'Who painted that picture?' he asked, as a test, pointing to a print on the wall. My sister Elizabeth had given me R. H. Wilenski's *French Painting* years before, and it rescued me now.

'Fantin-Latour, sir.'

'Of course. Now, you will remember that Ruskin says—'

'I have never read Ruskin, sir.'

'Never read Ruskin? Good gracious!'

I was fourteen. It was a great school, if you were lucky.

There were politics and politicians, dead and alive, everywhere. Walpole had carved his name in one of the schoolrooms. Chatham, Fox, Gladstone and Salisbury were represented in busts and portraits. Macmillan had contemplated appointing himself provost while still prime minister. Richard Crossman came to talk to us. So did Frank Cousins, former general secretary of the Transport and General Workers' Union and now Wilson's minister of technology; and Heath, just after de Gaulle vetoed Britain's entry into the EEC; and Sir Alec Douglas-Home, soon after he had lost the 1964 election (I introduced him). Isaiah Berlin came and delivered a talk on Romanticism. I thought it was the greatest lecture I had ever heard; it cemented for ever my discipleship.

Not all visits went so smoothly. On 7 February 1964, I recorded in my diary the appearance of Lord Lambton, who was, somewhat implausibly, a Conservative education spokesman:

Lord Lambton at the Politico . . . the usual excellent Provost's dinner. Lambton, in dark glasses, obviously rather strange . . . It was apparent that he was very, very drunk. A hilarious meeting followed, with sentences like, 'With the utmost deferentiation, Sir Claude [Sir Claude Aurelius Elliot was my austere and dignified predecessor as provost], we must open the gates for a dilutation of the Etonic system.' Rapturous applause. 'What people like doing is living, so we must teach them to do living!' Question: 'What do you

think of the proposals to make Eton into a Sixth Form College?'
Answer (archly): 'Where would the Fifth Form be?' Question:
'Do you think schools like Eton should put less emphasis on arts
courses?' Answer: 'I don't know anything about art, and I'm not
getting involved in your local difficulties!'

I suspect, in light of the events that later ended his political career, it was
not alcohol he had taken that evening.

Eton was beautiful. I had at least enough gaps in my self-absorption
to notice that. Some of that beauty has now been damaged by the box of
motorways that hem it in, though far from all. Then, you could take a
beautiful, handmade, wooden sculling shell out on the river in the evening, watch the flash of a kingfisher as he passed you on the way up to
Boveney lock, then bicycle back in the dusk from the old rafts building
across the water-meadows towards Henry VI's great unfinished chapel,
pausing for a glass of beer in the garden of Tap, the boys' pub, on the
way. Even if you were as pleased with yourself and as full of adolescent
turmoil as I was, you could not miss it all.

Robert Birley became an inspiration and mentor, infecting me with
bibliomania through exposure to Eton's then still largely uncatalogued
college library, with its Gutenberg Bible, its First Folios and its incu-
nabula. Many years later – as chairman of the Rhodes Trust – I worked
with Nelson Mandela to establish the new Mandela Rhodes Foundation
in South Africa. There I met many good people who had been helped
by Birley and his wife Eleanor when they went out to Witwatersrand
University to cause trouble for the apartheid regime after his headmas-
tership of Eton had come to an end.

My last year, sitting on top of a good many of Eton's easily accessible
hierarchies, was full of turmoil. Marsden was asked to leave by a new and
very different headmaster – the brilliant but damaged Anthony Chenevix
Trench. (On one occasion, such was my self-importance, I took it upon
myself to tell him that he could not go on beating so many boys, with the

result that he first wept and then handed me a tumbler of whisky.) I was full of fury and energy. Like many another teenager, it was obvious to me that I was surrounded by idiots. Why did no one applaud the fact that the national press had picked up every single issue of the Eton College *Chronicle* that I had edited? (I had called for co-education and the abolition of both beating and boxing at the school; I had published an opinion poll – with a tiny sample – that caused me to be invited to London to meet the experts at National Opinion Polls Ltd., complete with lunch at the Savoy Grill. All this, I now understand all too well, must have been more than a little irritating for the school's patient authorities.) Back at home, I judged that Chewton House was totally uncultured because no one there read Camus or Catullus. I was bursting with self-indulgent despair.

By then, my eclectic reading had exploded. I was consciously designing my own prince's education, designed to prepare me for the kingdom I secretly believed I would win, taking in what seems now an astonishing range of topics. I had a craze for obscure epics, including the Finnish *Kalevala*. I went through the inevitable Sartre and de Beauvoir phase. I investigated Ouspensky's *Tertium Organum* and tried to persuade myself that my Grenfell grandmother's enthusiasm for the Catholic mystic philosopher Pierre Teilhard de Chardin could be reconciled to the fact that Peter Medawar, Nobel Prize-winner, had used the logical techniques I had begun to understand utterly to destroy him in a famous review of Teilhard's book *The Phenomenon of Man*, published in *Mind* magazine – to which I subscribed. (I did the same with *Encounter*. They both went on the Eton bill for my long-suffering parents to pay.)

I chose a formidable and independently minded classical tutor, John Roberts, who gave me to read Richard Robinson's *An Atheist Values*, and Robert Eisler's *Man into Wolf* and E. R. Dodds's *The Greeks and the Irrational*. It tells one something of the strange freedom that Eton allowed, and still allows, within its traditional forms that, when he gave me Robinson, Roberts asked me to keep it under cover. He saw no risk in the Eisler, which is partly about the urges that drive *homo sapiens* towards bestiality. You didn't openly question God; that would be a form of bad manners. But you weren't afraid of Venus in furs.*

John Roberts – a serious though academic left-winger at Oxford – reinforced my father's lessons about the random ways in which people found themselves in high positions. 'The most intelligent couple in the Eton community,' he used to say in his solemn way, 'are Mr and Mrs Moulton.' They ran the Tap, the boys' pub. I had no reason to disagree.

I also fell in love with particle physics and the philosophy of science, from Lucretius to Schrödinger. I had a season pursuing Arthur, and followed him via Malory to Wace and Layamon. I drove my mother's green Mini to Glastonbury in the holidays. I filled my commonplace book with Greek and Latin tags, lists of books I planned to read and actually had read – J. S. Mill, Kafka, economics from Andrew Shonfield, Barbara Ward and Marjory Perham, Marguerite Yourcenar's *Memoirs of Hadrian*, John Braine and Cyril Connolly, Freud on Leonardo, a list of Shakespeare's plays, C. P. Snow, Euripides, Plato, Plautus, Gilbert Ryle (only some of *Dilemmas* – not a very long book – I noted honestly), Constantine Fitzgibbon's *When the Kissing Had to Stop* and Iris Murdoch's *Under the Net*. There was also John Buchan and *Scoop* and 'a Wodehouse or two', so I was not totally inhuman. I wept over the Athenian ships racing out of Piraeus to their doom in Sicily. I refought Marathon, Thermopylae and Salamis. And I wrote unsatisfactory poems in the style of Macaulay (plus rather savage criticism of my own poor efforts); melodramatic short stories; and furious, polemical (undelivered) speeches. One of the latter, pre-empting by a couple of years Herbert Marcuse's silly essay 'Repressive Tolerance', argued that liberal pluralism was just a more subtle method of control, but no different in intention from dictatorship. I tried to teach myself, still cripplingly shy when speaking in public,

---

* I did not hide Robinson well enough at home, however. My copy is fiercely annotated with counter arguments by my mother.

how to debate by reading and rereading Edwardian collections of great parliamentary speeches that could still be found then on the high, dusty shelves of the school library. Fox and Sheridan were the best.

I drove myself hard. I said to myself: 'You can do charm, you can work, you have some administrative capacity; if you are to be prime minister, you must now build a reputation for being clever.' I turned myself to those exams, and worked and worked. My victories were not elegant and effortless. I wrote '*Labor omnia vicit, improbus*' from Virgil's *Georgics* on my notebooks, as well as '*Trud, trud, y trud* – V. I. Lenin', which I believed to be the Russian for 'work, work, and work'. John Roberts found a Greek word for what drove me: *philonikia*, the love of victory. Coriolanus, lonely, proud and doomed, was a particular hero (especially as represented by Beethoven's overture). My heart sang with Marlowe's *Tamburlaine*:

> Is it not brave to be a king, Techelles?
> Usumcasane and Theridamas,
> Is it not passing brave to be a king
> And ride in triumph through Persepolis?

That was what I was going to do: ride in triumph. And, like Achilles, I would accept that the glory was worth any sacrifice.

As I got older, most of my holidays were spent in Greece. I became a full-blooded, Victorian philhellene, a sentimentalist for an imaginary classical world. High on the Acrocorinth, I remember sitting on a block of marble, looking at the red earth and out to the gulf, and thinking: 'Somehow this is all inside me, and will carry me to victory.' My absorption into the myth of Greece was intense, diverting the dangerous energy that sometimes carries teenagers into fundamental religion or nervous breakdown. Delphi and the Acropolis, Olympia and Bassae were places of extraordinary power in my imagination, and the reality was overwhelming. I can still taste the tea with lemon that I drank on my first evening at the Belle Helene – then the only hotel in Mycenae – before walking almost in a trance up the track and under the Lion Gate to see where Agamemnon had lived and died. It has not all left me: the charioteer of Delphi's gaze is still central to my idea of beauty; the *Bacchae* of Euripides to my understanding of the limits of rationality.

I won my glittering prizes, including the Newcastle, then still in its old form: you read the whole Bible in the Authorised Version (or at least I did), the Acts and one of the Gospels in Greek, studied the history of the Church in England, and did papers on the great Greek and Latin classics. Within a few years, though Eton still remains faithful to the Authorised Version and the Book of Common Prayer, a retreating Church of England had abandoned both. No sooner had I mastered Virgil, Horace, Homer, Herodotus and Thucydides than they disappeared as the central reference points for educated discourse that they had been since the Renaissance. My timing, as ever, was impeccable.

When I started classics at Eton, taught by Richard Martineau – whose slogan was 'all this modern scholarship is bricks without straw: read the texts' – all educated people knew the classical stories. They knew who you meant by Leonidas and Alcibiades, by Socrates and Alexander and Hannibal and Pompey and Nero, even if they had forgotten their Latin and had never known Greek. They also knew Joshua and Samuel, Jonah and Nebuchadnezzar, Jezebel and Martha, and what was wrong with the Laodicians, who were neither hot nor cold.

When I left, all these previously fixed cultural reference points were already becoming subjects solely for specialist scholarly study, like Egyptology or number theory. Split as I was – half conservative, half radical – I watched in fascination as modern analytical methods – often Marxist, like those of Moses Finley or E. P. Thompson or Geoffrey de Ste Croix – made the classics forever part of scholarship, not part of an English education. But I also mourned the passing of that old education. And I still do.

The focus of the battle waged over my head by modernists and traditionalists at Eton was the teaching of English. There was no English Department when I arrived. The subject was taught by classics teachers like the former first-class cricketer Claude Taylor, who introduced me to Conrad and guided me to the annual English literature prizes. I spent the money on collecting Kipling's many volumes. Richard Martineau was much more conservative. His idea of teaching English – a rather good one, I think – was to sit us down in the beautiful Fellows' Garden with Arthur Quiller-Couch's *Oxford Book of English Verse*. Then things changed. A pioneering teacher, Murray Biggs, was hired and a separate English Department was established. I argued strongly against. I believed we should be taught logic – so that we could think – and then left to read books by ourselves. With impertinence I now find embarrassing (although I also remain rather proud of it), I sat an English A-level by myself to prove you did not need to be taught the subject at all. In this, I turned out to be right. I was a volunteer skirmisher on the losing side in the war launched to defeat the old classical culture. Our defeat doubtless brought many benefits, but it also helped to divert many people down the dreadful intellectual cul-de-sac of postmodernist relativism which has wasted numerous clever people's energies for a generation. We did not know what rough French monsters would shamble towards Bethlehem to be born once Aristotle and Virgil had been toppled; but we did know that the old culture was surely going down.

Perhaps it is like Dutch elm disease, England's greatest environmental disaster of my lifetime, about which no one talks. It is too big to notice, or to mourn. John Clare could rage against the felling of a single beloved elm by ruthless agricultural developers, grieving in his greatest poem at the pain of his loss:

Thou owned a language by which hearts are stirred
Deeper than by a feeling clothed in word

In my lifetime *every* great elm went down; the loss was so total that we could not rage. So it was with the destruction and burial of the culture that would have allowed my father to talk freely to Archdeacon Grantly or Uncle Toby or Samuel Pepys. It has simply gone, like the trees that used to define the landscape of England; and there was nothing anyone could have done to stop it or them from going.

Lost communal culture does, however, leave some legacies. One is my fondness for fictional community. From Tintin on, I have always been a fan of secure constructed worlds of the imagination, into which one can safely disappear. I suspect that the unchanging nature of such fictional worlds provides a way of rediscovering childhood certainty. Not that the created worlds need be childish: some of the greatest works of literature provide them too – Homer, Jane Austen. They are bounded, comprehensible, coherent, like those islands of my child-hood, Shona and Colonsay, as well as the inland island of the Chewton Estate itself.

In the 1990s, I became a devotee of one of the finest such constructions of my time, Patrick O'Brian's Aubrey and Maturin stories, shrewdly described by A. S. Byatt as 'the novels Jane Austen's naval brothers might have written'. Encouraged by my friend, the excellent novelist and biographer Alan Judd, I struck up a correspondence with O'Brian, and Caroline and I became friends of his. We visited Patrick and his wife Mary in Collioure, in French Catalonia, where he had built his own house, and where he wrote. He said that when they had been very poor, living from hand to mouth, the local farmers had taken to leaving baskets of food on the doorstep, proud of their local *écrivain*. Now that he was rich and famous he had asked them to stop, but the village of Matisse knew about creative artists and knew they were always poor, so the bas-kets continued to arrive. He and I would lunch in his club, Brooks's, where, prosperous at last, he would order *un petit vin de famille*: that is, the best bottle of Haut-Brion on the list. But of course, as intrusive jour-nalists revealed when he became famous, it was not a *vin de famille* even in the imagination: he had reinvented himself after a disastrous first marriage and was no more Irish than I was.* I never understood why anyone thought it mattered; he was himself one of his best fictional inventions, closely modelled (at least, I think it was that way round) on the Stephen Maturin of his books. I thought he should be allowed to choose privacy, if he wanted it, although when Trinity College Dublin awarded him an honorary degree, celebrating an Irish inheritance that was entirely fictitious, it all became rather complicated.

He was a writer with a range far beyond the books that made his name and his fortune: a master short-story writer, a good biographer, and the author of an outstanding early novel, *Testimonies*. As I found later in the case of my patron and employer Victor, Lord Rothschild, it was sometimes difficult to discern where the truth stopped and started. Patrick said he had been helped by Caroline's great-great-uncle M. R. James in relation to scholarly work on bestiaries – all lost in the Blitz. But who knows? And who, really, cares?

At dinner at Palace Gardens Terrace late one evening, I was trying to keep my brother-in-law Duke Hussey, by then chairman of the BBC, awake (Patrick was a night person) with rather loud conversation. 'Did you know that Patrick wrote what the Spanish say is the best biography of Picasso?' I bellowed. At the other end of the table, Patrick stage-whispered to Caroline, 'Now, I think your husband is a very offensive fellow. Why does he say that only the Spanish say it is the best biography of Picasso?'

I introduced him to Douglas Hurd in the House of Commons dining room – one novelist to another. Douglas was in his pomp at the time – foreign secretary and recently a strong candidate for leadership of his party. They talked amicably for several minutes. 'Who was your charming

---

* Mary's background was similarly colourful. Before meeting Patrick, she had been married to a Russian: 'A very bad idea, my dear,' she informed Caroline. She also told us that when Patrick was working as Simone de Beauvoir's translator, the two of them visited the great feminist. Patrick and de Beauvoir were given whisky; the maid offered Mary and Simone's female lover fruit cordial.

friend?' asked Patrick, as Douglas left. At the height of the Scott Inquiry, I wrote to apologise for championing his books in public and thereby connecting him to someone whom the press had decided was a villain. I suspect he had no idea what I was talking about. Patrick had created his own world, and he lived in it.

Aubrey and Maturin in the double community of their fictional ships in Nelson's navy; Emma and Mr Knightley in an imaginary Regency England; Chewton and my childhood. These offered – and still offer – the dream of security. J. W. Roberts and logic, or the free individualism, destructive of tradition, that the 1960s celebrated, offer liberty and self-sufficiency. It is difficult to choose. It was difficult for the hippies, too: Tolkien was *their* author, creator of another imaginary universe, rule-bound and traditional in its own terms. The Professor of Anglo-Saxon Studies at Oxford University *and* the hero of the counter-culture is a pleasing juxtaposition. Perhaps my – and the hippies' – cultural schizophrenia is quite common. Perhaps it is universal. Gilbert Murray, the great classicist of my grandparents' generation, invented the concept of the 'inherited conglomerate'. He suggested that our ideas and beliefs are never consistent: we inherit all sorts of contradictory systems of thought and use different aspects for different purposes; like the Japanese, who are sometimes Buddhist, sometimes Shinto. On the one hand, I loved the old culture; on the other, I celebrated the radicalism of those who set out to destroy it.

The conflict started with my very first class at Eton, taught by a charming, old-fashioned master called D. C. Wilkinson. He read to us from Richard Jefferies's *Bevis*, with which I instantly identified, and told us that the internal combustion engine was an invention of the devil, destroying his beloved countryside. But how could that be? Moss and Fangio were my heroes!

Among my teachers, I admired both Martineau and Roberts. I read the mystical Christian poetry and novels of Charles Williams: *Taliessin through Logres* and *War in Heaven*. I still think

I saw a Druid light
Burn through the Druid hill,
As the hooves of King Arthur's horse
Rounded me in the night.
I heard the running of flame
Faster than fast through Logres
Into the camp by the hazels
I Taliessin came.

is pretty good. But I also cannot see what is wrong with Robinson's critique of the Sermon on the Mount: we are advised to be good only because we will get a handsome reward, or avoid punishment: ('This is prudence, not morality' he writes) nor with Medawar's attack on Teilhard: 'an active willingness to be deceived.' Then again, I mourn the last flickers of the old Church of England, providing a spiritual centre in every village, its churches, as Simon Jenkins rightly says, collectively the true Museum of England, but once much more than that. No more Kenneth Latter with his watch-chain and a full Chewton Church (and Methodist Chapel, on Chapel Hill); these days we have a faithful, unpaid, vicar in a mean little house (which the authorities want to sell) working diligently to keep something alive.

You are here to kneel,
Where prayer has been valid.

I shall mourn it when it is gone.

And I do not want the stories my mother told to be untrue. Like the one about the old nurse who tucked her up in bed when she stayed in a great house as a little girl. When she asked after her next morning, there was a shifty silence before she was told she had met the family's benign ghost. Or her tale of the Popham curse, a version of the story in Scott's *Rokeby* about how the Pophams obtained Littlecote House, but better.

She told of the knock on the old wise woman's door at night; the carriage with its armorials covered taking her to a dimly seen but splendid house; the baby boy she helps to deliver; the young aristocrat taking the baby and throwing it on the fire. The witch–midwife cuts a small piece of fabric from the bed hangings, determined to see justice done. But the magistrate, Popham, is bribed by the young murderer's father. So she curses not the family of the murderer but that of the corrupt magistrate: its first-born sons will never live. The witch was surely right: there will always be murderers; but if judges can be corrupted, what hope do the people have?

Therefore, I sometimes stood, and stand, with Bertrand Russell's attack on William James's plea for the Will to Believe ('What we need is the Will to Doubt,' countered Russell). But climbing alone on the slopes above Delphi in the midday heat I still felt as close to the great god Pan as ever I had to Poseidon in my childhood bed. Nonetheless, it was a time of fracturing belief, and of the loss of shared culture. A teenager exploding with intellectual curiosity and energy, well taught by masters who took diametrically opposed views on everything, did well at Eton in the early 1960s.

In retrospect, I can see that it was also around this time that I started to exhibit the political schizophrenia that was about to afflict the Conservative Party, and from which it has not yet recovered. One evening, my house master, John Marsden, knowing of and abetting my political ambitions, came into my room with a slim volume of poetry. 'I knew this chap in the war in the desert,' he said. 'Strange fellow. Used to read his Bible every night to perfect his English style. Professor at twenty-six. Wrote poetry.' So I came across J. Enoch Powell's Housmanesque poems, and swiftly added him to the pantheon alongside Macleod and Hailsham.

For the first – but not the last – time, I felt the attraction of sharp, paradoxical, logical argument that seems to turn common sense upside down. We get richer if the government makes no effort to interfere with the economy. The poor do better without welfare. The nuclear bomb is pointless. If the Second World War was truly our finest hour, then it was best for a patriot to have died in it. Nationhood is not a matter of allegiance to a common sovereign, but of the shared memories and blood of a thousand years.

All of this was not very Macmillanite.

CHAPTER FOUR

Oxford

I left Eton in 1965, not before time. Harold Wilson was in power. Drugs, sex and rock 'n' roll; hippies and swinging London. C. P. Snow's engineer heroes were old hat. The first chord of 'A Hard Day's Night' seemed to announce a new world. We didn't want to be F. E. Smith any more. We wanted to be Paul McCartney; or, if you looked like me, Bob Dylan. The Cold War surrounded us; Vietnam divided the world. Economically, Japan and Germany, let alone America, had decisively overtaken Britain. When we had driven across poor shattered France in 1957 to watch Fangio's last race as champion at Monza – he was beaten in his 250F Maserati by Moss in a Vanwall – we had marvelled at oxen ploughing and at the empty roads as we swept by in our Ford Zephyr. Now France was at least as prosperous as we were. Britain was, everyone said, in decline.

In 1963, *Encounter* magazine published an issue called 'Suicide of a Nation?' that was full of rather dull essays arguing that it was all the fault of the public schools (Elizabeth Young); the reds under the bed (Aidan Crawley); the House of Lords (Lord Altrincham); or insufficient public spending on his university research programmes (John Vaizey – who took a different view from Lady Young and sent his son to Eton). Malcolm

Muggeridge – in typical Old Testament style – blamed it on striptease and *Waiting for Godot*; Henry Fairlie on the amount of time people wasted writing articles like these in *Encounter*. But at least everyone agreed that everything was truly dreadful. Those years were genuinely a period of cultural shift, like the late 1980s and early 1990s. Not all the 'progress' we celebrated was as good as it seemed at the time – as the clever wordsmiths triumphed over the scientists and engineers – but the turmoil was undeniably exciting, the skirts were very short, and no one doubted that there were great issues for young Disraelis to confront: the defeat of totalitarian Marxism abroad and its fellow travellers at home; and the reversal of Britain's universally accepted decline.

Since testosterone drives more than ambition, as soon as I left Eton there came the first challenge to my previously single-minded pursuit of political glory, and also the best antidote to my old school's charm, which can be highly seductive. I fell in love. Alexandra 'Whizz' Dorrien-Smith – tall, with long blonde hair and legs that went on for ever – was the perfect sixties girlfriend. If Françoise Hardy herself was not immediately available, Whizz was just as good. And she came complete with another beautiful island: Tresco, in the Isles of Scilly; as good as Shona, as good as Colonsay, as good as Delos or Zakynthos. As an added bonus, the abbey and its famous gardens were usually full of Whizz's equally beautiful sisters. My brother was already in love with the eldest, while my cousin, Charles O'Hagan, fell for their mother – the source of all their spectacular looks – which complicated matters.

First love followed its usual course of despair, joy and ultimate disaster. I still have a whole suitcase of Whizz's letters, as we exchanged them every day and sometimes twice a day. (The postal service between Oxford and Cranborne Chase Girls' School was significantly better in 1965 than it is today, and her beautiful italic script made the correspondence much more satisfying than email.) But even love did not really divert me from my path: if anything, the joy of feeling loved strengthened my determination because there was the added dream of laying prizes at my beloved's feet. Whizz was the first woman with whom I shared the whole secret story of my ambition. By accepting me and it, she thereby strengthened me in my chosen course. Someone else believed in me (or said she did). Pride reinforced fear of failure.

Oxford in the 1960s, like Eton, perhaps like England as a whole, witnessed the end of those habits that genuinely – not as a conscious act of revival or nostalgia – led straight back to pre-war and Edwardian days. We wore gowns to our lectures: long ones, if you were a scholar like me; short ones for commoners (gowns for noblemen had gone, sadly for some). Osbert Lancaster's illustrations for *Zuleika Dobson*, the originals of which continue to hang in the Randolph Hotel, still had some echoes. Ornate college barges were used by oarsmen as changing rooms and clubhouses, including by the Corpus Christi crew for which I rowed. There was a Beefsteak Club, with premises above a bank near Carfax, where London club food was served to public schoolboys in a room like those in St James's. Female undergraduates were restricted to the women-only colleges. To call yourself a 'student', rather than an undergraduate, was a consciously left-wing gesture. There was much sneering in the twelve-hundred-strong Oxford University Conservative Association (of which I became president) when the national body (in which we grandly played little part) changed its name (rather understandably, in light of its acronym) from the Federation of University Conservative and Unionist Associations to the more innocent Federation of Conservative Students. Dons wore tweed jackets and smoked fragrant pipes during tutorials. College gates were locked at ten o'clock, forcing us to climb in perilously over the spikes.

But it was the sixties. The music, the drugs, the sex, the Vietnam War defined our world. Public schoolboys kept a low profile or disguised themselves. I chose Corpus Christi not only because it had been Berlin's undergraduate college and was full of classicists, but because I thought it contained no other Old Etonians. However, just as Randolph Churchill had forgotten Goschen, I forgot Cornes major. I suppose the Bullingdon existed; but if it did, it smashed its glass in private. The self-conscious public decadence of the Piers Gaveston Society was two decades away. I preferred to go with Karen Clare, my then girlfriend, on our very small motorbike to the first Dylan concert on the Isle of Wight in 1969, where the great man played in homage to the fact that Tennyson had lived at Faringford.

Karen was from Cheshire, and had a northern accent. I was aware of my parents' class-based anxiety about her, as was she. She was funny, clever, original, utterly free of neuroses and self-doubt, and brave. That I managed to go through Oxford without becoming contaminated by the self-conscious attempts to live in a re-enactment of *Brideshead Revisited* – an affliction suffered by rather too many of my contemporaries – is largely down to her; as is the fact that I finally achieved the degree I wanted. If anything, she reinforced my faith in my own destiny, since she believed powerfully that you could be whatever you wanted to be. Of all the regrets in my life, the one that returns to me most often is that our relationship ended badly, thanks to me. We said goodbye in Brattleborough, Vermont, when I was at Harvard, after Oxford. She made me dance away our grief, and my guilt, in her bleak room, not to the Grateful Dead or her beloved Janis Joplin, but to Vivaldi. I have never seen her since.

To most of my grammar school friends, I must have seemed the archetypical old school insider. Always the seventh child running along behind, infinitely fearful of ridicule, I certainly did not share that view. However, as I looked at those confident grandees in Christ Church or New College, I did start to think: 'You are going to need me one day.' I never expected to become a grandee myself; I would be the outsider come to lead them, like Disraeli or Heath. You might ask how an Old Etonian son of an earl could ever consider himself an outsider. All I can say is that six older siblings can produce some remarkable results. And horror of ridicule could still hurt. Robert Cecil, now Lord Salisbury, invited me to his twenty-first birthday party at Hatfield. As I arrived at the top of an immense staircase to shake hands with his grandfather, R. A. Butler's nemesis, 'Bobbety' Lord Salisbury, I realised that I was the only guest wearing a black, rather than a white, tie.

Other grand parties were more in tune with the times. The Conservatives held a ball in a tent at Blenheim. I took as my girl a spectacularly beautiful friend who designed and made her own clothes, largely, it seemed, out of silver tin-foil. She became rather the worse for wear and vomited into a powerful blow-heater. All over the great tent, people with puzzled expressions flicked particles off their lapels or shoulders. Eventually – and she was a tallish girl – I picked her up in a fireman's lift and carried her to a place of safety. Unfortunately, this caused her tin-foil construction to disintegrate. When I returned to check on her, after searching the dance floor for the remains of her outfit, I found that she had disappeared too. I did not see her again that night. Life was not all politics.

My Oxford, in spite of the Beefsteak Club, was the Oxford that Henry Fairlie had predicted years before in an article for the *Spectator*. Around 1958, he had written that we had not seen anything yet in terms of education. Now that the first full generation of children of the Butler Education Act of 1944 was coming through, we would see what Britain could produce. The public schools had better watch out. And he was right.

Oxford, when I went up in 1965, had a wider social mix than was achieved for the next forty years or so. Even now the statistics are tricky: that state schools in middle-class areas do well today does little for the bright child from a poor area; and less, I believe, than did the best grammar and direct grant schools, which were at least as good academically as the independent schools, and in many cases better. In 1965 their products felt that the world was going their way. They, not the public school boys, set the tone of the university. My friends and competitors were as likely – possibly more likely – to come from the great Lancashire and Midlands grammar schools as from my old school or Winchester or Harrow. They were confident, clever and at least as widely cultured as we were. Wilson's

Cabinet was a mixture of them and of Wykehamists; Heath's of both plus Eton. A surge of new, meritocratic ability refreshed Britain, even if a disconcerting number of the new television iconoclasts at whom we laughed turned out to have attended Shrewsbury or Charterhouse.

Nonetheless, old England still existed, deferential and attuned to all the nuances of class. One New Year's Eve – it must have been 1966 or 1967 – I quarrelled with Whizz and walked self-pityingly from her house in Ryecroft Street, Fulham, aimlessly wending my way through the celebratory chaos. After a while, even in the midst of my romantic gloom, I realised that I needed somewhere to stay. My sister Liz and my brother must have been out of town, or I was too nervous to wake them. So instead I walked to the Great Western Hotel at Paddington, a scruffy youth with no money, no identifying documents, no luggage, hair like Bob Dylan, but an upper-class accent. I explained that there had once been a locomotive on the Great Western line – 5057 *The Earl Waldegrave* – named after my family. If they let me stay the night, I would pay when they sent me the bill. So I found a bed for the night.

Such ancient attitudes had a less pleasant side, too. Late one night in Oxford, I pulled over in my Hillman Imp to let Karen, dressed in her usual not very formal way, jump out and get some cigarettes from a vending machine. A policeman appeared, shoved her against a wall, and began to search her, with unnecessary force and a string of expletives not in the vocabulary of *The Eagle*'s PC 49. I got out of the car and asked in my best upper-class accent if I could be of any assistance. The policeman faded into the night.

Oxford offered more prizes, and again I won some of them, including the Union presidency. (Whizz's presence at my presidential debate added sex appeal to my campaign, an effect I was not above calculating.) But again I knew the great days were over. Most of the serious left had withdrawn from the Union, accepting sixties dogma that it was elitist, although a few remained, and Tariq Ali and Paul Foot still returned to debate. Christopher Hitchens hung about in the bar. A fully signed-up

Conservative was still quite rare as president; most espoused an uncontroversial liberalism, like Robert Jackson.

Nonetheless, the post retained some of its glamour and I wanted it passionately. After my election, the Queen came to listen to a rather staged debate: in case of Trotskyite trouble, I had filled the benches behind her with ultra-loyalist American Rhodes scholars. I need not have worried: everyone cheered her, and themselves.

In my time, the Union was run by three remarkable men: Mr Walters, the charming professional librarian, who kept the beautiful library in order; Mr Duck, a man of reactionary views and Edwardian manners, who ran the dining room and always ensured that South African sherry was served whenever fashionable left-wingers came to speak; and Leslie Crawte, the steward, the boss. All three somehow kept the place going in spite of the best efforts of ephemeral undergraduate officers like myself. At the end of my term, I asked Leslie Crawte what he thought I would become. He gave the wrong answer: 'School master?'

Robert Kennedy came, and we all fell for him. I remember, as does everyone of my generation, where I was when I heard of his elder brother's death. In my room at Eton, into which burst the weeping Irish boys' maid Flo, crying, 'They've killed him!' But I also remember where I was when I heard of Bobby's death: in bed with Karen in our room in the tower of the crumbling Folly on Folly Bridge, where we lived with my friends Charlie Maclean and Johnny Grimond, as well as a mysterious member of the Keynes family (whom we assumed was already a spy) and many cats. We were listening to John Peel, who broke into the music to make the announcement, then immediately took the programme into moving mourning.

I founded a Macmillan Society, which held one meeting. The only object was to get Harold Macmillan, by now in increasingly vigorous retirement, to dinner, and we succeeded. He told us he was old and tired and would need a taxi at nine o'clock. Its meter was still running at one in the morning, when the great man left, with only us youngsters exhausted.

I went to tea with Selwyn Lloyd, who lived just south of Oxford and was kind to young Conservatives. Macmillan had sacked him as chancellor in the Night of the Long Knives, along with my father. Jonathan Aitken was there. At the end of the garden a sweltering figure (it was a very hot day) laboured with a shovel in a hole that we were told was to be a swimming pool. This was Peter Walker, in early training to be environment secretary. Bomber Harris was also of the party, though not a convivial presence: he showed us how to exterminate greenfly with the smoke from a cigar.

I gained a second in Classical Moderations, the first part of the Literae Humaniores course, taken after five terms but as formidable an examination as finals in most other courses. This produced a gloomy sulk for weeks. No double first for me. I worked for finals with concentrated fury: six days a week, eight or ten hours a day, only Sundays off, for the best part of a year. The effort paid off, thanks in large part to Karen's selfless support, and so I got my first in Greats. I received a letter of congratulations from the chief examiner. He seemed to think I was a Wykehamist. Did this mean I had earned a 'congratulated first', like so many of the glittering prize-winners of the past? Or was the letter meant for someone else; someone who *was* a Wykehamist? President of the Union, president of the Conservative Association, a first in Greats (perhaps even a congratulated first). The rosettes were duly pinned up; but not everyone was impressed. A wise friend, Caroline Younger, shocked me deeply by arguing that a good novelist or poet was more influential than any cabinet minister. When I asked her to lunch at the Union, she replied, 'Union of what?'

Throughout my time at Oxford, I was conscious of something coming to an end. For some decades, Oxford 'ordinary language' philosophy, following the 'linguistic turn' made by Frege and the later Wittgenstein of *Philosophical Investigations*, had dominated the English-speaking world. Also still at the university were the successors of the pre-war Vienna Circle of Rudolf Carnap: Old Etonian Freddie Ayer's lectures kept logical positivism alive; but it was the characteristically English voices of J. L. Austin and Gilbert Ryle that had made Oxford the centre of the philosophical world. Their roots lay deeply in Plato – the episte-mological Plato of the *Thaeatetus*, *Sophist* and *Meno* – and above all in Aristotle. Greats had rooted many of the best Oxford philosophers in the *Nichomachean Ethics* and in Aristotle's logic. In the background there was the great empiricist trio of Locke, Berkeley and, above all, Hume. P. F. Strawson (whom I had first heard at Eton) brought us Kant. No one thought what the French were doing was philosophy at all; as for Hegel and Marx, look where that ended! We were cautious, careful analysts and empiricists. Karl Popper, though bad mannered and not at all 'Oxford', was right. But Berlin was my man.

I had known Isaiah a little all my life, as a legend at least. My father met him when he was posted with the British Army Liaison mission to Washington during the war, and they became friends. (This posting, which won him a high American decoration, was another source of guilt for my father. Apart from an early episode in the anti-aircraft defences of Bristol – armed, he claimed, with a Bofors gun whose instructions were in Swedish – he had hardly heard a shot fired in anger.) As a result of this Washington connection, I was gathered up by Isaiah and his wife Aline, like so many undergraduates, and lunched in their beautiful house at Headington. When Karen and I hosted a party in the garden of Corpus after finals he came. 'What did you learn? What did you learn?' he asked. I muttered something about telling a good argument from a bad one. 'That's it! That's it! Spot the bunk! Spot the bunk!'

Later, I joined the two lobes of my brain together in a dinner party in the early 1980s by asking Isaiah to dinner to meet Enoch Powell for the first time. Both men of infinite courtesy in their own styles, they searched for a topic on which to agree. They finally settled on scepticism about Max Beloff.

'And now, the most extraordinary thing,' said Isaiah, 'Max has announced he has become a Tory!'

'You cannot *become* a Tory,' said Enoch. 'You are *born* a Tory. Except for the occasional socialist, who joins us to prove that the world is round.'

My own tutor, J. O. Urmson, encapsulated Oxford philosophy for me. His book on the *Nichomachean Ethics* is still the best introduction: forty years later, my youngest daughter Harriet, reading Mods and Greats, as I did, was given it by her tutor. His careful, analytical approach to language and its usages – derived from his own mentor J. L. Austin and the later Wittgenstein, but above all from Aristotle himself – represented the best of how a generation of Oxford students had been taught. He, R. M. Hare and Gilbert Ryle, with *The Concept of Mind* and *Dilemmas*, were my mentors. The Homeric Second World War glamour hung around many of these dons, as it did around others of the generation before mine. Urmson had won an immediate MC in the desert war, though we ignorant youngsters did not know it then. His famous article discussing the circumstances in which we may or may not criticise those who do not do things upon which we cannot, in ordinary morality, insist was born from experience that was unimaginable to us.

I took away ideas that my generation shared, if they did not revolt against them. They still seem good ideas to me. I still find satisfying the argument that words have meaning if they work in use; and that many confusions derive from what Ryle called 'category mistakes'. 'But where is the university?' asks the tourist, having been shown all the colleges and other buildings, not understanding that the university is a different category of thing from the colleges that constitute it. Ryle thought that confusions about the difference between mind and body were of the same sort. From others, I learned and still believe that there are no complete, overarching theories, even in mathematics, let alone anywhere else. I have my heavily annotated copy of Gödel's *Incompleteness Theorems* somewhere, which I may or may not have understood. It has an introduction by the philosopher–mathematician Richard Braithwaite, who was married to yet another high-achieving Lyttelton, the philosopher Margaret Masterman, a pupil of Wittgenstein.

Philosophy was about sorting out muddled thinking, often derived from the misuse of language, like the problems in *Dilemmas*. How we could think was limited by how we lived in space and time, as I thought Kant said. Noam Chomsky appeared to be revitalising Kant by demonstrating hard-wired grammar in our make-up.* Moral choices were always difficult: a good Oxford philosopher could always produce a thought experiment which showed that there might be – *pace* Kant, in his non-epistemological mode – occasions when it was right to break any rule, even truth-telling, even promises. 'Where is the axe?' asks the homicidal maniac. Answering honestly would be patently absurd.

Isaiah, by then no longer regarded by his peers as a serious contributor to philosophy, was, nonetheless, the embodiment of this pluralism in action. No simple hierarchy of rights, duties or moral rules could be made. Nothing was easy: we must simply try our best. His famous essay on Tolstoy, 'The Hedgehog and the Fox', divided human psychologies into two: those who sought overarching systems; and those who perceived separate experiences as ends in themselves. Isaiah suggested that all the greatest man-made evils of the world were driven by hedgehogs who tried to force us into ideological conformity. Plato (in his political mode), Hegel, Nietzsche and Marx stood on one side: Herodotus, Aristotle and Shakespeare were on the other, assisted by me. British empiricism, armed with its new technical weapons forged by analytical philosophy, was the best defence against the catastrophes of all-embracing systems in action, which spat people out if they did not fit. Fascism had done that; Communism was doing it now.

Moderate British Conservatism, with the works of Hume and Burke and Adam Smith the nearest it had to sacred texts, was the political equivalent of this philosophical approach: rooted in slow-moving institutions, plural, unromantic, careful, and quite different from American, French or German conservatism. Indeed, we Berlinite, Oakeshottianan,

---

* His fame, however, came from his opposition to American policy in Vietnam. When he came to lecture in Oxford the biggest lecture hall in the Schools building could not accommodate all his admirers: there were overflows and relays of loudspeakers. However, he lectured on epistemology: by the third lecture we were all back in one of the normal small rooms.

Popperian liberal Conservatives found few allies anywhere. When William F. Buckley, Jr turned up in Oxford and gave me space in his right-wing (in American terms) magazine *National Review*, I found my co-contributors decidedly odd. What was all this stuff about government being the enemy? Ayn Rand was not only a terrible writer, but ridiculous. Russell Kirk, with his *Conservative Mind* celebrating Edmund Burke and ridiculing libertarianism, was more like it. But the point of Conservatives should be that they do not think too much at all. Finding Kirk's book in my room, my Liberal friend Johnny Grimond said he thought that the whole point of Conservatives was that they did not *have* a mind.

For us Macmillanite young Oxford Tories, the state, successor to the just king, was the protector of the weak and the moderator of rampant capitalism. Those who came to be described in America as neo-cons were not our allies. This remains as much of a problem for David Cameron today as it was for English Burkean Conservatives in 1966: we have no natural allies. Certainly not in America. Nor, as I would discover later, after a few drinks in Brussels, could one avoid discomfort as German, or French, or Italian ministerial colleagues of the right relaxed into blood and forests, or Catholicism, or other dark, non-English doctrines.

People sometimes ask: 'Did you have something specific you wanted to achieve when you went into politics? Some great cause? The abolition of poverty? World peace?' The answer is 'No.'* I thought that what one had to do (and I thought it a very big thing) was to deal with the problems one faced through the application of as much intelligence as one could muster, guided by ordinary morality, just as in non-political life. Isaiah had taught me that there was no special political morality or science of statecraft. I still believe he was right.

---

* On one occasion this question of original motivation came up on Radio 4's *Any Questions*. The questioner asked the panel if they had achieved their childhood ambitions. 'No,' said the others. They still had world poverty to beat, and so on. I answered 'no' too: I was still not Stirling Moss. This frivolous answer won no applause from the audience, but it did get me a free day at the Castle Combe Motor Racing School, which was much better.

'Springtime at Chewton' by Tom van Oss. My parents, the first two of five daughters, and Rollo the schnauzer in pre-war grandeur at The Priory.

The Priory in its heyday. Its post-War ruins represented an abandoned past.

Magical Shona: Margot Howard de Walden with two of her tribes: Waldegraves (Jamie, Anne, Liz immediately behind her; Sue in front, me crossed-legged to her right) and Amorys.

The heavy horse drags timber down to the puffer.

John the boatman played the pipes on the last evening, and towed dinghies full of children during the day.

Sister Jinny giving instructions, my brother providing back-up, me in the war surplus bomb-loader.

Typing my newspaper. Bevan found no favour.

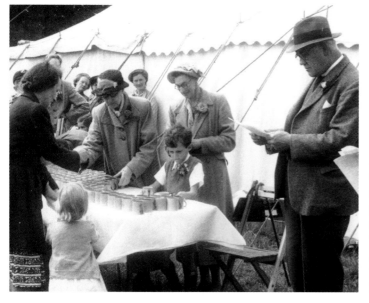

A world we have lost. Coronation mugs for the villagers. My grandmother to my right, beloved governess Val behind her, and Aunt Re behind me. The Rev. Kenneth Latter reads out the list.

My mother and sister Sue hold Sally's (*left*) two boys with Seward Heal and Reg Middle, gardeners, to whom I delivered socks at Christmas.

Mrs Emmett ('Mimi'), the cook, peers out of her scullery.

The war not far away: me with my B-24 Liberator.

Kenya Police uniform, with fine aiguillette. My mother is wearing home grown orchids.

Steering the *Curlew*.

Commanding my soldiers, perhaps to *Tannhäuser*.

(*left*) My brother the Coronation page, with sword and uniform.

(*above*) At Champéry. Struggling to keep up as usual.

(*above*) The AC Ace-Bristol's engine made a fine noise at 3000rpm …

(*right*) A worthy hero.

Ford V8 and the caravan which followed me to prep school, where my mother cooked us sausages on the playing fields.

My mother's worst day, she said, when her seventh child left for school. Jumbo the spaniel is cheerful, at least.

That era of the dominance of Oxford philosophy was ending as I arrived. One of those who was helping to move the focus across the Atlantic was a new and brilliant systematiser, a benevolent hedgehog in the mould of John Stuart Mill, namely John Rawls. Many thought he had brought us back to a more realistic and mainstream moral philosophy that actually engaged with the world: Oxford might quibble about words, but in Harvard they were showing us practical ways to make the world better through a system which, when you turned the handle for results, churned out answers that fitted the opinions of decent, liberal Americans perfectly. I do not believe even Rawls's benevolent system – which makes justice central and defines it as what sensible people would agree upon if their viewpoints were equally fair – quite works, any more than utilitarianism works, for the reasons Amartya Sen explains in *The Idea of Justice*. The problem, as Sen illustrates, is that reasonable people can have different ideas as to what constitutes 'fairness', so imagining an 'original position' in which people use the concept of fairness to design just institutions does not really help: who is to judge between competing concepts of fairness? Consequently, that Oxford, Berlinite mindset has stayed with me always, as it has with many others of my generation: never trust intellectual grand theories. In my undergraduate days, this protected me from the absurdities of the far left, with their Che Guevara T-shirts, and from the equal absurdities of the reactionary right. I caused some minor trouble for the national Conservative Party by supporting those who wanted military action against Ian Smith's unilateral declaration of independence in Southern Rhodesia: he and his regime were illegal rebels and should be suppressed, I thought. But I could not share the left's passionate opposition to the Americans in Vietnam, principally because it seemed that if you opposed the Americans, you had to support their enemies – the North Vietnamese Communists and their backers in the Soviet Union and China – regimes that were incomparably worse than Lyndon Johnson's American administration.

This careful English empiricism has a weakness, however: it does not make the heart sing. True, it does not launch aggressive wars, but sometimes wars fought with aggression are needed. It will fight back if attacked, most determinedly, and will surely outlast the ideologies that despise it. Jim Urmson had won his MC, after all. But it is not romantic. Moreover, it is difficult to explain. Select committees and the press, as I later learned to my cost, like simple answers: 'Is it right for ministers to lie?' 'Well, that depends' does not go down very well as an answer. And it sounds terribly arrogant to say that one's principal reason for entering politics is to keep out people who you fear are morally worse than you are.

Nonetheless, it is the truth: nothing is more important than to dissect and understand the moral banality of tyrannical doctrines. Putting Lenin back on the first train out of the Finland Station and supporting the boring, moderate democrats instead would have saved millions of lives; ridiculing Germanic mysticism about blood and forests would have saved even more. I suppose, if I had been educated in another time and another place, given my tendency for hero-worship and my personal ambition, I might well have been drawn to dangerous doctrines. The careful empiricism I was taught at Eton and at Oxford prevented any danger of that. 'Spot the bunk!' is still the best educational slogan of all, even if the bunk is dressed in the glorious rhetoric of Thomas Carlyle or set to the sublime music of Wagner.

CHAPTER FIVE

Harvard and the World

In my 1967 long vacation from Oxford I had travelled alone round the United States and a good deal of Canada on a $99 Greyhound Bus ticket. There is virtually no small town in America I have not visited. Intensely lonely, I consoled myself as I played the pinball machines with the only trace of home I could find: Procul Harum's 'Whiter Shade of Pale' on the jukeboxes. We New Elizabethans had been told that we were to be Greece to America's Rome; so, if my princely education were to be complete, I thought I had better go to Rome and learn about the imperial power.

A couple of years later, I won a Kennedy scholarship to Harvard (Isaiah Berlin was among the selectors) and soon I was on board the SS *United States*.* We steamed at full speed through the edge of a hurricane, past less powerful vessels hull down into the wind. Rainbow-coloured spray broke over us, and puffins flew in the shelter of the bow wave. As I could take a big trunk, I thought I might as well pack my dinner jacket. It turned out that I needed it more at Harvard than I had in Oxford. The rich and upper-class Harvard College, the undergraduate university, set

---

* A young William Jefferson Clinton had taken the same ship the year before, sailing in the other direction, to Oxford, on a Rhodes scholarship.

the tone; but the graduate school was already an extraordinary gathering of international scholarship.

Harvard in 1969, like the Oxford I had just left, was in a state of flux. Both universities had restored the *status quo ante bellum* in 1945. Oxford, with its gowns and its single-sex college gates closing at 10 p.m., and Harvard, with its men-only houses and gentlemen's clubs, had looked much the same in the early 1960s as they had looked in the 1930s. But both were now changing fast. Radcliffe was about to merge with Harvard College; the old Littauer Center was giving birth to the Kennedy School of Government. Not too long before, Harvard had operated a quota for Jews, which explains why Richard Feynman went to MIT. The Fly Club, the Hasty Pudding Club, the Lampoon and the rest continued to dine in the old-fashioned way. At one of these – dinner-jacketed, of course – I sat across the table from Norman Mailer as he rose to speak, swayed and promptly disappeared under the table. It was the first time I had seen this feat literally accomplished. I was given membership of the Senior Common Room at Lowell House, where the distinguished classicist Zeph Stewart was master and Rustam Kothavala, famous later as a proponent of gay rights as well as a leading geologist, was senior tutor.

My Oxford tutors had disdained political philosophy as a subject halfway to journalism. Even the 'Republic' option in Greats was seen as rather the vulgar end of Plato. That Plato, as Richard Crossman had pointed out in *Plato Today* in 1937, had been one of the godfathers of totalitarianism. It is true that Jim Urmson had once set me an essay on Hobbes – and told me to go and look at the picture of the great man in the Senior Common Room at Hertford College so I might understand how gloomy he was – but I think he did that as a bow to my known political hobby, and perhaps to steer me away from Hegelian nonsense. The theory of social contract, though second-order stuff, generated some philosophical interest; and Rawls, a respectable man, had resuscitated a form of it, thought Oxford. But that was all.

Harvard offered a quite different perspective and a seriousness of approach to political philosophy and the teaching of practical politics – which it coolly called 'government' – not seen in Oxford for many years. Perhaps the imperial power of the day always takes the philosophy of government seriously, as Britain had done in the era of Mill and Bagehot. But once the empire has gone, epistemology becomes the thing again, along with pure logic.

At any rate, at Harvard at the end of the sixties, I found in Samuel H. Beer someone who taught and wrote more incisively about modern Britain than any British don. In *British Politics in the Collectivist Age*, he expounded the theory that a patriotic trade union movement and a ruling class had forged a more or less explicit contract that promised the creation of the post-war welfare state in exchange for a united effort to win the war. This seemed the academic embodiment of what I believed I had seen in action on a small scale in the Chewton of my childhood on my father's estate: a new social contract which settled a stable, if hierarchical society on the basis of reciprocal obligations of a rational kind.

Other aspects of political philosophy had not troubled my Oxford education. So I learned a little Hegel and Marx, and – more interestingly to me – Machiavelli, which gave me the opportunity to attach myself to Harvey Mansfield Jr and to read Leo Strauss. I sat in classes for undergraduates learning economics, Ec 101, with Paul Samuelson as the textbook and Graham Allison's wife Elisabeth teaching us, holding our attention by her clarity of exposition and a very short skirt.

Other intense experiences were offered by America. I was lucky enough to end up living *en famille* with the world's outstanding scholar of Byzantine art and history, Ernst Kitzinger, and his wife Susan. They lived in a beautiful old colonial house, 7 Waterhouse Street, on Cambridge Common, with their beloved wire-haired dachshund Titus (named after Titus Groan in *Gormenghast*). Through the house flowed a huge tide of intellectuals of the first rank partly from that diaspora of genius gifted to the civilised world, like Ernst himself, by Hitler's persecution, some of whom had found prosperous homes in Harvard. Carl Friedrich and Karl

Deutsch, among many others, names on major books outside my English tradition, were friends of the Kitzingers. Lionel Trilling and his formidable wife Diana were often in the house; he was in Harvard as Professor of Poetry, delivering the lectures that became his powerful book, *Sincerity and Authenticity*. I found parallels between his thesis of the kind of cultural unity needed for the creation and reception of the great novel and my ideas about what was needed for a healthy society in politics. Perhaps what he called 'the singleness of mind' – the lack of a gap between the moral and social outlook of Austen's heroines and the idealised country-house society in which they lived – might be necessary not only for the production of *Mansfield Park* but for any decent civil society. This idea remained with me.

Some things at Harvard grated, however: the cult of the academic personality, in particular. Famous professors were surrounded by adoring acolytes. I rejoiced when J. K. Galbraith, then at the height of fashion, encountered Richard Crossman, the Wykehamist Labour minister, across a hall packed with Galbraith worshippers. The great man's lecture tackled the need for youth in government, which naturally went down well. Crossman, who was in Harvard giving the lectures that became his excellent little book *Cabinet Government*, sat with me at the back. He found the saccharine atmosphere unpalatable, and intervened to explain that the Nazis had won their first elections in the universities, and gave a short and brilliant account of disasters loosed upon the world by young leaders through the course of history. The sharp intakes of breath from the worshippers made me proud to be a troublesome Brit.

Asked to dinner by a grand Wasp hostess in Boston, she gave me a warning: 'Will you mind? There will be Jews present.' America's class system was, and is, no less complex than Britain's. In Boston, the Wasps were on top still; followed by the Irish; then the Italians; then the blacks. The British often do not understand who is who. Old Wilmarth Sheldon 'Lefty' Lewis, the Walpole collector, was hospitable to me at his fine old colonial home in Farmington, Connecticut, as well he might have been, given that he had persuaded my father to surrender much more of our family's Walpoliana than he should have done to the Farmington collection.* Lefty, whose wife was an Auchincloss and therefore related to Jackie Kennedy, had a set-piece story that he would recount after dinner about Jackie's wedding breakfast with JFK. It centred on the horrified reaction of the upper-class bride's family to the cigar-chomping, Irish politicos who were now their in-laws – though the Kennedys were often mistakenly assumed by the British to be socially grand. Taken by our family friends Don and Beth Straus to see Ethel Merman in *Hello, Dolly!* in New York, there could be no doubt however that Beth, and her friend Nancy Rockefeller, were the local equivalents of the ladies of the Cavendish or Mowbray families at home.

Outside on the streets, a more immediate play was being performed before us. The bombing of Cambodia and the National Guard's shooting of demonstrating students at Kent State University took the demonstration of opposition to the Vietnam War away from the pressure groups and politically active and moved the huge majority of the student body to take to the streets. Violent, balletic street warfare between visored, black-clad cops with their identifying numbers removed and similarly dressed opponents, such as the Weathermen and the Panthers, had already made Boston and Cambridge as familiar with the stink of tear gas as the Colonels' Athens of my teenage years had been. But after Cambodia the radical revolutionaries were swept aside by the genuine masses of the young, not only students, who met in their hundreds of thousands on Boston Common and elsewhere. It was impressive and moving – far more so than the dangerous games of the professional radicals, whose politics were as extreme as their self-publicising tactics were self-indulgent. A good many of the latter eventually ended up as Reaganite right-wingers.

One small incident – routine to many students in America at the time – taught me a valuable lesson: never be too sentimental about the forces

---

* My mother wrote of this episode in an obituary of Lewis in *The Book Collector*. As she says, Lewis's behaviour was not far short of that of a bandit.

of law and order. Caught in the wrong place in Cambridge as the cops arrived to chase the Weathermen – and indulge in a little class warfare on the side against the college boys – I was beaten up, left bloodied and briefly unconscious, before being rescued by my English girlfriend and fellow Kennedy Scholar Jane Bennett (subsequently a distinguished civil servant, appropriately in the Ministry of Defence). Full of English right-eous indignation, I was astonished to find my American liberal friends unimpressed by my heroism. American cops were not like your Dixon of Dock Green; if I put myself in a position where they might run over me, that was my fault.

Perthaps it would be a good thing for all aspirant politicians of the right or centre to find themselves on the wrong end of a police truncheon once at least, and learn how a policeman can hit you in places which hurt without leaving a mark. Sentimentality about how the ultimate instru-ments of state power – soldiers, police – act in reality is a dangerous thing. Being human, they are not always heroes and saints; if you launch a war, your side will not always behave like gentlemen. If you ask police to clear the streets, heads will get broken, sometimes just for fun. Those of us who grew up in the sixties were not just the generation of the pill and middle-class drug use. People far braver than I got knocked about in France and in Greece, while the most heroic of all stood up to the brutal regimes of South Africa and Eastern Europe.

Often, the aim of hard-left organisations like the Weathermen was to extract an incompetently violent reaction from a democratic government, and thereby radicalise ordinary people. As a tactic, it did not work very well; and it certainly failed in my case. It is hard to imagine now why intelligent people thought Che Guevara a hero, or Lenin, or Mao. But the bureaucracies of systematic terror these heroes helped to found were quite effective in persuading civilised societies to overreact, and damage them-selves in the process. In relation to Britain, by far the most skilful and cynical practitioners of this dark art were the leaders of the Provisional IRA; and by far their most successful provocation was the catastrophe of

Bloody Sunday, when murderous overreaction by the Parachute Regiment pushed a generation of Nationalists towards sympathy for the terrorists or even into their ranks. When that disaster happened, in January 1972, I sent an agonised minute to Lord Rothschild, for whom I was working in the Cabinet Office. It said that if this kind of action, which disgraced Britain, was necessary to maintain our policy in Northern Ireland, then that policy must change. I wonder if it is still on file somewhere.

The issue did not go away. In March 1988, by now a minister, I found myself in equally agonised conversation with Rothschild and his wife Tess as to whether the SAS were justified in killing an IRA active service unit in Gibraltar – the incident dubbed 'Death on the Rock' by the media. Both of them were very robust: having fought the Nazis, they were more realistic than I about the inevitability of horror in warfare. In that case, I came to believe they were right, and that the soldiers had acted correctly. When I became a minister in the Foreign and Commonwealth Office later that year, with responsibility for some of our counter-terrorist activity, I was asked to go to Hereford to talk to the soldiers involved. We sat down in the mess, my official FCO minder was dismissed, a couple of bottles of whisky appeared, and we talked all night. I was very impressed with the soldiers' intelligence and open-mindedness, as well as their clarity about the moral issues involved: they shared their critics' anxiety over whether they had done the right thing. These were no mindless thugs and I hope I reassured them: having agonised about the incident myself, I believed they were in the right.

Visits to Hereford could be alarming. Real bullets flew around the 'killing room' as the soldiers demonstrated their skills. On one occasion, I was driven on to a skid pan to simulate an attempted car-jacking by terrorists. Real bullets flew again. Beside me, equally pretending to be brave, was a rather pretty MI5 officer on a training course. As I emerged, proud of my (wholly artificial) cool, the sergeant said, 'You blew it, boss. Should have thrown yourself on the girl. To protect her.'

All of that was to come, though. My first tutorial in the reality of state-sponsored violence had been at the hands of that Boston cop in Harvard Yard in 1969. Of course, I learned more conventional lessons during my time in America, too. As far back as my Greyhound trip I had come to realise that Macmillan's idea of Britain as Greece to America's Rome was an illusion. In most parts of the country, people had barely heard of the United Kingdom, or indeed anywhere else outside their borders. An occasional item about the royal family, or a Beatles concert, did not really amount to intellectual suzerainty. Boston and Washington were different, of course, in terms of what and whom they knew; but the shock of discovering how small Britain was compared to the successor imperial power was acute. I began to wish that I had been born American, rather than British a hundred years ago. Like many others, I had a phase of imagining a true United States of Europe – not a mere trading arrangement, but a stage of decent size on which my genius might have room to flower. Its language would have to be English, of course.

I relished the freedom that sheer space gives you. In my Ford Mustang I could turn on to a great highway and drive continental distances. There is exhilaration in the sense of power which that freedom gives: you can just drive for a day and reinvent yourself in a new place. Even the weather is on a different scale. I loved the New England fall, of course, but also the winter, with real snow remaining for week after week. I would walk through it with Titus, proceeding like a small brown dolphin with his nose and tail rising and falling through the drifts on Cambridge Common. We would pass beggars – a phenomenon I had never witnessed in England. My education in the difference between a medium-sized and a continental power was completed when, at the end of our year in the States, Jane and I drove to San Francisco in the Mustang.

That June, Edward Heath astounded the pundits by winning the election against Harold Wilson. Unsurprisingly, this was hardly reported in Louisiana, where we were at the time, although there was a confusing mention of the election of Winston Churchill – Randolph's son – a name every American recognised. I was itching to return: surely Britain could not do without me much longer? But I had a round-the-world BOAC air ticket, with the first stop in Japan, and was equipped with an extraordinary range of letters of introduction, especially from uncles. (The list given me by Bernard Fergusson started with 'Lee Kuan Yew – Harry Lee – who got a first and runs Singapore with his wife, who got a double first.') Leaving Jane in San Francisco – after a night lying outside above the city under shower after shower of shooting stars – I set off alone westwards.

In due course, I found myself – a scruffy youth with hair as usual too long – staying in a cheap room in Rangoon, summoned to dinner with the ruthless dictator Ne Win and his French-speaking wife at their lakeside palace, a machine-gun-toting guard behind my chair facing out to the beautiful lake. This astonished and irritated a British Embassy more or less confined to its compound, whose somewhat supercilious young representative had contemptuously sent in my letter of introduction (from a Harley Street doctor on this occasion). It must have been galling to see me instantly swept away in a dictatorial black Mercedes.

I saw Pagan at a time when it was still swamped by jungle. I was the only Westerner there aside from an old British soldier who had arrived as we drove the Japanese out, fallen in love with the place, and somehow managed to stay for ever. I met several of Bernard Fergusson's Anglo-Burmese contacts, now persecuted and longing for news from the outside world. I ate, again the only European there, in the dilapidated Strand Palace Hotel, where nonetheless a card on the table advised gentlemen to dress for dinner. As far as I could see, I was the only person wearing trousers, let alone formal evening dress.

In Vietnam, I spent time with Harold Wilson's skilfully minimalist contribution to the war, a colonial policeman called Walter Pridgeon, who told me that his beat in the Mekong Delta changed hands at dusk: during the day, it was loyal to Saigon; after dark, to Hanoi. As we feasted on a huge hotpot containing the nameless parts of nameless creatures,

I boasted that I had a brother-in-law named John Dewar. To honour this connection, all present drank deeply of several bottles of the family product. Walter and I, led back to our Jeep emblazoned with the US 'hands of friendship' symbol, and much the worse for wear, drove straight into a ditch, out of which his comrades, only minutes from switching allegiance as dusk began to fall, uproariously and somewhat half-heartedly manhandled us.

I lunched in an old-style former French colonial club in Saigon, and succumbed to the sales pitch of a young man with a speedboat and water-skis. When I returned from the excursion, an old gentleman in a wicker chair announced, 'Last chap who did that never came back. Burst of machine-gun fire. *Finis.*' It was Graham Greene-land; Kurt Vonnegut-land; it was not the land described in their air-conditioned rooms by the keen young American CIA public relations people to whom other letters of introduction had exposed me.

In Malaysia, there had been savage intercommunal riots just before I arrived with my letter granting access to a kindly High Commissioner's Rolls-Royce. In idyllic, undeveloped Bali, I bicycled around paradise while in the distance black smoke rose from pyres on which the bodies of communists, slaughtered and dumped in mass graves the year before, were finally receiving proper cremations. Even in my innocence and ignorance, there was a sense of two empires – secretly for the most part, but openly in Vietnam – fighting a relentless war with one another. In Thailand, I was adopted by a beautiful Keren bar girl, whose American Air Force colonel was away bombing things. I met her family and fell in love with pre-modern, canal-crossed Bangkok, then still the Venice of Asia.

It seemed that most of the old British Empire had kept out of this semi-secret world war as I trundled up and down India on its still-magnificent railway system, learning to take with a pinch of salt the old gentlemen who would come up and say, 'Of course, it all ran much better when you chaps were in charge.' I knew enough to understand that such casual self-deprecation was born of thousands of years of cultural self-confidence that had seen many a transitory conqueror come and go, from Iskander onwards.

In Australia, I saw how culturally vibrant Sydney was becoming, but also spent wonderful days on horseback looking after sheep and cattle on the MacArthurs' beautiful, traditional station at Meningoort in western Victoria. In Nairobi, the Muthaiga Club seemed as permanent as the Selangor Club in Kuala Lumpur or the eponymous Port Dixon Club in which I had stayed in Malaya, though now with black club-men drinking pink gins and reading the *Financial Times*. There was Michael Blundell growing coffee and tea; Pam Scott with her Masai friends, and hyraxes in her thatched roof; and the Kenyan parliament's white Mr Speaker, Humphrey Slade, in his wig. At the time, it all seemed to have gone so right. How superior we British were. Had we not defeated our own South-East Asian insurgency in Malaya (with the help of my governess's brother, Alan)? These French and Americans with their messy wars had no idea.

Perhaps 1970 was one of the very last years when one could travel through the remnants of Britain's vast Australasian, Asian and African empire and see much of it little changed from when we surrendered it. The frail structures we had left behind persisted; it was as if the locals could not believe that in the course of a single generation we had utterly and completely left. Perhaps we were still controlling things from behind the scenes? Perhaps it had been better when we were undeniably in charge? America certainly seemed to be making a hash of succeeding us as the imperial power. Perhaps the American galleon itself might be well on its way to following ours into the sunset? Such a conclusion was sure to evoke a little *Schadenfreude*.

The conclusion was, of course, wrong, by at least half a century.

CHAPTER SIX

Heath and Rothschild

Edward Heath's premiership has almost been written out of history, at least by Conservatives. The winners write the first draft of history, and when Margaret Thatcher defeated Heath for the leadership of the Conservative Party in 1975 a new, resurgent version of the pre-war right defeated the liberal Conservatism built by Churchill and continued by Macmillan, Butler and the younger generation of Heath, Maudling and Macleod. I doubt that most of the Tory MPs who voted for Thatcher at the time understood quite what they had done; perhaps she did not understand it herself. Heath understood it very well: that understanding was the basis of his unrelenting subsequent bitterness. It was truly the end of an era.

At the end of 1970, when I returned to England, the final phase of that post-war liberal Conservative era, the springtime of Edward Heath's young administration, was in full bloom. The hope seemed real and practical. It was very similar to 1997, when I and the Conservative government I had served for eighteen years – sixteen of them as a minister – were swept away. Just like their Conservative counterparts twenty-seven years later, by 1970 Wilson and his Labour colleagues were widely perceived to be sleazy and incompetent. Heath, like Blair, was elected not so much because of an ideological shift, but simply to restore competence, decency and modernity.

The slogan in the 1970 election campaign was 'Action not Words'; efficiency was the watchword. The new management techniques that US Secretary of Defense Robert McNamara had transplanted from Ford's factories to the Vietnam War were now to be used to bring class-ridden, antiquated Britain up to date. Daniel Bell's *The End of Ideology* was a seminal text of the time. Businessmen and competent, non-ideological experts from Britain's equivalents of Ford – namely Marks & Spencer and Shell – would be brought into government. Much careful work had already been undertaken by David Howell and others during the years of opposition. Their pamphlets had names like *Beyond Efficiency.* We would build a modern classless economy, like Germany's, or Holland's, or even France's, and cement our membership of the modern world by joining the European Economic Community (which, obviously, we would lead, given our political skills). The latter epitomised the dream of moderate, liberal capitalism guided by a wise and meritocratic bureaucracy. We would rebuild Britain's infrastructure, with a new airport in the Thames Estuary at Maplin Sands and a Channel Tunnel. Out-of-date industries would no longer be bailed out. The pound would be free to float. There would even be a little denationalisation, for instance of the travel company Thomas Cook, which the taxpayer had somehow ended up owning. We would match France in our building of nuclear power stations. Britain would be renewed, rejuvenated.

At the time, my friend Simon Jenkins told me that none of these great schemes would be completed. I was outraged. Things were going to be different now! He was, of course, right, although twenty-five years later there was at least a tunnel.

One instrument of the reform and modernisation of Whitehall was to be the introduction of proper, modern, bottom-up programme budgeting. Departmental priorities would no longer be set by arm-wrestling contests between powerful ministerial barons, with small shifts in resources bargained over politically in Cabinet. The system was to be called Programme Analysis and Review: all departments must analyse their spending as if every last penny were new spending; then a central body, answerable to the Cabinet, would assess the results and present alternative strategies for collective decisions. This central body was to be called the Central Policy Review Staff. After various false starts, Victor, 3rd Lord Rothschild became its head in early 1971. I joined as a result of the kind of old-boy networking of which of course the modern world knows nothing. I was in the guest room of the House of Lords, having a drink with my father. I had just had a stately job interview at the Bank of England, and a less stately half-hour with Eric Roll of Warburgs. Neither seemed likely to lead to the kind of glory I took as my due. George Jellicoe wandered over. 'Victor's looking for chaps,' he said. As we left, I heard my father say, *sotto voce*, to Jellicoe, 'I am really not selling you a dud.'

An interview followed in Rothschild's flat at 23 St James's Place. What were my weaknesses? I do not remember thinking I had many. In spite of this, I got the job and met (and selected as my next hero) one of the most complex and difficult men of the age. He was a representative of things quite unknown to me, but for better or worse powerful strands in twentieth-century Britain: the Cambridge of the Apostles, and the spies; jazz; biological science; the Jewish aristocracy; serious money; secrets. Surely, if anyone understood that slippery grown-up world receding in front of me, it was Victor Rothschild. Was he not the descendant of the model for – and indeed the modern embodiment of – the all-wise Sidonia of Disraeli's novel *Coningsby*? And was I myself not going to be the modern Coningsby–Disraeli? My relationship to the English Rothschild family swiftly became intimate, because his youngest daughter and I were engaged later that year. When I asked his permission to marry Victoria, without looking up from his desk, Victor asked, 'And when are you going to buy a racehorse?' His cousin, the nineteenth-century prime minister Lord Rosebery, allegedly had three ambitions, all fulfilled: to marry a Rothschild, to become prime minister and to win the Derby.

At that time, Rothschild was embroiled in a bitter conflict with much of Britain's scientific establishment over the recommendations he had made in a report about the organisation of government-funded research and development. My father, who for many years had been chairman of the Long Ashton Agricultural Research Station, a government-funded centre run by Bristol University, spoke in the House of Lords in favour of Rothschild, who spent the two-day debate glowering from the officials' box. The debate concluded on 29 February 1972, a leap-year day when, traditionally, the woman asks for the man's hand in marriage. The Earl of Bessborough, winding up, ended his speech by saying that, in spite of the date, 'I understand that the daughter of the noble Lord, Lord Rothschild, has accepted the proposal of the son of my noble friend, Lord Waldegrave. I am sure that we all wish them both very good fortune in the future.' Hansard reads: 'Several Noble lords: Hear! Hear!'

My relationship with Victoria remains one of the fundamental pillars of my life. She went to study at the Sorbonne before winning a first at London University. I would fly over every night and back in the morning before going straight to work at 70 Whitehall. A customs official, who got to know me well, once said, 'I hope she's worth it, sir.' She was.

In the end, for reasons not relevant to this story, we did not marry. Instead, she became the wife of the distinguished playwright and diarist Simon Gray, but she is still one of my closest friends and godmother to my eldest daughter, Katie. Our early relationship redoubled the influence over me of the extraordinary, brilliant, talented, neurotic English Rothschild family. No one in that family is allowed to be anything other than brilliant; that I was apparently about to join it poured petrol on the flame of my ambition. As the Rothschild juggernaut powered ahead, I was like a novice driver slipstreaming Fangio in the motor race of life.

Much has been written about Victor for reasons both good and bad, by authors who should be taken seriously, such as Kenneth Rose, and by others who should not. If I had wanted an archetype of everything in English upper-class life that my own upbringing was not, attaching myself to Victor provided it. For instance, he was a conscious modernist. One of my former teachers at Eton, the mathematician and aesthete Norman Routledge, a fellow of King's, Cambridge, and a friend of Alan Turing, warned me not – on any account – to work for him. This was because, according to Norman, he had pulled down the prettiest house in England (Rushbrooke Hall) to build the ugliest (11 Herschel Road, Cambridge). Neither side of the trope was quite fair, but it was true that his estate in Suffolk boasted a modernist farmworkers' village designed by Richard Llewellyn-Davies, and that throughout every one of his several houses (and indeed, until they escaped, in the flats and houses of the children of his second wife, Tess) there was the same elephant-grey carpet, white walls and steel and leather furniture.

Inside the whitewashed walls of Herschel Road, however, were Cézanne's *Harlequin*, Braques, Klees and two astounding, full-size Nicholas Hilliards. Like my parents in their very different way, Rothschild had also made a conscious decision, with his second marriage to Tess Mayor, to shed his pre-war life: the demolition of the moated, Queen Anne Rushbrooke Hall was part of this, as was the donation to Trinity of his incomparable library of eighteenth-century books; his magnificent collection of silver and gold was on its way, except for a few astounding objects on the lunch table, to the saleroom or the museum. But everything that remained was remarkable.

My background let me hold my own, nearly, with the silver and the books, and indeed I could share Victor's intermittent regret at having given them away, since I felt the Waldegraves had suffered something similar with Lewis's acquisition of too much of our collection of Walpoliana. But I knew nothing of serious jazz. Victor was an excellent pianist, taught by Teddy Wilson; his sister Nica was the 'Jazz baroness' and friend of Thelonious Monk. Until I arrived at Herschel Road, I had never heard of Art Tatum.

I was astounded by the pictures, having grown up surrounded by Reynolds, Romney and Gainsborough, with Lear as the modernist. I had undertaken my own small rebellion as a child encouraged by my sister Elizabeth, who worked for a time for John Rothenstein at the Tate. She gave me a huge selection of the gallery's postcards, which I stuck in a thick exercise book, accompanied by solemn comments mostly lifted from Skira books about the Impressionists, or from Wilenski's *Modern French Painters* or Gombrich's *Story of Art*, both of which Elizabeth had given me, too – good presents for a precocious ten-year-old. I had attended the first big post-war Picasso exhibition (I still have the catalogue) and had prints of Van Gogh, Picasso, Utrillo and Ivon Hitchens (as well as Turner and First World War Dreadnoughts) on my bedroom walls at home and at Eton. I had always loved Klee and Chagall, too. So, I was awestruck by what I saw on Victor's walls.

It subsequently turned out that the *Harlequin* had been sold. When? Was what I saw always a very fine reproduction, then? Was it first the original, then the copy? It took me some time to learn that Victor was extremely unlikely to give a straight answer to such a question, even if I had dared to ask it. Secrecy, for him, was not an instrument of policy to be deployed when necessary, but a pathology.

Rose, in his biography *Elusive Rothschild*, carefully refutes the allegations of treason – that Victor was one of the so-called 'Cambridge spies' – with which conspiracy theorists blighted his last years. Those claims were always based on wishful thinking and envy rather than hard evidence: how wonderful a story it would be if Rothschild, the glamorous owner of the most famous name in the world, could be added to the dreadful list of Philby, Maclean, Burgess, Blunt and Cairncross. Wishful thinking, envy . . . and a touch of anti-Semitism, I suspect. I soon learned that anti-Semitism was alive and well in cultured Britain. When my engagement to Victoria ended, I found a letter at Chewton written by an old Wykehamist friend of my father. 'You must be pleased to see the back of the Jewess,' he suggested.

In vain did Sir Burke Trend, Sir Dick White and all the others whose knowledge of the secret world had not addled their brains say that it was nonsense. Even when later defectors – such as my friend Oleg Gordievsky, who had run the KGB station in London; and Vasili Mitokhin, who brought the KGB archives over to Britain with him – added their voices, it was not enough for some. Some people think the Americans never landed on the moon; many people think that the Americans or the Israelis destroyed the Twin Towers. It is a small matter besides these camels to strain at the gnat of believing that Victor Rothschild worked for Stalin.

In fact, he was intensely patriotic, proud of the deep Rothschild roots in modern Britain, from the first Jewish member allowed to take his seat in Parliament, to 'my cousin Rosebery', who was to be my model. His relationship with Zionism was complex: he did not resile from a hereditary commitment to the best aspects of Israel, such as the Weizmann Institute; but he had no religious belief (though, in order to respect tradition, the first of his two wives did convert). His powerful feeling for family, with which I entirely sympathised, led to his burial in an old, closed, East End cemetery where several early Rothschilds had been buried, with whose reopening for him I helped later as a minister. Nonetheless, he was inclined to claim that he had once told a waiter, 'Don't you know who I am? Take away this pork chop. Just bring me a ham sandwich.' He farmed pigs, and was criticised for buying a Mercedes. Of course, the Holocaust was always present. 'The difference between people like you and people like me,' he once said to me, 'is that your elderly aunt was not beaten to death by German soldiers at a railway station.'

He dreamed of a liberal, inclusive Israel, led by people like Teddy Kollek and Shimon Peres. Much later, he generously came to my aid with a letter to *The Times* when the Murdoch press were lambasting me after an on-air spat with Prime Minister Yitzhak Shamir of Israel. I think – admittedly with little evidence – that without the Holocaust he would have followed a wholly integrationist path, with tribal Jewish loyalties respected, in the way that Martin Rees, the great astrophysicist, says his are to the Church of England. But the Holocaust changed all that.

Holidays now became not my family affairs. Now they might be in Cecile de Rothschild's house in the South of France, to which I drove my yellow Alfa Romeo GT Junior 1600 (which my brother had given me); catching a cross-Channel ferry in the evening after work, driving through the night at 120 miles an hour (life was freer then) and arriving at breakfast-time, hallucinating, so as not to miss a minute with Victoria. Nor did I want to miss Cecile and the legends that surrounded her, a former French women's golf champion and, perhaps, lover of Greta Garbo. Most holidays, however, were spent at Victor's beautiful, coral-built house at Yeoman's Point in Barbados. Sidney Bernstein lived next door and he could be seen dictating to two secretaries while sitting on the beach. Ronnie and Marietta Tree, along with their supermodel daughter Penelope (who could water-ski on bare feet), occupied the classical house at Heron's Bay, where Tull the butler was alleged once to have silenced a boring guest at Rothschild's request by means of powdered Nembutal in his bullshot. At the Bernsteins' I met Alistair Cooke, the voice of America in Britain for so many years, who talked on in unbroken, measured sentences even though he had become trapped inside an umbrella that had folded itself around him at the lunch table. There was also Kitty Carlisle, the pretty girl of forty years before in *A Night at the Opera* and now an elegant and cultured *grande dame*. There were whisky sours and daiquiris brought by Babs, the Rothschilds' butler, as we watched for the green flash as the sun went down. The old, unspoilt Sandy Lane Hotel was our bar. It was not far off heaven.

In retrospect, I wince at my disloyalty to my parents. I was now spending every weekend at Cambridge or Rushbrooke: 'flat out at work' was my excuse, but that was only part of the reason why I spent so much time at the Rothschilds' rather than Chewton. Spies and Bloomsbury; Nobel Prize-winners and world-famous academics; masters of Trinity and provosts of King's. The glamour was irresistible. Anyone might turn up: from

R. A. Butler, now master of Trinity, to Leon Radzinowicz, the founder of modern criminology; from Sir Dick White to Dadie Rylands; from Elihu Lauterpacht and Alan Hodgkin to Artie Marshall (who, incongruously, had once been Victor's secretary) and Sidney Brenner. There was Lafitte 1928 (a more justified use of the term *un petit vin de famille*) and nineteenth-century brandy and the charm of Rifleman Sweeney, Victor's butler, whom he had stolen from Duff Cooper. This was a world beyond the imagination of Chewton House. Rothschild's friends Noel Annan and Gordon Richardson, the latter then governor of the Bank of England, became mentors of mine; both of them wise and clear-minded counsellors. Gordon's formidable wife Peggy persuaded me to become a magistrate on the Inner London Juvenile Bench, which taught me something about life in the big housing estates of the capital. Moreover, she and Tess introduced me, as my tutor in penal policy, to Barbara Wootton, the queen of the subject and the first woman ever to lecture at Cambridge University.*

It was at Herschel Road that the telephone call came from Robert Wade-Gery (a fellow member of the CPRS) telling me I had won my Prize Fellowship at All Souls. At my new college were to be found Berlin, Stuart Hampshire and Bernard Williams – all friends of the Rothschilds, too. There were also antique monsters: E. B. Ford, the geneticist, suggested that we should elect chimpanzees rather than women, because, he claimed, the former were just as closely related to males of *homo sapiens* as were the latter. And there was A. L. Rowse, holding forth at breakfast about the iniquities of the pre-war appeasers. Unlike many, I was rather fond of him: when I went to see him years later, on his death bed, he said sadly, 'The Germans destroyed our world.' I think he meant the old European world, the Europe of 1914. There was the delightful, if somewhat drunken, Professor of Oriental Religion R. C. Zaehner, who set fire to the college and had written a book on mysticism

---

* However, she was listed under a male name, with only a footnote admitting, 'These lectures will be delivered by Miss Barbara Adam'.

that contained an engaging and somewhat comic chapter describing his experiences while walking round Oxford under the influence of mescaline, which he had taken for research purposes. There was old Lord Salter, of Salter's Steamers, who had been Churchill's representative in Washington in charge of the vital issue of shipping during the war, as well as being Gladstone Professor of Political Theory. There was Roger Makins, Lord Sherfield, ambassador, permanent secretary and head of the Atomic Energy Authority (not to mention, according to my mother, the best dancer of his generation). There was Sir Patrick Reilly, who, as a senior official in the Foreign Office, had vetoed Kim Philby's appointment as the head of SIS. When I asked him how he knew, he replied that he did not: 'I just did not like the smell.' There was my particular friend Rohan Butler, a gentleman scholar whose 1,133-page volume on the French eighteenth-century statesman Choiseul ends, 'The diplomatic and political career of the future Duke de Choiseul had begun.' Sadly, death supervened before subsequent volumes could be written. There was Sir Edward Penderel Moon, in spite of his pre-modern name a brilliant and radical historian of India, much respected in the sub-continent. The warden was John Sparrow, perhaps the most systematic and thorough reactionary I have ever known, though charming with it. I was elected with another Old Etonian, Simon Hornblower, while Sparrow was on sabbatical. This allowed him to say, 'I go away for a minute and they elect nothing but Etonians!' Simon, however, was and is a serious scholar, one of the most productive and original classicists of his generation.

My arrival as a supernumerary family member at Herschel Road must have complicated life for Rothschild's children. Victoria became engaged to me. A few years later, when Caroline and I called our son James Victor, her younger brother – subtle, gentle Amschel, who became something of a younger brother to me, too – announced that he intended to call his next child Earl Waldegrave Rothschild. His older half-brother Jacob asked where my mother had been in the year before my birth (an implausible scandal, rather). Victor himself kept a picture of Victoria and me on the mantelpiece, both in profile: 'Spot the Semite,' he would say, as Victoria has an elegant straight nose.

It was not only her profile that was independent. She and I sent a small contribution to *Private Eye*'s 'Goldenballs Fund', which helped the magazine to fight the criminal libel prosecution launched by Sir James Goldsmith with the intention of shutting it down. Very swift and sharp pressure was brought to bear upon her for deploying the greatest name in English Jewry in opposition to Sir James. She paid no attention. I subsequently observed Goldsmith deftly outmanoeuvred by Heath, who by then was leader of the opposition after his defeat in the 1974 elections. Sir James's great cause at the time was not anti-Europeanism, as it later became, but the advancement of proportional representation, a voting system he believed would prevent the imminent communist takeover of the country which he feared. He came to Heath's Wilton Street home and made a proposition. He knew the Tories were short of money, so he would put this right in exchange for a commitment to PR.

There was a long silence.

Finally, Heath remarked that Sir James had done something no other man could have done. This was, in general, Sir James's view too, but he wondered in which particular respect. 'You have driven Nicholas Soames into accountancy.' Soames had indeed left Goldsmith's employ to study accountancy. Heath said nothing more. After a time, Sir James left. That was the end of that. Sometimes, deliberate obtuseness works very well.

So, here was another strand of Englishness, potent and influential throughout most of the twentieth century, the last act of which again I witnessed: the world of pre-war Cambridge, Bloomsbury and top-level science, all intertwined with a uniquely aristocratic Jewishness and the dangerous glamour of spies. If this was a novel world for me, how much more it must have been for Edward Heath, the builder's son from Broadstairs. Why had he appointed Rothschild, out of an alien culture, not even from Oxford, with virtually no Tory connections except those provided by the camaraderie of Whiggish wealth? Churchill, according to Victor, had once remarked, 'Sitting on your dividends, I suppose,' when the latter had taken his seat in the Lords (where he never spoke) on the cross-benches. Subsequently, he was often described as a 'Labour peer'. But Victor was no politician: he had just retired as head of research at Shell. He suited Heath for the following reason. If Heath represented one aspect of an approach to non-ideological politics where 'whate'er is best administered is best', Victor represented another: the 'scientific' approach. He believed there was a rational answer to every problem. There was, somewhere, an expert who would know the answer. Such people, always described by Victor as 'God-almighty in the field of . . .', surprisingly often turned out to be Jewish. International law? Lauterpacht. Business? Arnold Weinstock. Criminology? Radzinowicz. Biology? Brenner. Barrister? Lennie Hoffmann. Silver? Martin Norton. Almost everything else? Berlin.

This contradicted one of his favourite sayings: 'A clever goy is always cleverer than a clever Jew.' (Or was it 'tricky' and 'trickier'?) The *goyim* had Hubert Hart for analytical power, Hodgkin for neuroscience and Burke Trend for subtlety. I think Tatum and Monk were considered honorary Jews. I was submerged in the borrowed glory of Britain's intelligentsia.

A large part of the duties – and the fun – of the extraordinarily talented young team he assembled was to act as intermediaries between Victor, and hence the government, and this network. Victor's taste for secrecy, and hankering for mystery, sometimes led me, as one of his trusted emissaries, into strange and in retrospect probably dangerous territory. I remember being sent with an incomprehensible (to me) message to Lord Shawcross, then chairman of the Takeover Panel, about a particular deal. Was I acting as a messenger from the government? From Rothschild's Bank? From Victor himself? On another occasion, I was sent with an even more obscure – but clearly conspiratorial – message to the *Daily Express* journalist Harry Chapman Pincher, a friend of Victor and an expert in the world of shadows. Luckily, perhaps, I have forgotten what it was. Even more luckily, Victor did not involve me in the Peter Wright affair.

Chapman Pincher told what I believe to be the true story of Rothschild's relationship with the former MI5 man in his book, *The Spycatcher Affair*: the arranged, covertly approved, first book, *Their Trade is Treachery*, under Pincher's name, with part of the proceeds going to Wright, aimed at righting what Rothschild saw as an unfairness in the treatment of Wright's pension; and to provide him with some money. In return, Wright, who had been the convener of a Whitehall committee called 'Fluency' which had reviewed in great detail the history of Soviet penetration of MI5 and MI6, would provide a statement which Rothschild could deploy to lay to rest for ever the muttered rumours of Rothschild's involvement with the pre-war Cambridge traitors, and to suppress some of the gossip about his second wife, Tess.* I wonder whether any of the money for Wright actually came from Rothschild directly. He quite often helped people he deemed deserving: in his autobiography, James Lovelock, originator of the Gaia hypothesis and environmentalist *extraordinaire*, pays tribute to such assistance in his own case.

In the case of Peter Wright, though, Rothschild could not have anticipated the profligacy of the old MI5 colleague whom he had set out to help. Short of money again, Wright wrote his own own book, *Spycatcher*, which breached every trust, legal and moral, to which he had committed

---

* A more innocent example of covert action to right a wrong was the action he took to ensure that Paul Dirac was awarded the OM, which should have been his years before. This led incidentally to my own amateur interest in the greatest scientist ever produced by my constituency, Bristol West – and indeed Britain's greatest twentieth-century theoretical scientist – who wrote the Dirac Equation, predicted the existence of anti-matter, and shared the Nobel Prize for Physics in 1933 with Erwin Schrödinger. There was a typical Rothschild sequel, however. In his seventies Rothschild was having tutorials in mathematical statistics to keep his mind working. He was puzzled by a certain problem. He knew I was corresponding with Dirac (about a schools mathematics prize which I established in Bristol in his honour). Would I put to Dirac the following mathematical question (which I had to copy out), as from an anonymous friend of mine? The answer came back from Dirac that the problem was trivial. There was then another letter to Dirac, somewhat disloyal I thought, direct from Rothschild, apologising for my having wasted his time: this I did not see until Graham Farmelo went through the Dirac papers for his excellent biography long after the death of both men, and sent it to me.

himself. It told damaging half-truths and in the hands of genuine, if naive, campaigners against government secrecy it did considerable damage. No one suffered more than Robert Armstrong, the cabinet secretary, whose use of a remark originally made by Edmund Burke (though the thought is much older) that it was permissible sometimes to be economical with the truth, has dogged him for the rest of his life. Of course, this nonsense gave free rein to every 'intelligence expert' in the press to republish the very rumours about Rothschild's own loyalty that the whole exercise had been partly designed to quash.

As for the real traitors, he had indeed known some of them. Like him, they had been members of the Apostles, the Cambridge intellectuals' club, and his second wife Tess had owned the lease on a flat in London sometimes used by Guy Burgess. Victor had been a friend of Anthony Blunt, had given him the money to buy a Poussin, and had acted as one of his sponsors, helping him gain entry to the secret world. All of this is well documented in Kenneth Rose's book.

I have drawn some conclusions as a result of watching the latter stages of the continued damage done by the traitors. The first is that E. M. Forster's famous dictum that, given the choice, he would hope to have the courage to betray his country rather than his friends is idiotic. It was obvious, watching the collateral damage done to families, friends and acquaintances – and even to Forster's beloved college and its university – that by betraying your country, you also betray your friends.

The second is the hollowness of the defence that it was excusable to work for the KGB, as only the Soviet Union opposed fascism in the 1930s. Even then, let alone after the purges, the Molotov–Ribbentrop Pact and the joint Soviet–Nazi rape of Poland, you had to be wilfully blind not to understand that there was little to choose between the KGB and the Gestapo; or between Stalin and Hitler. And this is not just hindsight, nor a view only from the right: the liberal core of Britain, whose intellectual leaders were Keynes and Berlin, Orwell and Popper, understood it very well. The unpleasant truth is that there is a certain kind of intellectual, on both right and left, who feels a powerful *frisson* of pleasure by imagining himself or herself as part of a world of savage action; and in every generation, and for every cause, very clever people can be found to rationalise and decorate savagery with their cleverness. In Oxford in my day, clever people who would never have dared to raise a fist in physical action worshipped Mao, Castro and Guevara, just as Ezra Pound had salivated over Mussolini, and Christopher Hill, master of Balliol, had written on Stalin's death that Russia had lost a great historian (Lord help us!) and a man to whom all humanity owed a debt.

Combined with the arrogance of secrecy, of being the only one in the room who understands the mysteries, this intellectual sado-masochism makes a heady brew that will always attract adherents. I do not believe that such intellectuals' advocacy changes history perceptibly, because they come *after* the thugs have won power – horse-flies born from the dung. In fact, it is the power – Hitler's, Mao's, Stalin's – that attracts them. If Lenin had never made it back to St Petersburg, and democracy had won through in Russia, there would have been no Marxist middle-class students and no nonsense from Christopher Hill.

The secret world is seductive, and dangerous to those it seduces. In my experience, in Britain, it often – mostly – contains level-headed, decent, patriotic servants of our democracy whom we are right to trust. Those I knew – Sir Dick White, Sir Christopher Curwen, Sir Colin McColl or Dame Eliza Manningham-Buller – could stand as representatives of many others who are among the very best of our public servants, all the better for not seeking public recognition. I once asked White why we had not simply killed Philby when we knew he was likely to defect, and take still dangerous secrets with him. He had, after all, been responsible for the deaths of a large number of British agents in the field and the murder and torture of opponents of Stalin, not only in Russia. White glared at me with his very blue eyes: 'Because then we would have been no better than them.' I hope those who judge the morality of extraordinary rendition, drone attacks and such matters still think like that.

It is absolutely essential that those at the inevitably secret heart of state are free from direct political influence or control. They must inhabit a culture of service and be guided by normal morality. They deserve respect, but not too much: there is something wrong with a country if too many people and too much of the media are obsessed with spies and special forces. That is a phenomenon of decline. Britain, which has lost its global political power and declined in relative economic weight during my lifetime, has had a tendency to imagine a secret world where Britannia still rules, and we have projected on to it all sorts of fantasies and conspiracies in a bid to lighten our otherwise somewhat humdrum position in the real world. Such projection – which is extremely profitable for those who write its books and feed its conspiracies – is often damaging to those who actually serve us. And it finds an exact counterpoint in what some other nations – Iran, for example – think: that the subtle Brits still secretly rule the world.

This phenomenon – a culture of conspiracy providing solace for those whose position does not tally with their aspirations – is not unique to Britain, nor to the world of secret public service. Many others continue to share it as a way of explaining why the world never quite goes their way. When, in 1993–4, I was the minister in charge of publishing far more information about the real secret world, I asked whether our secret services might suffer a loss in prestige, and thus effectiveness, if our enemies saw how small their numbers and budgets actually were. 'Don't worry,' I was told, rightly, by the head of SIS. 'The Iranians will simply say, "Look at the figures those subtle British have published! How naive they are to expect us to believe such nonsense! Everyone knows there is a British spy behind every rock!" ' Much of the British press and public want to believe the same thing, so they can maintain the pleasant myth of post-imperial secret power. Similarly, at various times, Shia Muslims persecuted by a Sunni majority have sought refuge in the consolation of conspiracies; American neo-Nazis are convinced that the world is run by those who attend the Bilderberg Conferences, as I once did; young Muslims believe that Israel or America itself perpetrated 9/11 and 7/7 to provide an excuse for a Western war against Islam. A certain kind of Englishman, found on the right of the Conservative Party and now increasingly in UKIP, longs to blame Britain's fall from great power status on the all-encompassing, sinister influence of the European Union. Such people will be bereft of an explanation of Britain's historic relative decline if we ever leave that convenient recipient of blame; for them, all-powerful external enemies fill a vital psychological need.

For me, Victor Rothschild provided a dramatic embodiment of the perpetual search that partly drove my ambition: here was the romance of the mystery at the heart of state; here were the people who knew the meanings of the nods and the winks which signalled that the world was not what it seemed. Here were the insiders, the grown-ups, talking above the heads of the rest of us, who knew the truth – that there was a different world where Britain, or at least these initiates themselves, still ruled. I suspect that until the crash of the euro, the 'European project' provided similar comfort for a good many politicians and diplomats. It was a way of disguising Europe's continental drift into the margins of the world.

CHAPTER SEVEN

Think Tank

Several good books have been written – most notably by Peter Hennessy, and by former members Tessa Blackstone and the late William Plowden – about Lord Rothschild's 'Think Tank' (as the press instantly dubbed the CPRS). For eighteen months, from early 1971 to the end of 1972, for a young, politically ambitious person like me, it was a place and a time when bliss it was to be alive; and membership was the winning of another glittering prize.

The definition of 'youth' in the civil service of the early seventies was a dignified young man (and a few women) aged thirty-five or so – hardly what research scientists, or irregulars in the war, considered young. After all, George Jellicoe had liberated Athens at the age of twenty-six; Dirac had written his equation at the same age. I was taken on partly, I suspect, to punish the system: 'Look what I will choose unless you help.' My hair was still Dylan-esque, my suits had flares and I had no experience of anything except winning a series of academic prizes. My colleagues had more gravitas: Robin Butler, future cabinet secretary; Peter Carey, war hero and future permanent secretary; Robert Wade-Gery, fellow of All Souls and future High Commissioner in India; and many others. William Plowden, Adam Ridley and Brian Reading – all experts in their fields – were, like me, hired from outside (we became temporarily established civil servants). Dick Ross was the resident senior economist, charming, clever, and idle. John Mayne from the Ministry of Defence was – we chose to believe – Cabinet Secretary Burke Trend's spy. Had we turned him? I shared a room with Robin. My sister Susan, lady-in-waiting to the Queen, was much impressed when she rang me and he answered the phone as he had been trained to do: 'Waldegrave's telephone; Butler speaking.' How smart to have a telephone butler after only a week in the service!

There were some strange things about the old civil service. The curtains, for example. Robin and I were allowed no curtains. Middle-ranking officials had curtains that could not be drawn. Under-secretaries had curtains that worked. Our chief enemy was the establishment officer, Mr Moss. 'Could we have a fan, please? Our office is very hot.'

'There are 750,000 non-industrial civil servants. If they all asked for fans, the country would be bankrupt.'

There was a mess for officers – those of assistant principal rank, including me, temporarily established, and above; and a (cheaper) canteen for the other ranks. The food was identical. We had to inform the cabinet secretary if we planned to meet a journalist (a procedure that was reintroduced for cabinet ministers in 2011). Everything was very secret, and all files had to be locked up. Nothing could be taken home. The most powerful people in the building were the formidable ladies in the typing pool: woe betide you if you did not keep in with them.

On to this pre-lapsarian bureaucracy Victor Rothschild grafted his own unique way of working. 'One of my young men will come and see you,' he would tell a startled permanent secretary, cabinet minister, or great company's managing director, and I would duly turn up. If you produced what he considered a good memorandum (I wrote one such now released under the thirty-year rule, of which I remain proud, on Open Government), it would be sent straight to the prime minister, accompanied by a short note from Rothschild along the lines of 'Waldegrave wrote the attached. You may wish to accept his recommendations.'

When asked to review whether the Concorde programme should be scrapped, the Aviation Section of the Department of Trade and Industry refused to send us the relevant figures. Rothschild went to stay with a French cousin and asked General Toulouse, head of the French side of the joint project, to lunch. The figures were forthcoming. We told the Cabinet that the French would sue for damages if we unilaterally withdrew, so it would be cheaper to press on. However, our paper began, 'Concorde is a commercial disaster . . .' and we ridiculed the sales projection of 168 aircraft. Our paper, as always, was designed to catch the eye of a weary cabinet minister. It was printed, not cyclostyled, and accompanied by a Concorde tie paid for by Victor (a Hermès scarf for Mrs Thatcher): if we were to go on with the commercially doomed project, the message was that we should do so with panache. I was sent to see the fashionable business genius of the day, Jim Slater, to get tips on how to proceed with the marketing.

I was the link with our printers, the secret Foreign Office Press, run by an admirable craftsman called Mr Krojer. Rothschild – as a Roxburghe Club member and former owner of one of the finest eighteenth-century libraries in the world, particularly rich in his favourite Swift – cared obsessively about typefaces and punctuation. Our papers were always short, readable and beautifully produced. Technique mattered: I was sent to see the great mountaineer Chris Bonington, famous for the very advanced presentation skills he employed during his lectures. At Chequers, to the dismay of most of the rest of the civil service, we gave presentations to whole-day meetings of the Cabinet and, separately, to junior ministers. We told them how the government was doing, and what it should do next. Robin and I were in charge of this. We designed large charts that were not circulated in advance – against all protocol – so that departments could not brief against them in advance. 'How could we circulate them?' we would argue. 'They won't fit in the regulation secure envelopes.' I am ashamed to say that we pinned up huge 'end-of-term reports' ('Housing, 4/10; Environment 6/10') on the Tudor linen-fold panelling in the upstairs drawing-room at Chequers. When quite properly rebuked for this vandalism by the old gentleman who was the trustees' agent for the building, Butler told him we were only using holes that were there before. I knew then that he would one day be cabinet secretary and head of the civil service, KG, GCB, CVO and a peer.*

I used to drive down to Chequers in my Bristol 405 (having sold my Alfa and begun a love affair with our local West Country marque that continues to this day). Victor was driven in his stylish but rather elderly Bentley, at least until Heath mocked it and he bought a duller and more modern car instead. There were no armed guards in those days; indeed, there was a public right of way running past the front door. Terrorism put an end to much of this informality, terrorism, and in London, parking wardens. One night, driving home from the Cabinet Office, the 405 broke down on the Mall. I pushed it off the road by the gates into St James's Park. It was still there, untouched, unticketed, the next morning.

We became famous, and appeared in *Private Eye*, with Richard Ingrams (in an Afro wig) representing me. The whole great structure of Programme Analysis and Review was soon forgotten. Instead, we became a jack-of-all-trades unit in theory available to the Cabinet but in fact reporting to the prime minister. There was then a deep-seated belief that if cabinet government was to be genuine, and not become presidential, the prime minister should be prevented from building his own Department as Lloyd George had done in the First World War in what was called his 'Garden Suburb' and Churchill had repeated, in his war, employing Lord Ismay, his favourite scientists and others as his chasers and fixers. In order to avoid accusations of doing the same thing in peacetime, we had to sit on the far side of the blue baize door between

---

* On one occasion at Chequers, Rothschild wandered off to explore the house. He returned white-faced, having opened a door to find the prime minister in the bath.

Number Ten and the Cabinet Office, and had to ask for the key from Burke Trend's office.

It is hard now to remember just how thoroughgoing was the attempt to maintain the strict convention that all decisions were made collectively in Cabinet, with the prime minister merely the chairman. Even the existence of cabinet committees was kept secret, the theory being that knowledge of them would dilute trust in the Cabinet as the only constitutional decision-maker, accountable to Parliament. Much else remained secret, too. Denying the existence of the intelligence services and not publishing the names of their heads made some sort of sense. But, in theory, any knowledge any civil servant possessed by virtue of his or her job was also covered by the Official Secrets Act, and could not be divulged without fear of criminal prosecution. In our minds, iconoclastic and young, much of this seemed ridiculous; and, to us, Burke Trend was the embodiment of the old ways. Indeed, that great public servant did I think believed, like Ulysses in *Troilus and Cressida*,

> There is a mystery – with whom relation
> Durst never meddle – in the soul of state,
> Which hath an operation more divine
> Than breath or pen can give expression to.

That mystery surrounded and protected what he saw as the central pillars of our safety: the Anglo-American alliance embodied by the intelligence-sharing arrangements established uniquely with Britain and the Dominions in and after the Second World War; and the British nuclear deterrent. Young think-tankers might have bridled at all of this; Victor Rothschild, one of the most obsessively secretive people I have ever met, did not. He had received the ultimate accolade – clearance at the highest, nuclear-secret, for-UK-eyes-only level – as a result of a review of the British nuclear deterrent he had undertaken. Along with Wade-Gery, he was also involved in top-secret work relating to Northern Ireland. (At least it was secret until Heath asked him about it in front of the rest of us, much to Rothschild's chagrin.) His continuing connections to his old colleagues in the security services caused Burke Trend – who as cabinet secretary was the official overseer of all relationships between the prime minister and the secret world – much anxiety, for example over arguments about whether MI5 should be used to investigate corruption in the police.

Only one area was barred to us: tax. The Treasury had seen to that. Nor did we have anything to do with what Heath regarded as the central achievement of his administration: Britain's entry to the EEC. That was entirely under Heath's hand, though we were of course well aware of the divisions in Parliament and the country about it, and of the narrowness of some of the crucial votes. But we stuck our noses into pretty much everything else, from race relations to oil prices, throwing, as Robert Wade-Gery said, grit into the smooth running of the Whitehall machine; sometimes salutary grit.

As the days darkened and the government failed in the first attempts in Britain to bring the trades unions within a rational legal framework, losing desperate confrontations with power workers, dockers and coal miners, our little unit became ever more marginalised. Perhaps our most useful service to ministers came not in the end from our reports at all, but from the fact that our Chequers (and occasional Number Ten) meetings in 1972 and 1973 provided a forum in which the battle between two opposing ideologies could be played out. On one side were those who thought that inflation could be controlled by fiscal and monetary means; on the other were those who believed an incomes policy was the only answer. (In turn, the latter group was split over whether this should be voluntary or embodied in statute.) It was during those discussions, as unemployment rose towards the supposedly catastrophic level of one million, that the 'Butskellite' post-war consensus started to collapse.

Under Macmillan (and in a less competent way under Wilson between 1964 and 1970), an attempt had been made to build the institutions of national economic consensus. The National Economic Development Council – set up in 1962 by Selwyn Lloyd, a much-underrated politician – was to be the place where voluntary agreements would be hammered out by the great corporate interests of the nation, labour, capital and government (as 'Trades Union of All the People' – a phrase I put in one of Heath's speeches during the first election of 1974). At the time, it was thought the only alternatives to this were either full, totalitarian socialism (unthinkable in democratic Britain) or a return to the 1930s, using unemployment as the regulator and pitching us back into the class war and despair that were anathema to Macmillan, Butler, Macleod, Heath and, indeed, my parents.

With my usual intellectual schizophrenia, I was well aware that radically different but equally coherent analyses were also available. I used to visit the dreadfully eccentric – or so they seemed – and heterodox meetings of the Institute of Economic Affairs and hear Arthur Seldon and Ralph Harris proposing another model: a world where rational consumers steered a responsive free market towards the best possible outcome for all. But those ideas seemed as antique as the doctrines of the Anabaptists. In our rational, modern model, consumers would not be served by markets, but by a new corporatist institution. Hence, the National Consumer Council and consumerist legislation were born.

If the only options were a return to the 1930s or a planned economy, there was little doubt which side Heath would choose. In his book *The Middle Way* (1936), Macmillan had argued that planning had failed in Britain only because of the lackadaisical way it had been undertaken. So, in 1973, Heath decided to do it properly: he would control prices, incomes, dividends, and hence the level of employment, by statute. It failed, as it was bound to fail. The lesson was learned first by the Conservative Party and then, belatedly, by Labour: by a process of elimination of all the alternatives, that liberal economics was the only way. But in the early 1970s, sensible men and women thought that way led straight to social collapse. The chief constable of Strathclyde told Heath that there would be anarchy on the streets if the shipyards went down, precipitating the famous U-turn which renewed industrial subsidy. The policeman was wrong because he had underestimated the extent of welfare support available in the 1970s. But perhaps he was not quite as wrong as hindsight might lead us to believe. It is easy to forget how desperate were the battles between police and striking miners a decade later, before the market route was finally accepted.

In that crucible of conflict and governmental defeat in 1973–4 were formed the politics of Britain's next forty years. In those four decades confident statism died, as perhaps did the ideal of fairness and moderation. Arrogant, unanswerable trade unions, their leaderships sometimes tainted by Soviet money, were destroyed; but the balance of power also undoubtedly shifted against the weak. Communism, at home and abroad, collapsed and people dominated by vicious and incompetent totalitarianism were liberated; but no ideal could be found to inspire decent, collective action against the new monsters of reborn fascistic fundamental religion and a form of capitalism that responded not to consumers but to the interests of those with their hands on the cash.

I was at the fulcrum of genuinely dramatic history as the hope and light of the early Heath period turned into the disasters and defeats of 1974. I was a young observer, then a player, occupying a privileged position at the centre of Britain's politics, first at the CPRS, then at Number Ten, at a time when dangerous events were forcing fundamental change on to an unhappy and anxious Britain. This was what I had always hoped politics would be like: high stakes, which might all be lost; the adrenalin of crisis; the future of the nation at stake, and me right there in the middle of it all.

In the autumn of 1973 I stepped across the divide and went political, leaving the civil service and becoming Heath's political secretary, succeeding Douglas Hurd, who had been selected to fight a parliamentary seat. I was responsible for everything the civil service would not touch: relationships with the Conservative Party and its political planning committees; the party political content of speeches; the organisation of political tours; political advice. I inherited Douglas's room, to the left of the Cabinet Room as you enter Number Ten; the Private Office, under Robert Armstrong, was on the right.

I was thrown immediately into the thick of the crisis that ultimately brought down the government and with it Heath's career and his kind of Conservative Party. I have never been able to match Douglas Hurd's cool, analytical detachment in a crisis. I'm always more emotional. Passionately partisan and loyal to what I thought were Heath's and the country's best interests, I was all for straightforward confrontation with the miners once they had openly challenged the incomes policy by striking at the end of 1973. Rothschild had a more subtle suggestion. At the time of the Yom Kippur War and the Arab states' subsequent oil embargo against the West, he had argued that an exception could be made in the statutory prices and incomes policy for all energy prices (and therefore wages in the energy industries), and a special case made for coal as well as oil. Sadly, in late 1973, his influence was largely broken because of the release of a private speech in which he predicted that Britain would be half as rich per head as France or Germany by the year 2000. This was made on the same day that Peter Walker, for the government, announced that Heath's administration was facing no problems but the 'problems of success'. The prime minister's reaction was bitter and unforgiving, and his relationship with Rothschild never recovered.*

---

* When, some years later, I was acting as executor for Michael Wolff, Heath's wise and experienced senior speech writer, I found a draft minute from him to the prime minister in which he excoriated the latter's behaviour: 'Did we not, in opposition, say that we would allow open and honest argument?' Also in the files was a draft resignation speech for use by Heath if the crucial parliamentary vote on entry into the European Community went against him.

CHAPTER EIGHT

Defeat

So, into that last winter we went: the country rationed on energy and petrol use; industry working a three-day week; All Souls lit by candlelight (as it should always be); Number Ten lit by French-made Camping Gaz butane lamps. I argued that we should challenge the extra-parliamentary power of the unions in an early election, running under the slogan 'Who rules?' Heath was desperately tired after a long summer and autumn during which an unpleasant Commonwealth Conference (at which he was berated by African countries over Britain's trade with South Africa) was followed by the even more draining Sunningdale negotiations on Northern Ireland (which produced a fragile compromise foreshadowing by nearly a quarter of a century John Major's and Tony Blair's similar deal). He hung back from an early, confrontational election, seeing a far wider picture than I did. If he lost, he knew his historic Irish deal would collapse in the face of Enoch Powell's antique Unionism and Wilson's weakness in the face of the hard-line 'loyalists' it encouraged (and so it proved). His achievement of securing British entry to the European Economic Community would also be put at risk by Labour's opportunistic opposition and their promise of a referendum.

Worst of all would be the kind of victory (we did not doubt it would be victory) he would win. He hated the idea of winning on what he saw as the divisive 'Who rules?' question. He feared letting the right-wing genie out of the bottle, and a return to a pre-war, coercive Conservatism, with the unions suppressed by the victory of a party representing a hard, militant middle class. He did not want to see the end of the post-war attempt to make the Conservatives the party of one nation, outflanking class-based Labour. So, he delayed calling the election. And when he finally took the plunge, in February 1974, he agreed with his party chairman, Peter Carrington, that it was impossible to fight an election with the restrictions on broadcasting and the rest entailed by the electricity rationing of the three-day week. We would have to turn the lights on again. I thought this threw away our most powerful card: the sense of crisis, and that it would leave the country bemused.

At Gravesend, traditionally the last big public rally of the election (there were open rallies, with real people – and hecklers – in those days), came a cry from the back of the hall. I believe the questioner was genuinely seeking enlightenment, rather than merely trying to cause trouble. 'What can you do if you win which you can't do now with a majority of thirty?' he asked. We had no good answer. A series of upsets in the campaign – Powell's defection to the Unionists; an alleged muddle about what had been offered to the miners; a mishandled response to a clever apparent olive branch from the TUC – seemed crucial at the time. But they were far less important than the point raised by that Gravesend heckler. Still, it never occurred to me that we might lose.

We got more votes, but fewer seats, than Labour. Parliament was hung. The Liberals, Scottish Nationalists and Ulster Unionists held the balance; but Labour was the biggest party. Wilson was as surprised (and perhaps as alarmed) as anyone by his near victory. Heath, concentrating now on the common ground on Europe, negotiated with Jeremy Thorpe's Liberals, seeking full coalition. He refused offers from the Ulster Unionists that would have entailed the abandonment of the Sunningdale Agreement and

the betrayal of Brian Faulkner, the moderate Unionist leader, who had
bravely backed it. Wilson, like most opposition leaders, had led Labour
into an anti-European stance, and he was likely to give in to the hard
men in Northern Ireland – two issues on which we had Liberal support.
Right at the back of people's minds, however, there was another issue.
The prime minister, and Conservative Central Office, knew all about the
sordid scandal which ended in the the assassination of poor Rinka the
Great Dane that was about to come crashing down on Thorpe's head. An
absolute veto on the use of any of this material during the election had
been issued by Heath and Carrington – greatly, I believe, to their honour.
(Would the Campbells, McBrides and Coulsons have acted like this?) But
such knowledge did make Thorpe's demand for very high office, perhaps even the Home Office, as his reward for cooperation implausible.
Moreover, most of his party (though not some of his most senior colleagues, including Jo Grimond) was opposed to any serious negotiation
with the Conservatives. In any case, even with the Liberals, the majority
in the Commons would not have been secure, because of the hard-line
Unionists and of nationalist gains in Scotland. As in 2010, the incumbent
government, by not winning clearly, had lost. Heath stood down.

   In those few frantic days, I watched proceedings from my temporary
office over the front door of Number Ten.* There were no gates at the
end of Downing Street to keep out the people; indeed, there was a public
right of way directly under the Cabinet Office – through the passage that
connected Downing Street to Horse Guards Parade. There was a TUC
rent-a-mob in the street throughout the campaign, sometimes accompanied by one of my predecessors as president of the Oxford Union, Tariq
Ali. It was amusing to see who relished the old rough and tumble politics
and who did not. Lord Hailsham was of the former party. He stopped

---

* In the seventies, political staff were severely restricted in Number Ten during an election. I
was turned out of my grand downstairs office, and a new telephone line had to be installed in
my new one, paid for by Conservative Central Office. Ministers retained their positions until
the moment when the prime minister resigned, but party functionaries had no status.

his car at the end of Downing Street, placed his bowler hat on his rolled umbrella, and twirled it like an ensign of war through the mob, who – of course – applauded him.

What would I have answered then if Isaiah Berlin had asked again, 'What did you learn?'

First, I learnt that Heath's loneliness throughout 1973–4 gives a clue to the weakness of his government. To be effective, leadership has to represent a movement, a group, a structure, and you have to have friends who represent those things, too. Heath had friends in relation to Europe (as well as enemies); and plenty of people had supported him, as I had, because he seemed to represent modernity, meritocracy and honesty, in contrast to Wilson's deviousness. But there was no 'Heathism' and this was a source of weakness. I saw him one evening going alone up to his flat in Number Ten, seen up the stairs by Sir William Armstrong, the head of the civil service, who had acceded to an extraordinary role as a sort of chief operating officer for the government's central prices and incomes policy, and Robert Armstrong, the doyen of principal private secretaries. Once they had left, thunderous music emerged from the powerful stereo the prime minister had set up in the little flat where he lived alone. I believe that Heath's embitterment started then, as he came to think that the British Establishment, and particularly the Conservative Party Establishment – which he had conquered from far outside its traditional borders – had failed him. There were no strong and confident structures to rely on: just himself, and he could not do it all. Something like this, I believe, was what he felt, and it was, of course, deeply unfair to the Carringtons, Hurds, Whitelaws, Priors and the rest – including tens of thousands of loyal Conservatives activists – who had supported him.

It is perhaps another danger of the philosophy of the glittering prize – the conquest of the meritocratic *cursus honorum*, which had taken Heath from his humble origins to the top of Disraeli's greasy pole – that such conquest is an individual, solitary matter. No movement is represented by such an achievement; the long-distance runner is lonely. Disraeli himself, glittering prize-winner of all glittering prize-winners, was a lonely and somewhat ineffective figure once he had obtained power.

Heath did adhere to one other profound ideology, in addition to meritocracy itself: his belief that the destruction he had witnessed in Europe after the war validated the drive to unify the continent as a bloc, a new near-national federation. This commitment did indeed represent a movement, in the civil service, in academia, in the serious press (led then by William Rees-Mogg's pro-European *Times*) and in elements of each political party – particularly those who had fought in the war. But it sat uneasily with the Tory Party, one strand of which had always been a quiet but insular nationalism.

Heath once asked me, sitting in the back of the opposition leader's Rover, 'Do you think the British people have still got it in them?' This was a question of someone who was romantic about Britain, and who had found himself in a depressed and depressing country he did not understand. He had thought he had understood it better than the pundits: after all, he had never wavered in his certainty that he would win the 1970 election, in spite of the polls. Douglas Hurd had a framed copy on the mantelpiece of the office in Number Ten where he met journalists of the edition of the *Observer* published on the last Sunday of that campaign. Its front-page headline read: 'Labour 8% ahead: only a miracle can save the Tories now.' Heath had been right then; conventional wisdom wrong. On another occasion, after a Konigswinter Conference where he had made common cause in a European discussion with Shirley Williams and others, he said to me, 'Those are the people we should be working with!'

Heath was full of contradictions and oddities. He could instil passionate loyalty; but he could also be extremely offensive without apparent effort or, sometimes, purpose. He could be obviously vulnerable to hurt; but sometimes he seemed to have the insensitivity of a mule. He could be maddening to work for. 'It's not quite right,' he might say, handing back a speech you had written, as the speeding three-litre Rover arrived at RAF Northolt, where an aircraft was waiting to fly him to some great rally.

The speech had to be issued to the press while he was in the air, so what was one to do? It is true, however, that I never made a very good speech writer: I wanted to deliver the speeches myself.

I had first seen Heath in action when he spoke to the Political Society at Eton in 1963. He had led the complex negotiations for Britain's entry into the EEC brilliantly, forcing the French to use their weapon of last resort – the veto – a huge defeat for their diplomacy. The meeting at Eton had been a bravura performance, treating the audience of eighteen-year-olds wholly as adults; in command of every detail; clear and witty. Here, I thought, was the modern Conservatism I was looking for. Although he did not replace Iain Macleod in my affections, he was a formidable representative of the progressive party of which I wanted to be a member. I had never flirted with Labour – the combination of trade union bosses and fellow travelling with the Soviet Union made that party seem both reactionary and disloyal – but I had taken the sixties centrist/progressive ticket. My first grown-up political act had been to write to Macleod in support of his opposition to the imposition of controls on Commonwealth immigration; I was a passionate opponent of hanging; I applauded Roy Jenkins's liberalisation of the laws affecting homosexuals; and, as I have said, I thought military action should have been taken against Ian Smith's unilateral declaration of independence in Southern Rhodesia. So, although for reasons of friendship and family ties I had mourned Sir Alec's passing as leader, I had welcomed Heath's election, particularly as Macleod would be at his side.

Given the hopes I had placed in him, and the reasons for those hopes, it was hardly surprising that I could not allow myself to have any doubts about him, even by 1974. There was something about his unspoken assumption of your loyalty which made you respond. He took it that, if you were there, you were family: you understood, and did not need flattery or thanks; all that was a given. Of course, if he had misjudged, and you had not signed up in this unconditional way, you would see his behaviour as churlish ingratitude. But it was not so. I do not remember him ever thanking or flattering me in person; but he did both, movingly, in a little formal speech to my sister, Susan, doubtless knowing that I would hear of it.

I think this explains the great mystery of Edward Heath: how did the popular young army officer, the supremely effective chief whip whose care and charm helped to reunite the Conservative Party after Suez, the subtle negotiator who outgunned the best French *enarchs*, turn into the surly curmudgeon of later years? I think it was because his whole life had been based on a total commitment to and belief in a vision of a patriotic, liberal Conservative Party: he and it were family. So when that bond turned out to be conditional, premised on his delivery of continued success, almost everything he thought he understood turned out to be false.

There is a touch of this in the infinitely more successful, and much luckier, Tony Blair: he genuinely thought – and thinks – that he created a family called New Labour which loved him and represented all the best in Britain. But in fact his tactical skill and his luck – like Clinton's, Blair's period in office happened to coincide with the easiest economic conditions since at least the First World War – delivered victories, and it was the victories that Labour liked. He seems genuinely perplexed that many of the members of that party, and many others, do not love him. How would Blair have done as a progressive Tory leader – which is what he most likely would have been if he had been born in 1920 – facing the catastrophes of 1973–4? His indomitable optimism and political savvy would certainly have carried him through much better than Heath. But would he have been any more courageous about the dangerous issues than Wilson?

Heath was a romantic about the Union, though he appeared utterly alien to many Scots and refused to turn a blind eye to the injustices perpetrated by Northern Irish Unionists (at the risk of losing their support). And he was romantic about Europe. It is easy for my generation to be Eurosceptic, as we have never witnessed a European war. He was a romantic about rationality in politics (like Blair again) and constantly surprised by the reality and short-sightedness of special interests. He had a proper Tory scepticism about the magic of the markets: that 'magic' was in fact dependent on rational and disinterested behaviour from market players that he did not witness among the fashionable spivs of the day. He dubbed them the 'unacceptable face of capitalism'; their descendants are still around, and even richer, today. 'Do you think the British people have still got it in them?' – echoing Brecht – reflected his discovery that the national family did not exist in the way he had thought.

His later comments to me were more straightforward. When I accepted junior office under Thatcher I was cast out beyond the pale and he did not speak to me for years. One evening, though, we were wedged in the division lobby together. Even he had to say something. 'Well, you're not doing very well, are you?' he said. But was there a slight shake of the famous shoulders? And sometimes his sheer bloody-mindedness could almost make the heart sing, especially when everybody else was behaving with perfect political correctness. I attended one of many celebrations for his eightieth birthday, this one at the German Embassy. The Great and the Good of Europe were all present. Heath spoke of how there was now no leadership in Britain for the European cause. Much applause and *sotto voce* comment to the effect that it was wonderful to hear the voice of a true statesman again. But then he diverted: why had we declared war on the Serbs? 'They were always our allies when push came to shove against Germany.' Appalled silence, followed by: 'Poor old boy. Lost his marbles.' The provocation was quite deliberate, of course.

His dinner parties in London or at his house in the Close at Salisbury were not occasions of much merriment. On one occasion, I was one of a small group, apparently randomly selected, none of whom had been introduced to each other. Conversation languished, so Emma Soames, also a guest, tried to enliven the proceedings with a story. Her brother Nicholas had recently won the nomination for a tough seat in Glasgow. The selection meeting had not been quite like such an event in the Home Counties. As he was about to leave, a drunken figure had risen from the floor, grasped Nicholas by the lapels of his jacket, and asked, 'Are ye married?'

At that point Emma stopped, and said nothing more. Silence was prolonged and quizzical.

Driving her home later, I asked, 'Did you forget the punchline?'

'No,' she said, 'I was on autopilot and got that far without remembering that after Nicholas admitted to being unmarried, the response was, "Och, not another Tory poofter!" '

It had been rather brave to stop without offering any explanation, I thought. Incidentally, the Scotsman's allegation in relation to Mr Heath was not, as far as anyone I ever knew could discover, true.

Heath was arguably the last British prime minister to consider Anglo-American relations as not much different from relations with any other country: we should always do what was in our own best interests. The dangerous doctrine that we should normally fall in with whatever the Americans seriously demand because their hegemony (and the presents they gave us in intelligence and nuclear matters) will ultimately be good for us was not one he shared. Thatcher was brave during the Falklands conflict and called the bluff of an American administration that initially allowed its anti-British elements to rule the roost. In the end, Weinberger and Reagan himself realised that a Britain crippled by a humiliation at the hands of the Argentines would be of little use in the bigger play of facing down the Soviet Union. But it was also during the Thatcher years – aided by the devil's pact with Murdoch, which for the first time linked the British right to the American Republican right – that the doctrine of subservience became the norm, and on it went into the Blair years.

Heath's Europeanism was largely driven by his belief that a Europe with the UK genuinely at the top table gave Britain a better base for advancing its interests than did an Anglo-American alliance which, at least after the Casablanca Conference of 1943, had stopped having even the façade of equality. His fatal hesitation over when to call the first election in 1974 was due to his conviction that he was the only one who understood how much was at stake. His contempt for Wilson was not wholly unmerited, because the Labour leader would indeed give in on all the big issues. And the Conservative Party would indeed, in economics at least, revert to something much more like the party of the 1930s which Heath had fought over appeasement at the Oxford by-election of 1938, using high unemployment as an instrument of policy and drifting towards social reaction. That it did not wholly revert was due partly to the fact that no hard right party will ever gain more than 25 per cent or so of the vote in Britain; and partly to the fact that Thatcher knew this as well as anyone, which was why she presided over Cabinets that always included a wide spectrum of opinion, and was infinitely cautious in deed (though not always in word).*

'Making history is very tiring,' Robert Armstrong told me during that February election, observing my doubtless bedraggled state late one evening in Number Ten. It is, even for the supporting cast. Heath had phenomenal strength of will and reserves of energy. But those last months of 1973 and early months of 1974 broke him, and with him the liberal Conservative settlement that had existed since the war. Forty years later, the realignment of British politics which began in 1974 remains incomplete.

---

* In Clement Attlee's final year as prime minister, public spending stood at 36 per cent of GDP. By 1979, it had reached 42 per cent, and Mrs Thatcher left it there for another eight years. It eased back to Attlee's level only during the boom of her last two years. Adjusted for inflation, spending was slightly higher when she left office than when she had arrived.

CHAPTER NINE

Strange Times

They were strange times. In the autumn of 1973, Victor Rothschild took me on a very secret private mission to Iran, where we tried to persuade the Shah to give Britain privileged access to oil at a time when the oil-producing Arab countries were imposing restrictions on exports to punish the West for its support of Israel. Briefed by the SIS, I was told not to worry about the fact that every room in the Tehran Hilton (we were too secret to stay at the British Embassy) was bugged: by the time it was all transcribed and translated, whatever we had said would be out of date. I believe that Rothschild had had some role in the murky Anglo-American coup against Mohammad Mosaddegh that had returned the Shah to power in 1953, and he had a personal relationship with him. No significant oil was forthcoming, I think; nor did it avail Britain much that two of the world's greatest oil companies were British. As I remember, if we took powers to direct them to bring their oil to Britain, it came to our territorial waters – 'Land's End for orders' – and was sold on abroad.

Rothschild later served a further quiet national function. In the spring of 1974 William Armstrong, head of the civil service, suffered a breakdown. He arrived at Victor's office and talked apocalyptically of his control of the Blue Army in its war against the Red, then lay full length on the floor of Number Ten's waiting room, at the feet of an astonished delegation of businessmen. He retired hurt to Yeoman's Point, was restored to health – doubtless by Babs's daiquiris – and subsequently became chairman of the Midland Bank, which turned out not to be a good plan.

We know now – although we make little of it, in the British way – that there was very deep Soviet penetration of the British trade union movement in the 1970s. It was toughly resisted by many within that movement, but it was nonetheless real. Jack Jones, boss of the Transport and General Workers' Union,* was paid by the Soviet Union; and Arthur Scargill and Mick McGahey of the Miners' Union asked for Soviet cash and other support. Rothschild was keen to use his old contacts to expose all this, but Heath had little interest in such matters; and Rothschild's mentor Sir Dick White – uniquely head of first MI5 and then MI6 in the fifties and sixties – stopped such dangerous games. But it is worth remembering that at the time many believed in the increasingly demented CIA counter-intelligence chief James Angleton's fantasies. There were others who believed Hugh Gaitskell had been murdered by the KGB in order to insert Wilson in his place. (Labour was given the choice between a crook – Wilson – and a drunk – George Brown – said Anthony Crosland at the time.) And there were mad and farcical plots, culminating in the bizarre attempt in 1968 by Cecil King, proprietor of the then powerful Mirror Group, to establish Lord Mountbatten, no less, in power at the head of a national government.

Such talk of plots and conspiracies – the obsession with subversion and espionage – is always a symptom of weak government and loss of national confidence. Of course, there is sometimes real subversion; there is always real espionage; and on occasion there are dangerous secret enemies to fight – terrorists or representatives of totalitarian regimes. In its day, the Soviet Union expended immense resources on the subversion of British

---

* In 1977, 54 per cent of the British population believed that Jack Jones was more powerful than the prime minister. They were probably right.

institutions; and the Russians expend similar resources today, at least on espionage (almost the only aspect of government which that great people have ever really mastered). The Libyans did pour money and weapons into the IRA; Islamist terror is as real as Chinese cyber-warfare. Against all this, a nation must have efficient and honest secret services, as Britain does. But ultimately the best defence is the solidity of the open institutions on which a free society rests – Parliament, the law, the civil service, a free press – with enough reality in the implicit social contract that binds the interests of the nation together. The extraordinary conspiracy mania of the sixties and seventies was a reflection of – not a cause of – weak and muddled government, and of perceived failure to restore a sense of national pride. If, in Sir William Armstrong's phrase, the job of the civil service was 'the orderly management of decline', it is perhaps unsurprising that the body politic began to suffer strange nightmares.

So, into opposition we went. These were strange months for me, and disastrous months for Britain, between the first and second elections of 1974. Heath's defeat was followed by exactly the collapse he had feared. Wilson, astonished to be back in power, had no strategy in mind beyond the winning of a second election. To achieve this, his tactic was to restore as much surface normality to the country as quickly as possible. This meant surrender to both the miners and the hard-line Protestants in Northern Ireland, and a spate of ephemeral policy initiatives of which little more was heard after the October election.

Robin Butler, who acted as private secretary to both, told me the difference between Heath and Wilson. If the former made a policy speech, it was preceded and followed by intense meetings, thumpings of the table, calls for immediate action. The first time Butler presided over such a speech for Wilson in 1974, he asked when he should schedule the follow-up meetings. 'Follow up?' queried Wilson. 'I've made the speech. No need for anything further.'

It was a dire period in British government. Inflation roared ahead: the chancellor, Denis Healey, announced a triumphant reduction to 8.4

per cent, but that was the *quarterly* figure. The stock market crashed; a banking crisis damaged the City; the atmosphere was febrile. Heath, now installed uncomfortably in a modern flat near the Tate Gallery, appeared to be in a state of shock, but he remained formidable. Within the Conservative Party, the battle between the Macmillanite consensual approach to management of the economy and revived economic liberalism – intellectually centred at the Institute for Economic Affairs and increasingly championed by Sir Keith Joseph – became open.

Breaking all tradition, Joseph and his business supporters established a rival research centre – the Centre for Policy Studies – in direct opposition to the Conservative Research Department, the party's official centre of doctrine, chaired by the pro-European, Keynesian Chris Patten. The best Heath could do was persuade Joseph to include the moderate Adam Ridley, a former CPRS member and Treasury official who had now gone political, on his board.

Like many others at the time, I was muddled and divided. Enoch Powell had always appealed to my romanticism, with his brilliance as a classicist, his remarkable war (he had joined as a private and ended up a brigadier) and his biblical use of the English language. Nonetheless, I was proud of Heath for sacking him in 1969 after his 'Rivers of Blood' speech, which, whatever its intention, legitimised the politics of racism. My loyalty to Heath was intense; but the intellectual rigour of the free-marketeers attracted me. I had come to know and like Keith Joseph at All Souls; and the passionate speakers at the IEA were counter-cultural and exciting. (It is astonishing to recall now how strange their free market ideas seemed then, and how marginal were their proponents.)

For me, though, there was – and still is – a problem. While these people were arguing for what seemed to be a much more effective approach to economic management, they also seemed to be proponents of reaction in all other matters. Why was economic liberalism always accompanied by extreme social illiberalism? Powell, for all his stirring language, was a prime example of this. How could he exclude the free movement of labour from his cherished dream of free movement of capital in a free trading world? Why could the 'piccaninnies' of his speech not grow into the new labour force we needed? Why did those who were arguing persuasively against the soft corporatism of collective economic management under Macmillan and Heath almost invariably come from that wing of the party that was pro-hanging, soft on South Africa, against the sexual liberalisation of the 1960s, including the legalisation of homosexuality, and reactionary about feminism? Why on earth did belief in the freedom of markets not extend to freedom of behaviour? All of these questions meant it was easy to remain loyal to Heath, even though I was having serious doubts about his economics.

On the other hand, if one was against hanging, and for the equality of the sexes and freedom of expression, why did one have to sign up to Jean Monnet's programme for the unification of Europe? In general, I shared the views of Chris Patten, Ian Gilmour, Roy Jenkins and Jo Grimond on how to live; but by committing themselves so wholeheartedly to Europe they seemed to be risking the destruction of the very traditions of secular, pragmatic, common-law-based English exceptionalism that had made our progress on social liberalism possible. Our political and social institutions had served us well – certainly far better than those of Germany, France or Italy – in the nineteenth and the twentieth centuries. So why were we supposed to surrender them?

Thus, a very odd sort of division appeared in the Conservative Party (and other parties, too): on one side, socially reactionary and incipiently anti-European free-marketeers; on the other, socially liberal and pro-European *dirigistes*. It is worth remembering that the former were only incipiently anti-European at this stage: Keith Joseph, Margaret Thatcher and Nicholas Ridley were all strong supporters of the 'yes' vote in the referendum on EEC membership in 1975; Enoch Powell had shifted by then, but even he had been a supporter earlier. Therefore, on this issue, I was 'ahead' (if that is the right word) of the subsequently dominant position of the right of my party, though I shared little of the rest of their ticket. I refused a position in the all-party organisation that was managing the 'yes' campaign as I felt it was impossible to campaign for the European Community while also saying that it did not infringe our sovereignty. 'Pooled' sovereignty was a meaningless slogan, I could see. And the Treaty of Rome was explicit: there would be ever closer union. The treaty had one thing – and one thing only – in common with *Mein Kampf*: very few people had read it. I had, however, so I knew that the objective was fairly explicitly stated in the founding documents: a political union, with a single currency (which ultimately meant a single fiscal policy), a parliament, and all the trappings of nationhood. It was at least as much the dishonesty which repelled me – not Heath himself, who was among the frankest about all of this, but the pro-European Establishment, whose approach to dissent was a little like that of the old Soviet Union: if you did not agree with them, you were a case for the men in the white coats.

If the 'yes' campaigners had said, 'This is what we want! A single great new nation of Europe, to stand as equal with America and Russia,' a majority of the British people might even have signed up to the European integration project. But they did not say that. Instead, they said, 'Nothing will really change. Britain will still be Britain. Just trust us.' Because that was palpably false, Britain never committed itself to an honest and fundamental change.

In 1974–5, someone in Britain could have led the way in arguing for a socially liberal, anti-European, free-market programme. Those principles were not – and are not – incompatible. Yet the only voices we heard were those of social liberals pushing the pro-European, anti-free-market agenda, and those of social reactionaries campaigning against Europe and for a freer market. I might have fulfilled my teenage dream of stardom if I had been the one to point out that there was, for want of a better phrase, a third way. As it was, I left London and drove, accompanied by Victoria and two other beautiful girls, to Isfahan, via Lake Van and Shiraz.

That, of course, was after Heath had lost the second election of 1974 and then the leadership itself.

*   *   *

During that spring and summer of 1974 I was at the centre of events in
the Conservative Party because I was now in charge of Heath's private
office in the House of Commons, behind the Speaker's chair. Michael
Wolff, happily, was senior speech writer and adviser; Tim Kitson was
the PPS; Douglas Hurd, now an MP, was still close. Chris Patten's star
was steadily rising as he continued to oversee the Research Department.
Of course, I should have kept a proper diary to record it all for posterity.
Instead, I scribbled down bits and pieces in an elegant black Smythson
notebook, which starts with the things Rothschild wanted me to remember ('Seating at Chequers') and ends with notes from my time running
Heath's office ('Karajan – will help with conductor'; 'Ask Toby Aldington
about new dockers deal').

The Chinese made it clear that an invitation to Beijing accepted
by Heath as prime minister still stood, so, in May, we went. By then,
China's leadership had come to see the Soviet Union as their principal
opponent: those who were staunchly anti-Soviet in Europe, like British
Conservatives, were therefore allies. Labour, with its fellow travellers,
and British trade unions, some of them with friends in Moscow, were
enemies. Heath was a mere youngster in Chinese political terms, and the
consensus was that he would surely soon be restored to power by the
incomprehensible procedures of the British Politburo.

The extent of our welcome became apparent only after we arrived,
exhausted and bedraggled, at Beijing airport: as far as the eye could
see were dancing children carrying banners proclaiming, 'Solidarity
between the People's Republic of China and the Conservative Party of
Great Britain'. The visit continued in the same extraordinary vein. The
Cultural Revolution had just ended; Deng Xiaoping had been recalled
but was still a marginal figure; Zhou Enlai chaired the delegations for
talks, morning and afternoon, leading officials whom Heath said were
the best he had ever negotiated with, even better than the French. We
travelled west to Kunming, where we saw what were clearly ethnic

Chinese pretending to be Tibetans in theatrical displays of loyalty; we attended an awful operatic performance with Madame Mao as our host; we visited ground-nut schemes and schools (at one of the latter, Heath established that the old man teaching basic English to small children had taught Chaucer before the Cultural Revolution). We saw half-finished road tunnels that were now proclaimed to be nuclear fallout shelters, prepared against Russian attack. We ate immense feasts and saw officials disappear, Norman Mailer-like, under the table, drunk on the sweet wine made of cashew nuts followed by the appalling Mao Tai spirit, made, I think, from sorghum. Wherever we went, clapping crowds lined the streets; Douglas Hurd, who had retained some Mandarin from his time as a young diplomat at the British Embassy in Beijing, said he could hear the loudspeakers in the background telling them to do so.

In the back of the limousines, with their little curtains to shade the great Party men from the eyes of the people, Douglas and I talked of our own unhappiness: his first marriage was breaking up, as was my engagement to Victoria. Personal sadness heightens your perceptions, so my memories of a China that has utterly disappeared remain very sharp: the populace on foot or on bicycles; the smell everywhere in Beijing of night soil, though the sky above was a piercing, pollution-free blue. The even more pervasive smell was fear.

A large press corps from Britain followed us around, searching for evidence that the Cultural Revolution was about to break out again. The Chinese were amazed at the BBC's union rules, which meant three men operated each camera; all of theirs were hand-held. We learned of the cool pragmatism of Chinese officials. Zhou Huan-Wha, the deputy foreign minister, who travelled with us, when faced with excited journalists who had seen local officials' names crossed out or criticised on the walls of buildings, said that he had heard that even in Britain one was allowed to criticise the government. Every question about human rights or freedom was parried with: 'And how many people do you have in Britain?'

We had arranged a gift of Père David deer, now extinct in China, from

Woburn to Beijing Zoo, and also gave our hosts a Darwin first-edition facsimile (this was the first item on the television news for three days running). The Keynes family had suggested the latter as a suitable present for Mao, said to be a Darwin enthusiast, but they refused to surrender the presentation copy of *Das Kapital* that Marx had sent to Darwin. The book is, satisfactorily, unopened, the pages not separated.

We were determined to return with some giant pandas for London Zoo worth several marginal seats, we believed; so we would address the not-very-hidden microphones in the guest houses, saying, 'What the British people really like are pandas! Pandas are just the thing in Britain!' There was no response until almost the last night, when Zhou Huan-Wha came to visit us and asked, 'Are the British people at all interested in pandas?' Hence, in due course, Chi Chi and An An arrived at London Zoo, where they lay on their backs and sulked, causing analogies to be drawn with the later behaviour of their donor.

There was much teasing from our hosts about whether we would meet Mao: sometimes they said yes; mostly no. Finally, at a moment's notice, Heath was summoned. Being by nature a negotiator, he refused to go unless he could bring all his staff too. This was an unprecedented demand which caused considerable consternation, but in the end we all went and I shook the hand of one of the world's greatest political criminals. It was a firm handshake, from a bigger man than I had expected. He retained the hand of Maurice Troubridge, our press officer, for some time. 'This is a very dangerous man, the Chairman says,' announced the interpreter. It was, possibly, a joke. As, perhaps, was the question, 'What is all this fuss in America about Nixon? Everyone knows Americans like to play with tape-recorders.' To the carefully prepared questions about China's policy towards Hong Kong, twenty-five years before the end of the lease on the New Territories, came the reply that 'the children' would settle that matter, with a nod towards Deng Xiaoping, in the corner of the room, who was already seventy-one.

This surreal visit ended appropriately with a journey in a luxurious train, complete with its own observation carriage, back to Hong Kong and the yacht of Y. K. Pao (who liked to call himself Chairman Pao), the great shipping magnate, where I water-skied behind one of his beautiful speedboats.

I was still engaged to Victoria, though there was the beginning of an understanding, unspoken by both of us, that we would never marry. Later in 1974 we sailed with her parents on the SS *France* to America. When we arrived at the Carlyle Hotel in New York on 8 August, we were just in time to switch on the television and see Nixon's resignation speech. Victor had travelled on the great ship incognito under the name 'Mr Fish' (this was when the terrorist known as 'The Jackal' was trying to kill prominent Jews), but not *too* incognito: 'Monsieur Fish, milord,' the waiters would say at our table. Then the US immigration authorities came on board in New York to escort us through with no question of queuing (a courtesy I was never accorded during my time as a secretary of state). 'Fish', incidentally, was in homage to the fine illustrator and draftsman Lawrence Fish, who had drawn the mechanisms of German fuses which Victor had made safe during the war.

Back home, throughout that summer and into autumn, the party rumbled and grumbled. Powell had already deserted to the Ulster Unionists. ('Another cause for him to betray; another leader for them to desert,' said Hailsham.) If he had remained a Conservative, he would have been the rallying point for opposition to Heath. As it was, Joseph and the emerging – but still relatively loyal – figure of Thatcher led the charge for a different approach to economic policy from the base of the CPS. A sudden flurry of rumour led us to believe that Peter Walker, a centre-left Conservative who had been a successful environment secretary in Heath's government, was plotting a coup to replace Heath with William Whitelaw before the October election, fearing that a second defeat was inevitable and would deliver the party into the hands of the right. Nothing came of it.

I was a member of a faction that also included Ian Gilmour, Chris Patten and Jim Prior. We felt that we should acknowledge the country's deep anxiety over the perilous state of the economy and the collapse of national morale and appeal beyond normal party lines for national unity. The flavour of our manifesto should be non-partisan, and argue that we needed a new national settlement that would bring together the best from all parties. I believe that this reflected the national mood at that time, and it countered the demands of many disaffected backbenchers and others in the party for a shift to the right and towards a more partisan approach. This latter battle was also being fought in the selections for parliamentary seats, from which Heath and Whitelaw (as chairman of the party) had, like all party leaders, attempted to see that leading dissidents were excluded. This line began to break and the right-wingers win through. I remember the gloom in our office when we heard that Ian Gow and Alan Clark had been selected for safe seats.

Just before the autumn election, with the manifesto prepared, I carried Heath's bags to the United States, where he addressed the Council on Foreign Relations and breakfasted with Henry Kissinger, who told us, 'If there is another anti-American President of France, the US will be compelled to take action.' What action was not clear. Heath himself had complemented his Europeanism with a certain stiffness and detachment in his relations with the US which had reached near crisis-point the year before when he had refused the US permission to use British bases in Cyprus for the resupply of Israel during the Yom Kippur War.

While we were in the States, the printers leaked the manifesto to the press, and Labour pretended to think that its appeal for national unity was reminiscent of the National Front.

The second election of 1974 is one of the unsung successes of Conservative campaigning since the Second World War. Labour, and most commentators, predicted a rerun of 1966 after 1964 – a clear and overwhelming victory for Harold Wilson. But the nation had long since fallen out of love with him, and the Labour Party he led was as deeply divided between the hard left and social democrats as the Conservatives were between Heathites and Josephites. Labour won, but their overall majority was only three, though they had forty-two more seats than the Conservatives, a far narrower victory than had been predicted. By holding Labour to that margin, Heath gave to his successor a position which provided the basis for her future victory. Within one Parliament, the erosion of his majority by lost by-elections forced James Callaghan, Wilson's successor, into a weak and unpopular pact with the Liberals, which in turn led to Callaghan's defeat on the floor of the House, to a shattered Labour Party and to the Thatcher–Major years.

Willie Whitelaw, now party chairman, was a Wykehamist and the holder of a Military Cross (like his predecessor in that office, Carrington). A subtle and intelligent man, he knew that the British do not like their politicians to appear too clever. His deliberate comical obfuscations pre-dated Boris Johnson's by thirty years, and were a delight. There were people, he claimed, led by Wilson himself, going round the country stirring up apathy, which was a disgrace. On another occasion, he was challenged about a report from the Law Commission, which had argued that long sentences were no deterrent to criminals. What did Whitelaw think? He thought on the one hand this; on the other hand that.

'That is not what your candidate for Little Tiddlehampton says,' cried the reporters. 'He says you should put it in the wastepaper basket!'

'That's what I say,' answered Whitelaw. 'Put in now! Take it out later!'

For a moment or two during that long night in October 1974, in the upstairs room at Heath's Sidcup constituency office where we listened as the first results started to come in, it even looked as if we might win. I remember Heath looking across the room, away from the group of frenetic staffers surrounding him and towards Victoria, who was sitting quietly on her own, the sole outsider to all this. He caught her eye and shrugged faintly as if to say, 'Only you and I know this is all nonsense.'

His approach to his own position displayed the same mixture of courage, stubbornness and reluctance to face reality as had his attitude to calling the first election of 1974. After the surprisingly good result of October, if he had immediately offered himself for re-election, promising widespread policy reviews and accepting the need to shift some way towards the economic liberals in the process, he might have retained his leadership. But he did none of those things. In fact, he barely hid his contempt for his opponents. Keith Joseph, honest, anxious, and intelligent, proved that he was not himself leadership material in a series of brave but politically disastrous speeches, one of which his enemies spun as recommending birth control for the lower classes.

At All Souls, a seventeenth-century drinking song, 'The Mallard Song', is sung at the Gaudy in the Michaelmas term. In 1974 the Lord Mallard, the fellow who led the singing, the brilliant Alan Tyson, classicist, psychoanalyst and editor of Beethoven's manuscripts (among other things), availed himself of his right to interpolate an ephemeral verse dealing with current events. There had been a bomb scare at the college,* and Tyson's verse went:

On Thursday night with much aplomb
Three Fellows sought a ticking bomb.
They discovered no explosives
Except a weekend speech of Joseph's.

Next up, in what appeared to us to be a doomed procession of contenders, was Edward du Cann, inexplicably the chairman of the backbench 1922 Committee for many years and a man with a controversial reputation in the City. His merchant bank, Keyser Ullman, had collapsed during the 1973–4 secondary banking crisis. His supporters unwisely met in his offices in Milk Street in the City, leading Maurice Trowbridge

---

* It should be remembered that through all this economic and political turmoil there was always the background drumbeat of the IRA's bombing campaign, which culminated in the murderous slaughter of youngsters in two pubs in Birmingham on 21 November. I went with Heath to see the appallingly burned survivors in hospital.

to label them the Milk Street Mafia. Genuine Tory grandees (and small fry like me) would have left the party if du Cann had been elected. In those days, powerful City voices who declared, 'You cannot do business with so-and-so' still carried a veto. Not so now. For better or worse, today we have to rely on the Financial Conduct Authority.

Finally, there was the rising phenomenon of Margaret Thatcher. There is no question that Heath both admired *and* despised her. He admired the fact that she was an outsider, like himself, from a background only slightly more prosperous than his own. He despised her, certainly in part, I am afraid, because she was a woman; but he also had very little time for her new-found ideological stance. As education secretary, she had followed the standard departmental line without complaint, continuing the bipartisan comprehensivisation programme. She had also been a strong pro-European, and campaigned energetically for a 'yes' vote in the referendum that took place just after she became leader. She had not been an important player in the Cabinet's struggles in 1973 over whether to move to a more *dirigiste* incomes policy.

There was then the historic irony of why she had become a popular figure with the grass roots of the party. During the autumn election of 1974 she held the shadow portfolio for the environment, which included the perennially vexed issue of local rates. The old rating system relied on rate poundage – a percentage tax – on a valuation of domestic property undertaken at supposedly fixed intervals for this purpose. Such revaluations were supposed to correct changes in the relative values of properties. They did not increase the total amount raised by domestic rates, but shifted more of the burden to more valuable properties. Broadly, therefore, each revaluation tended to result in increasing rates for areas where property values were rising – the Home Counties, and their equivalents elsewhere in the United Kingdom, for example – and for those who had improved their homes, and falling rates in the (mostly Labour-voting) big cities. This was anathema, for obvious reasons, to grass-roots Tories. Of course, the value of the property was the only determinant; the income of the household did not enter into the calculations. So a widowed pensioner now living alone in the home where she had raised her children would pay the same as the four adult wage-earners who lived next door. The Treasury saw domestic rates as an efficient tax: they pushed the widow to sell, releasing her property to those who really needed it and providing her with a pension fund in the process. But such arguments held little sway with Tories, even among the new economic liberals who had safe Home Counties seats. I discovered early that economic liberals rarely behave in the way their theories say they should when their own interests are involved.*

During the summer of 1974, lobbies and the party's own grass roots pressed Heath to abolish domestic rates. One particularly aggressive lobbyist, David Petri, who called himself the chairman of the National Association of Ratepayers' Actions Groups, more or less camped in Heath's outer office, from which I tried (and usually failed) to expel him. In the end, Heath buckled and agreed to add a commitment in the manifesto: we would 'abolish the domestic rating system and replace it with taxes more broadly based and related to people's ability to pay'. Thatcher was thus handed an extremely popular policy to sell, particularly in the Tory heartlands. There was no elaboration on what the new 'more broadly based' taxes might be, so there was no danger of future losers rallying against the pledge. If there was a single episode which rocketed Thatcher into the public, and above all the party's, eye, it was this. If there was a single pledge that kept the bedrock Tory vote solid, especially in England, it was that promise to abolish the rates. The irony will not be lost on readers. The pledge to replace domestic rates was Heath's gift to Thatcher; without it, she might never have become leader. It also helped to limit the scale of Labour's victory, laying the ground for Thatcher's parliamentary defeat of Callaghan and the latter's subsequent defeat at the 1979 general election. The gift, of course,

---

* Daniel Kahneman and Amos Tversky won the Nobel Prize for Economics for saying the self-same thing in 2002. I think I was robbed.

then came back to haunt her. The Community Charge, or poll tax, was how the pledge was fulfilled.

The only person present throughout this story, from start to finish, was me: I was the private secretary who failed to eject Mr Petri; ten years later I was the parliamentary under-secretary who oversaw the design of the poll tax.*

By the beginning of 1975, Heath had manoeuvred himself into a much weaker position. Stubbornly resisting, as ever, he had missed the opportunity for a swift leadership election that he probably would have won, as either Keith Joseph or du Cann would have been his main opponent. Then, inch by inch, he had conceded some policy-making ground to the liberal economists, and had finally made Thatcher jointly responsible for economic policy. He had also agreed to a review of the party's election rules, to be carried out by Sir Alec Douglas-Home. He had taken some steps to broaden his appeal in the parliamentary party by appointing Kenneth Baker as an additional PPS, alongside Tim Kitson. But all attempts to get him to use the social skills he had once deployed so deftly as a popular army officer and successful chief whip seemed doomed to failure. I would mention a backbencher who might be swayed by a little courteous treatment. Heath would wave away the idea: 'I have spoken to him. Last year. He's a great friend.' (Often, in reality, he was not.) Meanwhile, his handling of honours was admirable but suicidal. Until I became his private secretary, I had not known how brazen requests for honours could be. Backbenchers' letters had a structure to them along the lines of: 'I myself think the honours system outdated and absurd. However, my constituents, my family, my elderly dachshund dog are all

---

* In my maiden party conference speech, as a delegate from the floor in 1976, with Heath glowering on the platform behind me, I tried a self-deprecating joke: 'When I started working for Mr Heath, he was a prime minister with a majority over all other parties of thirty. When I stopped working for him, he was a backbencher in opposition.' It raised a few laughs. But the following Sunday's *Express* showed me it is foolish to prime guns that others can then fire at you. 'That young Waldegrave is supposed to be smart,' they wrote, 'but has it occurred to anyone that when he started working for Mr Heath . . .' Perhaps, given my unique connection to the Poll Tax, I should now claim to have disposed not only of Heath but of Thatcher, too.

now stupefied – and taking it personally – that I have been passed over for so long.' Heath would throw them into the waste-paper basket, and another monetarist would be born.

He would also stubbornly resist any attempt to woo the public. Not so his great rival. I attended 1975's FA Cup Final (West Ham 2, Fulham 0) with Heath. It was not his idea of fun. As we all emerged from the grand dining room and came into public view in the FA's box, I noticed that Harold Wilson stubbed out his Havana cigar and extracted from his pocket his 'trademark' demotic pipe.

Fate, as it likes to do, kicked Heath hard when he was down: his yacht, *Morning Cloud IV*, was lost in a freak storm, drowning a godson and several other good friends. In the chaos of journalists' telephone calls to his outer office, I took all the phones off their hooks, leaving just one on which we awaited a desperate call. When I came to replace them I found the Élysée Palace still holding on one, hoping to speak to the prime minister, which Heath no longer was. So much for the fabled French official efficiency.

Tim Kitson brought the result of the leadership ballot into the big Commons office where some of us had gathered, and handed Heath the piece of paper showing that Thatcher had won the first round. There are two versions of what he said next: Kenneth Baker's, 'So we got it all wrong then'; and mine, 'It has all gone wrong, then.' The version I remember is subtly but importantly different from Baker's. His means 'we', and indeed 'you – the staff', have messed up the election. Mine means that he was still thinking with the clarity that made him nearly great: that everything he had inherited, from Churchill, Macmillan, Butler and the other architects of post-war British Conservatism, was about to end. I may be reading too much into this, but I know that he was so stubborn, and so ungracious and sour in defeat because he understood that the contest was not a matter of personalities, nor even of superficial policy differences. He realised that his defeat meant that a sea change was coming over the British right. It would be the end of the attempt to maintain what my old

Harvard teacher Sam Beer had called the social contract, forged during and after the Second World War, and a reversion to far freer economics in which the government would not regard full employment as a possible – or even legitimate – object of policy. It would be the end of the dominance in the Conservative Party of those who feared above all else being seen as the successors of the hard-faced inter-war men who had made economic policy in the twenties and thirties. And it would begin the inexorable rise of anti-Europeanism in the party, which had the potential to undo what Heath regarded as his greatest achievement. To simplify, it meant a very big shift to the right, towards attitudes against which Heath had been part of a broad alliance in the party ever since that famous Oxford by-election in 1938. That alliance had been defeated on his watch, and his anger derived from the fact that he knew in his heart of hearts that it was his fault.

Meanwhile, I was in turmoil: passionate in my loyalty to Heath; intellectually troubled by his stubbornness, or his courage, in refusing to alter in any way. I have always been an instinctive loyalist – to Macmillan, to Douglas-Home, to Heath, to Thatcher and (more or less) to Major. It is probably a weakness in a politician. Shortly after Heath's defeat, I paid a visit to the Eton Political Society and delivered a bitter speech (which I released to the press) accusing Thatcher of disloyalty. Had Heath not defended her in the famous fracas about her abolition of free school milk? This speech does me some credit for my loyalty (my mother wrote to me, 'Even the ranks of Tusculum could scarce forebear to cheer'), but not much for my political sense. Nevertheless, Thatcher was kind to me when, boiling with self-righteousness, I tendered my resignation as head of the leader's office before I could be sacked. She merely observed that the abolition of free school milk – an unpopular policy she had seen through as education secretary – was not her idea but the Treasury's. I expect that was true.

The great tectonic shift that swept away the old liberal Conservative Party was probably inevitable. Even within the Labour government, it shook anciently entrenched attitudes. In a year or two, Anthony Crosland, the environment secretary, was telling local authorities, 'The party is over'; Peter Jay was writing monetarist speeches for his father-in-law Jim Callaghan; and Shirley Williams was warning the universities that the first-ever cuts would be coming soon. Nevertheless, all sorts of plausible counter-factual history can be imagined. Enoch Powell sourly but probably correctly observed that if the leadership election had been held either a little earlier or a little later, Thatcher would not have won. And it is alleged that moderate backbenchers, wanting to warn Heath that he should stand down in favour of Whitelaw and/or improve his manners, voted for Thatcher on the first ballot in the belief that she could not possibly win, thereby propelling her to the lead that put paid to both Heath *and* Whitelaw.

If Heath had won, and held on, it would have been a hard and unrewarding victory, at least at first. All parties swing against Europe when in opposition in Britain, and those strains would have become ever more acute in the Conservative Party. But Wilson's and Callaghan's governments descended swiftly into sleaze, incompetence and their own conflicts with the unions, so that it seems likely that any viable opposition would have had a good chance of defeating Labour in 1979, no matter who was in charge. Moreover, Thatcher's manifesto was markedly moderate in policy terms – no mention of privatisation or confrontation with the unions – and many Heathites were still in prominent positions in her shadow Cabinet. Perhaps Heath, standing on a similar platform, would have been similarly victorious. We shall never know.

Thatcher, however, did possess one great advantage in 1979: a sense of newness, of a last chance for a fresh start; and neither Heath nor Callaghan could offer that.

CHAPTER TEN

Escape

Fleeing the sunken ship, avoiding the EEC referendum, dashing off to Persia, I was young and ambitious enough to feel I had emerged from the wreckage without too much damage, and that there was nothing in the mild Euroscepticism that was becoming fashionable which much bothered me; nor did I really mind the shift towards my old friends in that den of iniquity, the Institute for Economic Affairs.

A little book I wrote in 1977 mostly shows my contempt for economics of all kinds. Instead, it is a celebration of politics of the community: the lost world of childhood. It unexpectedly surfaced again in 2013, in a *London Review of Books* review article by the distinguished historian of political thought Colin Kidd, who described it as 'a neglected classic'. Neglected, certainly: Professor Kidd may have been the first person to have opened it since Peter Utley, the Conservative thinker whose wisdom was somehow enhanced by his blindness and who reviewed the book generously in a *Daily Telegraph* leader when it was published.

And some big, simple things remained clear. I had never flirted with the murderous nonsense of Communism, nor been taken in by the alleged moral, as opposed to sectarian, differences between Leninism,

Stalinism and Trotskyism. Alone in Britain, the Conservatives were wholly sound in their opposition to the desperately dangerous late Soviet Empire, whose relatively early dissolution I predicted in my little book. Communism was not only wicked and incompetent, I thought, but intellectually trivial and the sponsor of truly banal art to boot. As the novelist Milan Kundera said when it finally collapsed, Communism was totalitarian *kitsch*, but *kitsch* with teeth.

At home, whatever the economics, both Labour and Conservative governments had been destroyed by the brute power of the anti-democratic trades unions. Indeed, many fundamental freedoms – such as the freedom not to join a trade union – were violently suppressed by thugs who were accountable to no one. Witnessing this, I was in no doubt about whose side I was on. The fall of Heath had shaken me personally, but politically I did not question where I wanted to be or what I wanted to do: I wanted to be in Parliament on the Conservative benches; and I wanted to reach the very highest office. My superstitions were still intact: I must never for a second acknowledge self-doubt and I continued to believe that if I did something to the best of my ability, that would be good enough for success. Also, sometimes, I would touch every third lamp-post, or not tread on the gaps between paving stones – through fear not of the bears, but of failure. There was no other prize worth winning. How could anyone have any other ambition?

Now some god up there, glancing down for a moment, decided I had had enough bad luck for the time being. Give him a break! It was a big one, the biggest. My long engagement to Victoria was over, its ending handled by both of us with a skill based on our understanding that though our friendship was unbreakable, we had better come clean and admit that we were never going to marry. So we freed each other from our promises. Consequently, even though we had split up, I was there when someone said to Victoria, 'There's a girl called Angela Gorgas who looks exactly like you. Have you met her?' Life can sometimes turn on such trivial comments. We decided to investigate the phenomenon and duly met Angela at a dinner party. She did indeed look a little like Victoria, but more interestingly another of the guests knew someone who had a flat near mine in Linden Gardens. Did I know him? As a result of that conversation, a few days later I found myself round the corner in that flat, looking at a girl in blue jeans and a T-shirt which read 'Leith's School of Food and Wine'.

This is not an *histoire sentimentale*. Rather, it is an attempt to describe a certain kind of political ambition and its origins, and to give an account of the weather of a certain kind of public life. But it is futile to pretend that the people one loves do not affect everything else. What I found in Caroline Burrows was no lesser support for my attempt at glory than I had found in Whizz, and Karen, and Victoria. Nor was it irrelevant that she was – and is – astoundingly beautiful. But in her I also found that sense of completion, of the resolution of things, that unlucky people say occurs only in novels. It does not. It happens in real life too, which is why Jane Austen wrote the truth as well as fiction.

Caroline and I were married in 1977, and the happiness she spread surrounded not only me but my parents, who had quietly known that Victoria and I were in danger of making each other unhappy. As I have explained, I inherit the despondent Waldegrave gene. But if ever that gene met its match, it was in Caroline, whose capacity for practical love has created everything that is best in my life since I first saw her kneeling on the floor of my neighbour's flat that lucky day.

Tolstoy begins *Anna Karenina* by proposing that 'Happy families are all alike; every unhappy family is unhappy in its own way.' That is not really true. I have seen a good many happy families, including my own at Chewton (in spite of the tensions my father created). I have not seen many founded on such generous and practical love as Caroline provides. Walking along Linden Gardens one evening very early in our relationship, I prepared to cross the street to avoid a drunken tramp who was lying on the pavement. She did not. She knew him.

'Come on, Charlie, this is no good. Do you need help?'

'Oh, hello, Caroline. Sorry, I'm a bit drunk.'

Practical steps followed to help Charlie.

So it went. Later, our friend John Wells was dying. To help his wife Theresa, Caroline delivered food from Leith's every day. Before he died, John said that he had never seen a greater example of practical love – a phrase so apt that I have repeated it when describing Caroline.

On her deathbed, my mother said, 'Caroline has been like another daughter to me.' She meant it.

If this makes Caroline sound saintly, here is another of my mother's deathbed remarks, said of a dear old priest who visited her rather regularly: 'He is a saint. And, like most saints, he is a bit of a bore.' Caroline is not a bore. As we walked back early one morning from a splendid party at the Ritz in Paris to the British Embassy where we were staying, she in her spectacular Chloe dress and precariously high heels, workmen on the scaffolding we passed simply downed tools and applauded.

Her capacity for happiness and kindness has kept me sane. Others too: after selling Leith's, she trained as a psychotherapist, winning her degree scroll and mortarboard in her fifties. I was once sitting after dinner at All Souls listening to one of those conversations in which people say, 'All this talking therapy is nonsense. People should just pull themselves together.'

A fellow intervened: 'Not so. After my father died, I was shattered. I went to a bereavement counsellor. She saved me.'

I knew, although I should not have done, that the counsellor was Caroline.

She is an autodidact, the good nuns of the Sacred Heart at Woldingham having taught her how to play tennis and smoke (to alleviate nerves before examinations), but not much else. To live with an intelligent adult who is reading things for the first time, especially things that you think you understand because you won a prize writing about them at the age of fifteen, is a wonderful re-education. Moreover, she has a craft, and is a master of it, recognised by her peers. A particular pleasure derived from being taken, say, to a Roux Brothers restaurant by Victor Rothschild and from observing his consternation when the great chefs emerged from the kitchen wreathed in smiles not to greet him but to embrace their friend Caroline.

Her smile lights up a room. The sight of her in the street in the distance on a rainy day still makes my heart leap. It is not true that love inevitably declines as the years pass.

My family were generous to me because they rejoiced in Caroline. They bought us 66 Palace Gardens Terrace, just over the road from Linden Gardens, and we lived there until we sold it to buy flats for our children in 2010. As babies, all of those children had come back from St Mary's Hospital to that lovely street, filled as it is with glorious white cherry-blossom every spring.

Just before I met Caroline, in the certain knowledge that even the first of my political ambitions – entering Parliament – would not be fulfilled for at least another four years, there had been no avoiding the fact that, having no private income, I needed to find a job. Journalism did not seem to fit with my ambitions. Years before, sat next to R. A. Butler on the sofa after lunch at Victor Rothschild's house in Cambridge, the great man had turned to me with a difficult opening line for any nervous youngster: 'They all said, you know, that I should have been prime minister.' Who were 'they'? And what on earth was the proper reply? Later, thankfully, he was less enigmatic: 'Do not become typecast as an adviser.' This was powerful advice, and I tried to act on it. Even worse, to my mind, than an adviser was a commentator. Forgetting that some of my greatest heroes had earned their living by the pen, I refused Henry Keswick's generous offer of the political editorship of the *Spectator*.

What about the City? Well, I took a rather lofty view of money. God would provide, normally via my long-suffering father. Had not F. E. Smith told his (even more long-suffering) father to keep quiet and pay up after his Oxford debts caught up with him? So, in spite of the good advice of Peter Walker to make money before going into politics, as he himself undoubtedly had, I spurned the Square Mile (which did not, it is true, pursue me with much vigour). Instead, Victor Rothschild recommended me to Arnold Weinstock, managing director of the General Electric Company as a young man deserving his patronage. As far as I was concerned, this would allow my princely education to continue: I needed to know about industry and the real world. However, I soon learned that it was not going to make me rich. 'How much are you going to pay me to come and learn about my company?' was Arnold's opening shot.

In 1975, GEC was the largest private sector company in Britain, employing around 160,000 people, with roughly the same number of shareholders (Weinstock was particularly proud of this). It was the inheritor of some titanic names from Britain's – and indeed the world's – industrial past: Associated Electrical Industries, British Thomson-Houston, English Electric, Marconi, Radio and Allied, as well as the old GEC itself. It was the principal industrial employer in Stafford, Rugby, Coventry, Trafford Park and many other places. It had a large research centre at Wembley. It made huge steam turbines and their alternators for power stations, fighting it out with, and often winning against, the United States' General Electric and Japan's Mitsubishi in world markets. It also went toe to toe with Siemens and Philips. It made telephone exchanges, medical equipment, torpedoes, avionics, Hotpoint washing machines and Schreiber furniture. It was a key shareholder of the company that made the nuclear islands of nuclear power stations. In the back of one of its factories were the remains of Whittle's Power Jets test beds. As the British-owned shipbuilding, steel and car industries declined and fell, only GEC and Rolls-Royce (which went bankrupt in 1971 but was rescued by nationalisation) remained in the first division of the world's engineering companies.

At first, I 'worked' in Weinstock's office. This mostly consisted of helping him think up names for his racehorses, helping him with the

Times crossword (neither of us was much good at it) and accompanying him to meetings with French and British government ministers. I was also commissioned to write a private history of Britain's nuclear industry, explaining how, at virtually every key point, the British government had taken the wrong decision: five rival prototypes squandering resources; then a crazy, nationalistic decision to build steam-generating heavy-water reactors, followed by advanced gas-cooled reactors – on the grounds that pressurised water reactors, which became the world's standard, were not British. I enjoyed this.

I went with Weinstock to meet Tony Benn, who as industry secretary was making yet more mistakes on nuclear matters. He was accompanied by his political adviser, the very left-wing Frances Morrell. Arnold, who knew how to manage the theatre of a meeting, announced that he had come to meet Her Majesty's government, not the Labour Party: either Morrell left, or he would. If Benn had not been so dumbfounded, he might have thought of objecting to me.

The government had to negotiate with Weinstock over defence supply, civil nuclear energy, power transmission, telecoms and power generation – and he was a much more accomplished negotiator than most ministers. It was an intensely political company, although not in a party sense: the only time Weinstock offered financial support to the Conservatives was when Labour committed itself to nationalisation of the aerospace industry; and on that occasion he also gave money to the Liberals. He wanted a dramatic advertising campaign like the one he remembered on behalf of Mr Cube, when Labour had threatened nationalisation of Tate & Lyle, the sugar company, in 1951. He and I pored over draft advertisements showing poor little aeroplanes, *à la* Mr Cube. Michael Heseltine's suggestion that we should hire a couple of youngsters he had found, Maurice and Charles Saatchi, was spurned. Our campaign is not remembered.

Quite often Weinstock would, with unspeakable but deliberate bad manners, greet visitors with his feet on the desk and then spend most of the meeting rummaging in a drawer for a fresh cigar. He also made terrible Jewish jokes. As I had been with Rothschild, but to a much lesser extent, I became a supernumerary family member. Weinstock was the youngest of a large family, as I am; like me, he lived as elder siblings died. One of my duties was to accompany him to an annual lunch at the Connaught with visiting elder brothers. These meals were festivals of his awful Jewish jokes. I accompanied Arnold and his shy son Simon to the Mozart festival at Salzburg.* Weinstock was a tremendously knowledgeable Mozartian and close friend of the great conductor Ricardo Muti (in spite of the latter claiming to be a Communist), but I mostly remember Simon's horror as his father sent back a prawn cocktail via the fawning waiter on the grounds that it had only three prawns in it. On another occasion, when we took his daughter Susan out to lunch, I put my foot in it: 'Do you know,' I said, 'when I became engaged to Victoria, I discovered that her bank statements went first to her father.' There was a chilly silence round the table.

Weinstock had immaculate eighteenth-century taste: not just Mozart, but beautiful harpsichords and good pictures by Arthur Devis and others in his Wiltshire house. However, when he played up to his idea of the caricature of the Jewish businessman, he could be wonderfully absurd. If he got a wrong number, he would demand to speak to Sir Ian Vallance, the head of the still-nationalised telephone company. 'Ian, your machine gave me the wrong number. I'm not paying for that!' Actually, the machine in question was almost certainly made in GEC's Coventry factory. He would proffer a credit card in a grand restaurant to an obsequious waiter. Then withdraw it with, 'Well, then, if you're willing to share your profit with American Express, how about sharing it with me?' and produce cash. Rather like the trader in *The Life of Brian*, he regarded a failure to haggle as a failure of normal human intercourse. However, with his own money – never the shareholders' – he could often be generous. His

---

* Simon contracted melanoma and died tragically young in the same year as Amschel Rothschild, 1996.

superlative stallion Troy won the Derby in 1979, Willie Carson up. It was the two-hundredth running of the race and the Queen's horse came second, to national disappointment. It was probably the greatest day in Arnold's life. A little later, a useful cheque for an oddly exact sum – say £135 – arrived for Caroline and me, with a note from Arnold which read, 'You will remember that on the day Troy was entered for the Derby, you placed a bet of ten pounds. Here are your winnings.' It was an elegant way to give a present to a friend, and gambling winnings are tax free. I have to admit to HMRC, however, that it was all – except the cheque – fiction.

Heath was a great negotiator in a complex, multifaceted, official setting, with an iron memory for detail. But Weinstock, ably backed by the other members of the triumvirate with whom he ran the company – David Lewis, the lawyer, and Kenneth Bond, the accountant – was even better. 'There is always another deal,' he taught me, 'especially when they tell you that this is the last deal that will ever be available.'

I remember an evening when – under great pressure from the British government to do the deal – we were supposed to finalise the sale of a civil nuclear power station to the Romanians. (Ceauşescu was flavour of the month at the time, the theory being 'He might do a Tito and break with Moscow', along with that other perennially dreadful argument, 'If we don't sell it to him, the French will'.) A horde of Romanians and bewildered Foreign Office minders arrived in Weinstock's office. I sat at a table at the far end of the room, on which lived a large silver box of fine cigars; these soon disappeared into Romanian pockets. Meanwhile, behind his huge desk, Weinstock was in his element. 'It must be signed, Lord Weinstock! There is the communiqué! The delegation leaves tomorrow!' He had no intention of signing anything that night or under any pressure of artificial deadlines.

There is no reason at all why GEC should not still exist today. Some blame Weinstock for not investing or researching enough, but the figures do not bear this out. He certainly missed some opportunities: for instance, he thought Sir Ernest Harrison's Racal, the fore-runner of Vodafone, was a 'bucket shop' and that mobile phones were toys. But so did McKinsey and Company, who predicted that a total of around one million might ultimately be sold in the United States.

He did 'fail' to oversee the huge merger in the US which some thought was essential: we looked at National Cash Register Inc.; and we did acquire the Picker Corporation for its medical equipment, including the MRI scanner invented at Nottingham University. But Weinstock thought a US mega-merger would be too dangerous and expensive, and he may well have been right: the record of British, or indeed any foreign, industrial takeovers in the intensely protectionist US market was – and is – mixed, to put it mildly. Instead, he put his efforts into building Anglo-French companies, on the basis that, for all our differences, the two economies were of the same scale and had broadly similar interests. An insane British government prevented him from agreeing a fifty–fifty deal with the French to build the next generation of pressurised water reactors for both countries, and put paid to tens of thousands of British jobs in the process. But British politicians thought they knew better. They chose rival (inferior) reactors and in the end sold the whole industry to the Japanese and the Germans.

The destruction of Weinstock's company at the end of the century by some second-rate investment bankers who bought overpriced American paper companies for cash is one of the great tragedies of modern British industry. 'Even they can't get the shares below a pound,' he told me not long before he died, as he watched the bubble they had made of his life's work burst. But they did.

Weinstock blamed himself for the fall of his company because he had appointed Jim Prior chairman, and Prior, he said, was not strong enough to sack the underperforming management. Perhaps I was partly to blame for GEC having an ex-politician as chairman, because I had, earlier, suggested that he appoint Lord Carrington when he resigned as foreign secretary over the Falklands (Weinstock was dining with us that night). But neither Weinstock nor anyone else had any reason to criticise Carrington's performance as chairman.

Weinstock, though intensely and proudly Jewish, and a little more observant (though not much) than Rothschild, was the least Zionist of men. In fact, Israel was a perpetual irritant to his business. (It was claimed that GEC observed the Arab boycott of sales to Israel in order to sell to Saudi Arabia and elsewhere.) I suspect he, like Rothschild, would have become wholly assimilated were it not for the Holocaust.

In 1976 I was about to be installed as the boss of a little 'training company' – Walsall Conduits, it was called – when I was selected as parliamentary candidate for the Bristol West constituency. Consequently, as the by-now minority Labour government might fall at any moment, Walsall Conduits was put in more experienced hands. This was a shame for me – as well as a lucky escape for a fine West Midlands firm – because running a company under Weinstock's tutelage would have been a wonderful training. Of all the formidable people I have known, even though some will say he was past his prime by the time I worked for him, I believe that he understood action better than any of them, including Thatcher. The feet on the desk, the insouciance, the terrible jokes – it was all a pose. When he needed to move, there was no gap between thought and action, any more than there is for a good pianist playing a Mozart sonata. He understood how to devolve, but also how to cross-examine those to whom he had devolved; he would never be bounced; he had an overall vision into which individual strategies and tactics fitted, though this did not preclude swift opportunism if something unexpected turned up. In one respect he was very like Thatcher: he had his team – Lewis and Bond in my day – and when they retired he was unable to find replacements, though he tried harder than she did. He knew it was impossible for a single man to run a great organisation: a team was essential, and a team which spread a doctrine. In some far-off factory I left the light on as I walked out of a room. 'Turn that off or Arnie will be after us,' said my companion. Once, at Stafford, where we made the big steam turbines that still produce most of Britain's elec-tricity, I was guided from one part of the immense site to another by an elderly supervisor. He wore a white coat with tabs of rank in the old-fashioned way. We passed a huge portrait of the first Lord Nelson of Stafford – the great boss of British Thomson-Houston, one of the many companies absorbed into GEC. 'He did a lot for Stafford, did Lord Nelson,' said my guide. Then, looking round to see that such heresy was not overheard, 'They will say the same of that Weinstock one day.' They do not, however, because his pygmy successors saw to it that the Stafford site went with all the rest, and indeed with a huge swathe of British engineering

After the period in his office, I did gain some real industrial expe-rience – as a junior clerk in the purchasing department of GEC Gas Turbines at Whetstone, south of Leicester. The site also contained part of the National Nuclear Corporation, and thousands were employed there. No trace remains; it has all been sold for housing. My friend in this very menial task was an autodidact member of the Communist Party who knew enough about Shelley and Orwell not to give up on an Old Etonian; others put their heads round the door just so they could say they had seen the strange creature. The factory had another celebrity, too – a man who had rescued the portly prime minister, Harold Wilson, when he had tumbled out of his dinghy while on holiday in the Scilly Isles. Some said his Labrador had pushed him overboard.

I lived in gloomy, traditional digs with a suspicious landlady and fry-ups for breakfast, until rescued by the local MP, Nigel Lawson, who with great generosity offered me his constituency house in nearby Blaby, as long as I agreed to address his constituency Conservative association. At the meeting I sat next to, and greatly admired, his first wife, Vanessa. She told me she maintained her independence from local Conservatives by never eating their food. For each course – prawn cocktail, Coronation chicken, Black Forest gateau – she would find a new excuse: 'Oh, my favourite! But I'm afraid I had it for lunch. Oh, how I love Black Forest gateau, but sadly I am allergic to cherries.'

Nothing, not even the reality of constituency dinners, dimmed my belief in my own destiny. The Labour government was disintegrating. There could be an election at any time. I must have a parliamentary seat!

CHAPTER ELEVEN

Not Typecast as an Adviser

I still find it easier to believe in the frivolous and mischievous gods of Olympus than in any of the stern, unbending lawgivers who passed through Jerusalem at one time or another. Heath, assisted by me, pledges to abolish the rates, which leads to disaster for him by helping Thatcher. Thatcher, assisted by me, does abolish the rates, which leads to disaster for her. A later comedy has me believing that I have triumphantly held the moral and honourable line against the appallingly amoral would-be arms-trader Alan Clark, my ministerial colleague. 'Let every last paper be published to the widest possible inquiry!' I tell Robin Butler. In the popular version of what follows, my reputation is destroyed and Alan Clark becomes a famous whistle-blower.

And so to my selection for a parliamentary seat. I have put forward my name for Bristol West, only a dozen miles from Chewton. Then Keith Joseph intervenes, to recommend his protégé (and my friend, subsequently) Brian Griffiths. Alderman Cyril Hebblethwaite, the chairman of Bristol West's Conservative association, has missed Keith's latest

Damascene conversion, to right-wing austerity. He remembers him only as the secretary of state for health and social security who forced him, in his other role as chairman of Avon Social Services Committee, to double and then redouble expenditure: a dreadful left-winger. Cyril is therefore in no mood to accept Joseph's recommendation. It is a close contest, but Miss Griffiths BEM swings her group of ladies behind me because, she subsequently tells me, she bought some curtains from Chewton Priory in the sale after the war. ('There were no curtains in the sale,' said my mother later.) As a result, I am adopted as Bristol West's candidate for the next election, whenever that may be – a more or less local boy who owns a Bristol car. Richard Needham came second (just). Such twists of fate make one think the gods like pointless jokes. But they settle lives.

Now my journeys in one or other of my Bristol-engined cars – Aceaca, Bristol 402 or 405 – became even longer as I drove along the three sides of a triangle: Whetstone, London (where Caroline was) and Bristol. Sometimes Caroline and I would meet at the Crest Motel in Luton, where I would find her surrounded by hopeful commercial travellers, astounded by what they hoped was their good fortune, and not at all pleased to see me. Then the election came.

I received over 50 per cent of the votes for the only time in my career.[*] Bristol West had never been anything other than a Conservative seat. The widow of my predecessor but one – Biddy, Lady Monckton – whose husband Sir Walter had been the great legal fixer of his day, supported me, as did Ursula, Lady Wraxall, the widow of an even more antique pre-decessor, Colonel Gibbs. There was a Constitutional Club, presided over by the Duke of Beaufort, with premises in the city centre; a Citizens' Party, under whose banner the Conservatives fought local elections; and a powerful Conservative and Unionist Club. Terraced family homes in the Bishopston Ward, between the prison and Gloucester's cricket ground, were full of old-fashioned upper-working-class or lower-middle-class

---

[*] When I lost in 1997, that had declined to 34 per cent.

white Tory voters of robust views. So it had been perhaps since the streets named 'Beaconsfield' and 'Alma' had been built and named. By the time I left, Bishopston was a multiracial community, with many student lodgings, and no longer a source of many Tory votes.

Constituency work is hard, and in a real sense thankless. At general elections, swings are almost always uniform, however conscientious an MP has been over the previous four or five years. You can probably contribute to the loss of a seat; but the conventional wisdom is that a good MP is only ever worth a few hundred votes. A few spectacular counter-examples can be found, but normally it is the party label after your name for which people vote, or refuse to vote. The effect of MPs' surgeries on one's view of humanity must be a little like the effect of prolonged exposure to the insane on a psychiatrist: madness becomes the norm. If every Friday evening or Saturday morning you sit listening to people with extremely intricate and mostly insoluble problems, you may well make the mistake of believing that everyone is complaining, all of the time, about everything. You tend to forget the 99 per cent of your constituents who have better things to do than visit their MP.

There are, of course, consolations: sometimes you manage to help someone who really needs it; you get to know one small patch of the nation in minute detail (a decisive argument, to my mind, in favour of smallish, single-member constituencies); and occasionally you hear, usually from modest, elderly people, the most astounding life stories. One day a neighbour in Clifton, where we had a little house, asked us to meet an old gentleman she had befriended: 'He claims to have known Lenin and been a friend of Matisse. I think he was a very famous architect, once. He is called Berthold Lubetkin.' Every word of this turned out to be true: Lubetkin had indeed known Lenin and Matisse (and everyone else who mattered in the 1920s and 1930s in Moscow, Paris and London); and he was arguably one of the most influential modernist architects who has ever lived. He was living out a quiet retirement just round the corner – though the calm soon disappeared if you asked him what he thought of British architecture or town planning over the previous fifty years.

It is the failures which really stick in your mind, though. A young Muslim girl came to see me in a bid to escape a forced marriage. On that first visit she was dressed in Western clothes, and she explained that she wanted to marry her Western boyfriend. Her parents had beaten her. Bristol's approach to multiculturalism at the time meant that she had been allocated a Muslim social worker, who happened to be a cousin of her parents. I told her of the women's refuge and promised police protection. Would they really protect her, year in, year out? she asked. The last time I saw her she was in traditional dress, accompanied by her family. She said she wanted to withdraw all complaints against them and had split from her non-Muslim boyfriend. I knew I had failed her.

But there were more positive experiences, too. I made many good friends, one truly remarkable man, John Miles, among them. He was the convener of the joint shop stewards at Filton, the great hub of aircraft manufacture where Concorde was built. During the election, the local Conservative candidates were asked to meet his committee at the aerodrome. One of my colleagues gave, it seemed to me, an embarrassingly patronising talk. John puffed on his pipe thoughtfully (smoking, in the city of the Wills family, was almost *de rigueur* at the time). Afterwards, he approached me. 'I think you are unfair to Hegel and Marx in your book,' he said. 'Can I come and see you?' Our correspondence continues to this day. Like my Communist friend at the Whetstone factory, John is an extraordinary autodidact who has read his way through public libraries wherever he has found them, even to the extent of borrowing my little book. One thing that first encounter taught me: never patronise an audience. I learned it just in time. At a little pub meeting in Hotwells not long after, the constituent sitting quietly at the back was Professor John Vincent, the formidable historian and philosopher, who became another firm friend, as did his wife, Nicolette. Later, reminding us both who the enemy really was, Socialist Worker Party members attacked his lectures, closing them down. The university was pusillanimous, I am sorry to say, in his defence.

Bristol in the seventies and eighties also introduced me to two formidable people who demonstrated the divisions in the Labour Party. One of my neighbours, representing Bristol South East, was Tony Benn, by now very left wing (though he had not always been so). The other, in Bristol South, was Michael Cocks, the Labour chief whip, who was not among Mr Benn's admirers. Not long before, the Conservatives had sent a candidate by the name of Dicks to fight Cocks, which delighted Michael. Walking in procession up Park Street in Bristol's grand Remembrance Day parade one year, I was alongside Michael. Tony was just in front, well within earshot. 'Do you want to know when I realised Tony was potty?' asked Michael, addressing Tony's back as much as me. 'It was on this occasion a few years back. As we came past the Boy Scouts – you see them drawn up there? – Tony said to me, "Doesn't the power of the state terrify you?" Potty! Quite potty!' I kept out of it, and both remained friendly acquaintances. Labour chief whip though he was, Michael used to give me sensible advice in the House: 'Throw away that young fogey waistcoat' was one wise tip. On another occasion he said I had been mumbling at the despatch box, with my head down. 'I will go and sit three rows up, and you keep your head up and look at me!' he said. So he abandoned the formidable seat of the chief whip, at the end of the front row, behind the table, and sat instead among his alarmed junior colleagues, to help a wicked young Tory, but a wicked young *West Country* Tory.

The birth of 'Thatcherism' was a strange, prolonged affair. In fact, a case could be made that no such creature ever truly existed. The Conservatives were elected in 1979 on an opaque and moderate manifesto written largely by Chris Patten. We were propelled into power, not decisively, after the so-called 'Winter of Discontent', when mostly public sector unions defied not only the Labour government's calls for pay restraint (insisted upon by the International Monetary Fund, from which Britain had been forced to borrow) but all normal rules of decency and citizenship. Young thugs manning picket lines decided who should be allowed into hospitals; the dead went unburied; rubbish piled up in the streets. Britain, at least in the bigger cities, seemed near to Third World breakdown. Prue Leith, Caroline's employer, helped to precipitate the dustmen's strike in London by refusing to pay the bribes the men demanded. Sir Nicholas Henderson, our ambassador in Paris, in his valedictory telegram, said that it was an embarrassment to represent Britain abroad. Inheriting Turkey's nineteenth-century title, we were known as the 'Sick Man of Europe'.

Prime Minister Jim Callaghan had begun to stem the growth of public expenditure a little and to talk the language of liberal economics, known as 'monetarism' at the time. This validated the incoming government's adoption of a similar policy, although a good third of the Cabinet was Heathite, Macmillanite or 'Keynesian'. Some of them, like Ian Gilmour, were indeed well-informed believers in the old programme of economic management: build consensus with unions and business behind government-brokered demand-management policies, with full employment the principal measure of success and inflation restrained by agreed norms for pay and prices. Others, like Jim Prior, Christopher Soames and Francis Pym, were instinctive social conciliators. Some were simply contemptuous of what they saw as the vulgar Poujadism of Thatcher's culture and language.* This rag-tag internal opposition became known as 'the wets'. As Heath's former private secretary, I was clearly identified as one of them. Very young, and not truly economically literate, I was nevertheless elected secretary of the Conservative backbench Economics Committee, part of a well-organised 'wet' slate, beating a right-wing candidate. We newly elected wets, or some of us, founded a dining club, as

---

* Pierre Poujade (1920–2003) founded the Union de Défense Commerçants et Artisans to protest against taxes on small businesses, deploying the rhetoric of the common man's opposition to metropolitan elites sixty years before the old Dulwich public schoolboy Nigel Farage adopted the same tactic.

was then the tradition, which met first in our kitchen at Palace Gardens Terrace and then in Tristan Garel-Jones's home in Westminster, which was within division bell distance. This became famous enough to be given names by journalists – the 'Blue Chips' or the 'Dirty Dozen' – and doubtless quite a few ruder nicknames besides.

At first the group comprised just the two Pattens – Chris and John – myself, my Euro MP cousin Charles O'Hagan and Garel-Jones, but it grew quite rapidly to include Robert Cranborne, Jocelyn Cadbury, Michael Ancram, Robert Pollock, Richard Needham, Peter Fraser, Robert Atkins, Douglas Hogg, Matthew Parris and John Major. A skilful group portrait painted by Cranborne's sister Rose Cecil catches the internal dynamic well: Chris Patten and I are central; as is John Major, though he is curiously shadowed. John Patten, always the most careful to avoid offence in argument, and the first of us to win office, is leaning against the door: hating confrontation, especially between friends, he was normally to be found with the wives in the kitchen whenever tempers rose, which they often did when I was in full flight. No women; quite a number of Old Etonians. In spite of these handicaps, though, not a bad group.

In microcosm, what happened within our group reflects why Margaret Thatcher's – or perhaps more accurately Geoffrey Howe's – economic policy won through and why the decisive budget of 1981 did not split the party more fundamentally. I do not mean to suggest that we were influential; rather that we were having the sorts of arguments that were taking place throughout the Conservative Party, and indeed around the country. This process was crystallised in our group in the battles between myself and Chris Patten. I believed that the consensual style of economic management clearly no longer worked; that there was nothing for it but to try a dose of economic liberalism, by which I meant that fiscal policy should provide incentives for private sector growth, and monetary policy should be used to control inflation. This meant tough control of public expenditure in order to allow room for tax cuts, which in turn would provide incentives for business and for those in work. The unemployment level would be an uncontrollable residual, though it would come down eventually, when the private sector created new jobs. Chris was deeply sceptical of all this: how you could keep down the price of goods by making *fewer* of them?

We produced a pamphlet, which I edited, entitled *Changing Gear*. In it we argued for more social intervention – training, help for the unemployed and so on (that part was written largely by Cadbury) – but did not attack the Howe–Thatcher economic policy head on. A similar approach was adopted in far more influential quarters: Whitelaw, Carrington and Hailsham all – crucially – stood by Thatcher as their friends and fellow former Macmillanites Gilmour, Soames and Norman St John Stevas gossiped and plotted with varying degrees of disloyalty. There was constant talk that Thatcher was about to do a U-turn. Our friend Mark Boxer gave Caroline and me the original of a cartoon representing this expectation: the grand host and hostess say, 'We had better start asking the Wets to dinner again!' as they read a newspaper headlined 'U-Turns'.

But overall the party remained solid, in spite of extreme anxiety not only in the Commons but around the country. It did so partly because the grandees remained loyal, and partly because many of us who did not care for the right-wing language – and sometimes policies – on social and cultural matters accepted that there was 'no alternative', to use Thatcher's phrase, to a rough and brutal rebalancing of the economy. That rebalancing was made far more savage by the fact that it had been postponed for so many years, and by the arrival of North Sea oil revenues, which helped to drive the pound to two dollars for a time and thereby decimated much of Britain's older exporting industry.

After John Patten, I was the second of our little group to become a minister – namely, parliamentary secretary for higher education – alongside Rhodes Boyson, the genial, right-wing former comprehensive headmaster, and under my colleague from All Souls Keith Joseph, the education secretary. When I exclaimed, 'That is a hot seat!' on being told I would be in charge of university cuts, Joseph replied, 'They are all burning.' And so they were.

There were often riots and demonstrations when I visited universities and polytechnics. I always tried to defend the cuts on the basis of the need for national economy: we had to do more with less if we could; and in any case there was simply less money to spend. I tried to avoid saying that what went on in universities was of low value, a distinction in argument not always maintained by either the right-wing press or some of my colleagues. However, it seemed essential that the cuts should be shaped, not merely imposed across the board; and it was for the universities themselves, not ministers, to do that. A brave and intelligent chairman of the body that distributed the money, the mathematician Peter Swinnerton-Dyer, sought to protect the best and cut the less good. Paradoxically, those hard-hit second-rank universities, famously Salford in Manchester and Aston in Birmingham, that were prepared to take their futures in their own hands and made tough decisions about what to fund and what to close down recovered quickest. Those like my constituency university, Bristol, with much less swingeing savings demanded, simply cut across the board on the basis of 'fairness' and perhaps displayed lesser leadership.

I had proposed Swinnerton-Dyer's appointment to the University Grants Committee on the basis that he had courage and believed in excellence. He was no Tory, however, and was thought to be an opponent of the deployment of cruise missiles in Europe – a US-led NATO policy which Thatcher viewed as a touchstone for reliability. I was summoned to Number Ten to explain myself. Not for the last time, I discovered that by sticking to my guns with a good argument, the prime minister would listen. She relented and allowed the appointment.

In one matter I made my own policy; and for a time it succeeded, until it was swept away by Kenneth Clarke during his time as education secretary in 1992. I resisted the demand from the polytechnics that they should be removed from local authority control and all become centrally funded universities. I thought they should have a different mission from the research-based universities, closer to the vocational; and I thought it was a bad idea to remove all tertiary education from its local roots. (Bristol University, founded by the nineteenth-century city fathers for the children of Bristol merchants, now contained fewer Bristolians, claimed Michael Cocks, than either Oxford or Cambridge.) I therefore suggested a partnership of local authorities and the central government to sponsor the polytechnics, to the wrath of those running the latter, who wanted the prestige of the title 'vice-chancellor' and the freedom to escape from tedious pressure from local councillors about the importance of their local economies.

At All Souls the debate on the cuts took characteristic form. Joseph had sent a letter to all universities and colleges challenging the concept of academic tenure. Surely it was wrong to give jobs for life? He left the College Hall (I did not) while this issue was debated in a college meeting. It was regarded as a trivial interruption when one junior fellow wondered why we were debating the letter at all since (a) we received no money from the government and (b) none of us had tenure. (We were all elected fellows for seven years at a time.) Another academically very distinguished fellow, although not one given to regular speeches, made a brilliant, but rather long, intervention. Many of his colleagues were indeed wasting our money and their time, and they should all be fired at once, he proposed. But who would be on the committee who would select those who should be fired? The self-same inadequates, the very ones who should be fired, who were invariably on all the committees! He gave a long history of how universities had always sacked the wrong people: Maxwell, sacked by Aberdeen; Gauss, leaving Göttingen without a diploma; and so on. The one relieving factor of an unpleasant introduction to ministerial life in a hard time was that, however rude the academics were to me, they were always far ruder to each other.

Thus, with my hands on the greasy pole for the first time, I immediately learned that my childhood visions of an ascent to the heights, wafted upward on waves of applause, was not quite what happened in real life. And thereafter it continued much the same: my first job when I moved to the Department of the Environment in 1983 was to find a place to bury Britain's nuclear waste. Protests accompanied me wherever I went. The remarkable chairman of the Central Electricity Generating Board, Sir Walter Marshall – who as a brilliant young Welsh physicist had adopted what he took to be a Central European accent on the grounds that all serious physicists spoke that way – proposed a typically original – and typically wayward – solution. It was no good trying to hide the stuff apologetically in remote sites, he said. It should be left in full view, to prove it was safe. How about directly under the Palace of Westminster? Geologically no good – shame. Where else, then? Who might step forward for a sweetener of, say, £50 million? The answer was obvious: an aristocrat with an enormous house to maintain who could market the waste site as a tourist attraction and would know precisely what to do with the £50 million. Of course, the house would have to be built on a sound geological formation, preferably very deep clay. Was there such a volunteer? Yes, there was: the Duke of Bedford, who offered his Woburn Estate. The plan was nearly genius, but I was not as brave as the Russell family. So the waste remains unburied to this day.

If I made myself unpopular with the anti-nuclear lobby, I made myself similarly unpopular with the nuclear industry by authorising the prosecution of Sellafield for leaking waste. Tony Benn had said this was impossible, because of the power of the secret state, represented by Sellafield. But the roof did not crash down on me; no representative of the said secret state took me aside for a word, quiet or otherwise. The chief executive of British Nuclear Fuels did come to see me and said it was intolerable: he had been interviewed by the police. Sadly, because I liked him, I had to tell him that such things tended to happen when you broke the law.

There were some good moments. When I arrived in my first office – in the appalling 1960s tower block Elizabeth House, by Waterloo Station, which housed the Department of Education and Science – I found I had been allocated a somewhat scruffy black box for my official papers. I had been dreaming of the legendary red boxes for many a year, but, thinking I must be too junior for such an honour, I hid my disappointment from my private secretary, Brian Glicksman. However, I then experienced the first of many stylish kindnesses from the first of a wonderful series of private secretaries. Brian knew very well what I was thinking, and two days later I arrived to find a fine new set of gleaming red boxes standing elegantly on my desk, with my lowly office inscribed in gold upon them. A new set had had to be made, for some reason I forget, and Brian had ordered them, without feeling the need to consult me.

He did something else for me, too. He was about my age, so I suggested, 'Surely you should call me by my first name, rather than "Minister"?'

'No,' he said, 'I am working for you because of your office, not because you are William Waldegrave.'

It may sound a little pompous, now, and I suspect Mr Blair's Government did away with such constitutional niceties in order to be cool: but Brian Glicksman had the better doctrine.

There was another pleasure. While I unshakeably despised the totalitarian systems of the Communists and the Fascists, I never felt much triumphalism at the victory of one domestic party manifesto over another, though I certainly wanted my team to win. All plans are contingent, and can be improved, I thought (and think). What I did feel was almost physical pleasure the first time I sat at a table, Union Flags in front of me, representing Britain's government. At that moment there was just the faintest echo of those long-gone phantom cheering crowds. No one can dull the pride nor diminish the romance of representing the country you love.

I was a minister in the era so beautifully satirised by Anthony Jay and Jonathan Lynn in *Yes, Minister*, that definitive account of the subtle relationship which then existed between ministers and civil servants. That world was destroyed for ever by the Blair government. Journalists write about Sir Humphrey as if he still exists in the twenty-first-century world of short-term contracts and bonus payments in Whitehall, just as cartoonists still portray civil servants in the bowler hats that were already antique in the 1960s. Neither now exist in Whitehall.

I explained earlier that my respect for the old mandarinate – the real-life Sir Huberts of *The Eagle* – was deeply ingrained. My early contact with Whitehall had reinforced it. When I had worked in the CPRS, Robert Armstrong, Tom Bridges and other civil servants of equal intelligence and moral quality had been behind the baize door of Number Ten. Victor Rothschild, himself a temporary permanent secretary, also had exaggerated respect for the great men – Trend, Armstrong, Dunnett, Greenhill – whom he would invite to weekly sandwich lunches (supplied by the Mirabelle), accompanied by 'cider-cup', an extremely potent concoction made by his butler, Rifleman Sweeney. I would sit in the corner, trying to remain invisible, pretending not to take notes. In one such meeting Sir James Greenhill, the head of the Diplomatic Service, when asked his opinion on how we might tackle inflation, said, 'Increase the Territorial Army.' He saw with more clarity than most that there would be no chance of a stable economy until Parliament reasserted its authority over the unions, and that doing so was likely to involve a contest of straightforward physical power. In due course, though happily without the need to deploy the Army, Territorial or Regular, that is what happened. The police did the work in the coalfields and at the power stations; many heads were broken, not all with justification (as is always the case in physical conflict); and power returned to its proper constitutional place.

During my time as a minister, I was served in my private offices among others by Helen Ghosh, Kim Darroch, Simon Fraser and Andrew Cahn – each and every one of them later, deservedly, a permanent secretary. Another, Dominic Asquith, became a heroic ambassador to Iraq and Egypt, and nearly died in Libya. I believed in the civil service – by which I meant the senior, policy-making and advisory bureaucracy that ran the central departments. They were proud of rank, which in those days ran from permanent secretary to assistant principal to executive officers. It was more than a little reminiscent of the divisions between commissioned and non-commissioned officers in the forces. Nonetheless, the more powerful the department, the more like a college common room or a continuous seminar was the atmosphere. Particularly at the Treasury (always a tiny, elite department) and the Foreign Office (which had its own ancient ranks, 'chief clerk' and 'head of Chancery', for example, all of which have now been replaced with titles borrowed from private enterprise, to show modernity), complete openness between seniors and juniors was the rule in all discussions. When I was a minister there, the Foreign Office had a system of swaps running with the Quai D'Orsay in Paris. Saying goodbye to the excellent young man the French had sent us, I asked him what was the main difference between the two departments. 'That I am talking to you, Minister,' he said.

Clear and coherent marching orders won respect, as did hard work. One minister was removed from office in my time because his senior civil servants complained that he did no work whatsoever, regardless of how much or little they put into his red box, partly through idleness and partly because of his incapacity to reach a decision about anything. Indeed, apart from being the carrier of the political or ideological message of the governing party (where that is relevant or clear), ministers' other main duty is simply to make a decision – *any* decision – when all opposing arguments have been considered. When I became a senior minister, Peter Carrington, with characteristic but not wholly ironic self-deprecation, told me how I should behave. 'All the decisions where there is a rational balance of argument will have been taken by civil servants or your junior ministers,' he said. 'The ones that reach you will be evenly balanced. So you may as well toss a coin. But then don't change your mind.'

I therefore have little time for ex-ministers who complain that their bold schemes were constantly thwarted by all-powerful civil servants. It is not the duty of any big organisation to obey every whim of the boss, especially in public life, where political bosses can be very ephemeral and most have very little experience of anything outside political debate. Tony Benn regularly complains about civil service obstruction in his memoirs, but those mandarins knew that he did not have the backing of either the prime minister or other senior colleagues for many of his policies, and they acted accordingly. In 2013–14 there was another wave of these perennial complaints, this time from Conservative members of the coalition government, and the usual solution was proposed: more political appointees. As if the introduction of even more young enthusiasts armed with nothing but finely honed debating skills would improve the situation. By contrast, ministers with a clear understanding of what they want to do – and cabinet and prime ministerial backing – seem perfectly capable of pushing through radical reforms, whatever the opposition from within their own departments, now just as in Thatcher's day.

Nor is it true, as some say, that ministers are simply presented with officials with whom they find it impossible to work. In 1992 John Major asked me to establish the new Department of Public Service and Science. I was given Sir Peter Kemp as my permanent secretary, once a vigorous and effective official but in my opinion not the right man for that particular role. So I asked Robin Butler, the head of the civil service, to replace him. I suggested that Richard Mottram, currently at the Ministry of Defence, might be a better fit, and the transfer was agreed. Sir Peter went to his grave saying that I had sacked him, but that was not quite true; I had no power to do any such thing. (He left the civil service because there was no other job for him to do, according to Butler.) Nevertheless, as this incident shows, it is perfectly possible, if you have a good case, to exercise decisive influence over the most senior civil service appointments, including your permanent secretary and your principal private secretary. No more than that is necessary. In fact, to go further and make senior civil service appointments from among one's own friends, as Blair did when he appointed Jonathan Powell 'chief of staff' in Number Ten, inevitably leads to the disasters of 'sofa government' that followed. Following that course results in no procedures, no proper records and a demoralised public service, and runs the even greater risk of political and other corruption of our civil service.

Our traditional structure, with uncorrupt and non-ideological civil servants working for ministers who have powerful incentives to lead them properly since they themselves are directly accountable to the savage bear pit of the House of Commons, is one of the many great legacies of our Victorian forebears. Those who imagine that the German or the French or the American system works better have usually had very little experience of friends in those systems explaining how much greener the British grass seems from their side of the fence. Meanwhile, those who sing the praises of the private sector seem to have missed what has happened in the banks over recent years, here and abroad, and have failed to noticed such catastrophes as the demise of poor GEC. Competitive private enterprise can and does work beautifully when there is a functioning market. But an essential part of such a market is the creative destruction of firms when they cease to be economically viable. Government cannot allow the collapse of a department in the hope that something better will come along to replace it. Nor can government abandon its responsibilities because they are too difficult to meet, as a private company can withdraw from an activity in which it is finding it tough to make a profit.

I therefore retain my allegiance to Sir Hubert and Sir Humphrey. The problems with which politicians and civil servants wrestle are inherently difficult and sometimes insoluble, though it is difficult to get elected if one has the honesty to say so. 'Just say "yes"!' has a better ring to it than 'It is mostly a matter of saying "no"!' 'Vote for change!' is more of a sure fire winner than 'Vote for me! Most things are quite out of anyone's control!' The pressures of expectation to which competitive democracy contributes, together with the intractability of the problems themselves, are the causes of our frustration, not Whitehall, which serves us well. There is no quick fix on offer from abroad, or the private sector, or the latest management gurus. All you can do is soldier on, try your best, and not make a rod for your own back by promising more than you can deliver.

CHAPTER TWELVE

Encountering Greatness

For many months, I had been trying to persuade the prime minister to meet some vice-chancellors so that she could hear first hand what they had to say, and so that my credibility with my ministerial constituency might be improved. Finally she agreed. The appointed day was a week after the sinking of HMS *Sheffield* on 4 May 1982. The Falklands War, Thatcher's future and that of her government hung in the balance; Exocet missiles for a moment seemed to threaten catastrophe. I assumed the dinner would be cancelled. It was not. So it was that the prime minister, Keith Joseph and I proceeded to the Bloomsbury headquarters of the great men. They opened their mouths to speak, but she was quicker, and explained vigorously to them how they should go about their business. I had provided a phrase for a draft speech to the effect that there were some stagnant pools amid the ivory towers. I am rather ashamed of it now, but it was deployed that evening. Private secretaries brought in urgent notes for her to read. As we left, and I ushered the stunned vice-chancellors to safety, she grasped my elbow.

'The trouble is, William, there is no proper air cover,' she said. This was not bad leadership.*

I am temperamentally a pessimist, so I could see all sorts of hazards in fighting in the South Atlantic, though I do not believe I ever wavered in thinking we were doing the right thing. I had not predicted the impact it would have in my constituency. One of the very best councillors in Avon County – a man of progressive views who was a key ally of mine – had for some time been thinking of defecting to the newly formed Social Democrats. He came to see me on that first Falkland weekend to tell me that I need have no worries: he would stick by Mrs Thatcher for ever now. There was equally strong support in the multiracial end of my constituency. West Indians and Greek Cypriots knew all about the independence of islands, though the Cypriots asked why we had not driven out the Turks in similar fashion. Poles were intensely patriotic, concerned only that the Argentinians did not seem to be Communists. Sikhs remembered their martial traditions. Only the white English upper middle classes were in a funk.

Childhood romanticism and pride stirred: the glorious pictures of

---

* I must admit that this is not exactly how I remember this incident. I have a clear memory of an earlier, preparatory lunch at Number Ten, on the very day when confirmation came through that the Argentinians had landed. I remember a vigorous discussion of university affairs, dominated by the prime minister, and her comment, as the somewhat shell-shocked university grandees left, that there *would be* no proper air cover – a far more prescient remark, indicating that even then she knew what she was going to do, and how dangerous it would be. But unlike my other sharp memories, when researched, this one starts to dissolve. Or does it? There *was* a lunch on that day at the beginning of April, according to Thatcher's diary (now kept at Churchill College, Cambridge). But it was about information technology; Kenneth Baker is recorded as bringing along a group of businessmen; Arnold Weinstock was there, too; but there is no record of my attendance. So is my original memory correct? Was the story reported to me by Weinstock? Was I at that lunch, unrecorded, because I was Weinstock's protégé and the subject of IT was relevant to universities? Have I conflated the lunch and the later Bloomsbury dinner? Or, as I firmly believe, was there a preparatory university meeting with a few vice-chancellors in Number Ten, unrecorded, on that same Friday? The diary records are far from complete, surprisingly. I told my preferred version of the story at an Old Etonian occasion in 2011, before I had researched it. Jonathan Aitken borrowed it, and some others, for his book *Margaret Thatcher: Power and Personality* (2013). Historical truth is slippery. 'I often think it odd,' says Jane Austen's Catherine Morland in *Northanger Abbey*, 'that history should be so dull, since a great deal of it must be invention.'

sleek frigates racing southwards; the heroism; the horror of burning ships and men; the young Etonian VC who was killed in action; a military junta defeated. Some of the humiliation of Suez, when a British prime minister had to humble himself and submit to the orders of big brother in Washington, was erased. One day I was in the division lobby when the prime minister bore down upon me, flanked by PPSs and toadies. I had to say something. It was at the time when US Secretary of State Alexander Haig, a vain ex-general whom I had met somewhere, was trying to broker a sell-out to the Argentinians. 'Where do the Americans stand, Prime Minister?' I asked.

'I don't know, William. But I know where they are *going* to stand.'

The heart sang.

We would have won the 1983 election even if *Canberra* had not steamed back to Portsmouth with a huge banner hanging from her upper decks bearing the legend 'Maggie Rules OK'. Labour had committed electoral suicide by choosing Michael Foot as leader; the economy was beginning to respond to the harsh medicine of Geoffrey Howe's 1981 budget measures; the polls had already turned. But the Falklands victory changed the nature of the relationship between the British people and Thatcher. Even her bitterest opponents now began their criticisms, 'You have to hand it to her . . .' The upper-class critics were silenced by her sheer courage. Sour old Enoch Powell had said at the beginning of the campaign, 'Now we shall see what the Iron Lady is made of.' At the end, he rose in the Commons and said, 'The analysis shows the material to be ferrous matter of the highest quality.' Something had changed for the better.

As it turned out, there was risk from all this in the future. A precedent full of danger had been set for those who came later and wanted to show *their* capacity for leadership by finding their own Falklands. Eden had wanted to show he could act like Churchill and led us into Suez; Blair wanted to show he was equal to Thatcher and followed the Americans into Iraq. *Facilis descensus Averno.*

Thatcher showed greatness over the Falklands. The phenomenon was very near to me, easy to observe: this thing for which for nearly forty years I had been striving. And for the very first time, seeing it so close to, I began to have doubts that I would ever have it. At the same time came an even more central doubt: did I really want it? It is hard to describe how fundamental were the changes I watched occurring in myself, driven by this first little cloud of self-doubt, as yet no bigger than a man's hand; and partly also by something altogether different.

Ever since I could remember, one conscious, constructed goal had been the magnetic pole around which everything I did was centred. At Eton, I had consciously followed what I thought were the paths to glory. At Oxford, shy and insecure when speaking in public, I forced myself into the Union Chamber, genuinely never believing I would win the ultimate prize of its presidency. I worked six days a week for a whole year for my first. I tried to map out my princely education – civil service, Number Ten, industry, the book. Of course, being a romantic and having enough of my family's dual capacity for gloom and ecstasy, I fell in love several times and managed to suffer for it despite the best efforts of the generous women I have described in these pages. ('You *enjoy* being unhappy in love,' my redoubtable friend Caroline Younger once told me.) I was not such a political fanatic that I missed the sixties, but always at the absolute centre of my being was the belief – more like a superstition – that if I kept my single-minded concentration on the great objective, it would be achieved.

There was another aspect to this superstition, though. I would repeat to myself, 'I must not admit to the possibility of failure, or I will fail.' But also, 'In the meantime I must not admit to any success, or it will be taken away from me.' I have always been bad at accepting praise, not because I do not like it – on the contrary – but because doing so runs the risk of attracting the attention of one of those bored Olympians, who might then send something horrible, to teach you to mind your manners.

There is a passage in the third volume of Philip Pullman's magnificent cosmological trilogy, *His Dark Materials*, in which Will finds he cannot use the Subtle Knife to cut through from world to world any more because he has lost the single-minded concentration to do so. 'His mind left the point.' The knife shatters. The reason is Will's love for his mother. In an even greater book, *Anna Karenina*, Tolstoy provides the definitive account of what such single-mindedness means in the accomplishment of a task when he describes Levin working in the fields at harvest time:

> The longer Levin went on mowing, the oftener he experienced those moments of oblivion when his arms no longer seemed to swing the scythe, but the scythe itself his whole body, so conscious and full of life; and as if by magic, regularly and definitely without a thought being given to it, the work accomplished itself of its own accord. These were blessed moments.

In 1980 our first child was born, after Caroline had undergone painful operations and treatment and we had faced the very real fear that longed-for children might be impossible. Brilliant surgery and careful doctoring did their best. Month after month we looked for circles in the test tubes of pregnancy-testing kits, trying to persuade ourselves that cloudy blobs, or tricks of the light, were definitive circles. But they never were. Then, at the dawn of the new decade, at Home Farm, Rushbrooke, where Amschel Rothschild lived, we set up the tubes one more time. And there was an utterly, magnificently, clear circle.

From that moment, driving home gingerly on the icy roads, everything was different: all those imaginary childhood cheering crowds were replaced by a far more powerful reality, just as they were for silly Gordon Comstock in Orwell's *Keep the Aspidistras Flying*, or for billions of others before and since. It is the oldest discovery in the world, but I made it all over again. Looking at our first child when she was born (to be followed, to the astonishment of the doctors, by three more), I knew that there would never again be a single, selfish objective in my life; she, then they, trumped everything. It became clear to me that my single-minded ambition was not the same thing as real singleness of heart.

It shows how I was loved, in both childhood and adulthood, by people more generous than myself that their love had always reinforced my ambition: they were always with me on what Mr Blair calls 'the journey'. I was also doing it for them, and I was well aware that I could not do it without them. But the 'it' remained. What happens – what happened to me at any rate – when a child is born is that you cannot pretend, even to yourself, that you are the most important object in the universe any more. A new universe has been born, autonomous.

That was the main thing. But the other – the little cloud of self-doubt – grew alongside it. Although I had heeded Rab Butler's advice not to become an adviser but to participate in the action, I was beginning to acknowledge to myself – usually in the dark hours of the morning – that even after all my efforts I was not quite well-enough equipped for the task. There was something missing. After I left politics, people would often say, 'You were too nice for the top' or 'You were too honest for the top.' They were quite wrong, though kindly intentioned. What I lacked was that confidence, which can look thick-skinned but need not be; that certain grace in action that does not, I am sure, banish anxiety, but frees the will for decision-making by quietening anxiety. Lionel Trilling discusses the same quality, using the word 'authentic' to describe the undivided singleness of the old shepherd Michael in Wordsworth's narrative poem: there is no question of his self being divided. He quotes Edward Young's famous question that describes what happens to most of the rest of us: 'Born Originals, how comes it to pass that we die Copies?' The most successful people of action – not just in politics, not even especially in politics – are not copies. Some, as Charles Moore shows convincingly in the case of Thatcher, simply do not reflect at all. Others, like Macmillan, live their lives not without self-analysis, but nonetheless succeed in deploying judgement and courage without too much fuss or self-doubt. They are like Jane Austen's heroes. They manage the same single-minded absorption that Levin found in his swinging scythe when they act.

I am more like one of those maddening people in *Jude the Obscure*. I envy what appears as the cool common sense, the capacity for far-sighted decision-making without too much fuss or bother, that my friends Chris Patten and Douglas Hurd and Jack Straw and Ken Clarke seem to possess; and what they have many perfectly ordinary people in other walks of life have, too. By contrast, I am in the camp of Keith Joseph and Rab Butler and Victor Rothschild – of all sorts of clever and admirable people who have to work hard to overcome self-doubt.

It was always a conscious act of will not to give in to anxiety, and I succeeded in doing so only at the cost of grinding my teeth and making those around me suffer. There may be another joke of nature in all this. Perhaps people go into applause-seeking careers, like politics or journalism or acting, because they want to prove – to themselves and others – that they can overcome the very neuroses that make them ill-suited for such roles in the first place. Perhaps we would do better to select our politicians by lot, as the Athenians did.

Would it have been different if I had not spent a whole decade as a junior minister, a number two? If a Whitelaw or a Carrington as prime minister had given me Cabinet rank in 1984 or 5? I do not think so. Something was missing in me, and I began to understand that. In truth, this was the central episode of my life. Slowly I began to admit to myself – though to no one else – that everything was ultimately going to be in vain: that the dreams would not be fulfilled; the weather would never be truly favourable, because the weather was not the problem. Not that ambition disappeared: I was realistic enough to know that plenty of people who fell short of greatness had reached high office, so perhaps luck would carry me to the foreign secretary's or the chancellor's office, too. And perhaps I might survive there, if fortune remained on my side. Then anything might happen.

The fundamental change was this. Previously, I had always believed that I *deserved* to fulfil the destiny of which I had dreamed. Now, if it came, I knew it would be by luck and not by merit. I had once thought like Churchill – that although we were all worms, I was a glow-worm. Now that belief was gone, along with 'authenticity' and singleness of mind. Like my ancestor the admiral, I had often wondered whether I would have courage in action. Everyone who has been lucky enough to avoid war must have asked themselves the same question. Now I saw true leadership in extreme crisis, close up. I saw Thatcher's courage over the Falklands, and over the miners' strike, and her capacity to withstand the relentless pressure that never leaves the holder of the highest office, and I had to recognise that I could not have done what she did. I would have sought compromise, and I would have been wrong (or so I then thought).

And then came that other unavoidable question: did I really care any more? I had learned that happiness had nothing to do with what I did. By now, I had discovered that I was only ever as happy as my least happy child. The events that broke my political career came later. But even if I had never encountered Alan Clark or Richard Scott, and my trajectory downwards had been more graceful, that trajectory would have started in the mid-1980s, towards the end of my fourth decade, when most journalists were still predicting great things for me. Even then, I knew they were wrong.

There is a passage in Cecil Lewis's wonderful account of flying in the First World War, *Sagittarius Rising*, in which he describes how if you flew at exactly the right altitude above the battlefield, you could actually see the great artillery shells stopping at the top of their trajectory before plunging downwards. So it was with me in the mid-1980s: I was poised to start my descent.

In the meantime, though, I was a minister, and I could not admit my doubts to anyone, including Caroline. But she knew that I did not enjoy the pressure, and she often had to take the strain when I wrestled inwardly with those doubts. Of course, there was no time for quiet reflection. There was always the next problem, the next big debate, the next ministerial reshuffle to anticipate with hope, the next pressure to resist. Quite a lot of the job of being a minister is handling the pressure of people lobbying and trying to sow doubt in your mind about what you are defending, to try to make you change your mind. If it is simply a matter of spending money, you usually have to say 'no'. If it is a matter of holding the line for an agreed policy (irrespective of whether you personally agree with it), you have to stick to your guns even when they are in danger of being overrun. Again, you find yourself saying 'no' much more often than you say 'yes'.

Lobbying takes many forms. Almost as soon as I became a minister, I was tested by what I took to be the offer of a quite spectacular bribe. I was given the job of closing teacher-training colleges, of which it was alleged there were too many. Many belonged to the various Christian denominations, and the suffering had to be fairly spread. The Cardinal Archbishop of Cardiff, splendidly robed and well supported by priests and other attendants, came to berate me on behalf of the Roman Catholic Church. Having done so, he asked if he could speak to me alone. Nervously, his acolytes and my officials left. He asked if I was aware that there was a member of my family who was a candidate for beatification. (Sixteenth-century Waldegraves had been determined adherents to the old faith.) Was a deal being proffered? The Roman Catholic college duly closed, and I heard no more about my potentially saintly ancestor.

As planning minister, I received, as planning ministers always do, unremitting pressure from the development lobby, which argues that only the Town and Country Planning Act stands between Britain and growth akin to that of China (or whichever country happens to be surging ahead at the time). In my day, the lobby was led by a friend of mine, the great philanthropist John Sainsbury, who ran the family firm very well indeed. Denis Thatcher sometimes joined in. 'We retail families . . .' he opened a conversation with me once, leaving me speechless, but unmoved.

More subtle was the approach of Cyril Stein, the boss of Ladbrokes, who had a big stake in a city-centre development in Bristol that stretched into my constituency. Outside the city, at Cribbs Causeway, to the north, an application for a huge out-of-town shopping development had also been submitted. If approved, it would provide stiff competition for Mr Stein's proposed development. While the Cribbs Causeway proposal was still going through the tortuous application process, the Marriage Guidance Council asked for my help in finding some subsidised office space, because Mr Stein had turfed them out of their old inner-city site as the area began to be cleared for his new development. I wrote to the great man, as a constituency MP, to ask if there was anything he could do. He and his man of business came to see me almost the very next day. 'Now, Mr Waldegrave, we know we are seeing you as the local MP and not as planning minister. But we can reassure you about the good people of the Marriage Guidance Council. There is a very wonderful planning application in for Cribbs Causeway, in case you have not heard. If that goes through, there will be plenty of empty shops for them to use. The whole city centre will be bankrupt! You needn't worry at all. And here is a personal cheque for the Marriage Guidance Council from me. It is a cause that my wife and I have always supported.'*

The pressure to relax planning laws was always intense: huge fortunes often hung on ministers' decisions, while powerful and effective lobbies fought against development on behalf of Britain's green spaces and architectural heritage. As the Thatcher government struggled to get the economy moving, the post of planning minister, following that of universities minister, further educated me in the rough and tumble world of democratic politics, and tested whether I possessed the necessary toughness. So far, it seemed that I did. I concluded that our underlying growth rate had little to do with the planning laws, since large areas of the Midlands and northern England, and a good deal of Scotland and Wales, were begging for development. It was just that it could not all be in the parts of south-east England where it was easiest to sell the houses. The battle is rejoined in every recession, and the arguments never change.

---

* Other meetings were sometimes arranged for more surreal reasons. Willie Whitelaw had once peppered Sir Joseph Nickerson, the king of Lincolnshire's seed merchants, when out shooting. 'Please,' Willie said, 'see him. But do not give him anything!'

Twenty-first-century ministers should remind themselves that the recession of 2008 was not caused by the planning laws, and its effects will not be resolved by their abolition. They should remember that over the last two hundred years, the long-term underlying growth rate of the United States, occupying an under-populated continent all of its own, deploying for the majority of that time no land-use planning laws at all, and enjoying virtually no constraints on space, was 2 per cent. And the United Kingdom? 2 per cent.

Revitalising long-dormant environmental policy sometimes landed me in trouble with the free-marketeers, though the best liberal economists have always understood the argument for the protection of 'the commons' and for shifting responsibility for clearing up pollution on to those who produced it. I became adept at defending policy – such as the government's refusal to clean up the deposits of sulphur from the big coal-fired power stations (built by GEC) – while at the same time trying to change it. Thatcher could be a stalwart defender of environmental action if it was based on good science, sometimes to the surprise of those who forgot she trained as a chemist. Liberalising the rented sector of housing, on the other hand, was a piece of pure Thatcherism in which I thoroughly believed. The act I steered through Parliament, with my friend Jack Straw eloquently leading the opposition to my rack-renting wickedness (but subsequently not very anxious to reverse the legislation when in power), certainly brought more investment into a more flexible housing market.

I believe I was also right to press on with Kenneth Clarke's nascent reforms as secretary of state for health after Thatcher offered me the clear option of retreating and winning plaudits from the toughest trade union of all, the British Medical Association. And though it went against my natural inclination, I could go on the offensive when I had to. I was right to trigger the uproar of the 'War of Jennifer's Ear' in the 1992 general election campaign after Labour contrasted the fates of two little girls – one treated in the private sector, the other in the NHS – with painful grommets in their ears in one of their slick, but not wholly honest, party political broadcasts. As always when politicians use allegedly genuine cases, the facts were not quite as portrayed by Labour's advertising company, and by attacking the errors I managed to divert the press away from the message. In the last week of the campaign Labour abandoned its NHS focus and lost momentum as a result. But I did not enjoy being at the epicentre of the storm: I was not tough enough to see it through properly, and both I and some of my sturdier colleagues knew that I had been bruised by the battle.

After the 1992 election, John Major offered me the Department of Social Security. I begged to be excused. An Old Etonian with a house in W8 cutting benefits? I did not have the stomach for that fight. Major was understanding and offered me two alternatives instead: stay at Health or become chancellor of the Duchy of Lancaster, with responsibility for his personally endorsed policy that was designed to give a greater voice to ordinary citizens – the Citizens' Charter. To the latter, to my great pleasure, was added responsibility for science policy.

I had turned down a big ministry, knowing it might break me; and I chose to escape from Health as well. I knew that my trajectory was now flat, unless I had some luck. But in due course it was not luck which turned up, but my colleague Alan Clark.

CHAPTER THIRTEEN

Parliament and the Press

I was never sentimental about the House of Commons. I never thought it 'the best club in London'. Pugin is an interesting and original designer, and much of the neo-Gothic detail inside the building is very fine. But Barry was not a subtle architect: the building is essentially a long, straight barn with decoration. Some of the technology is interesting: the first big building to be hung on a metal (cast-iron) frame, it boasts an early attempt at air-conditioning based on the wind-tower, Venturi-effect system; the middle pinnacle was specifically designed to help circulate air. But it is a gloomy place to work. There are two fine libraries, normally full of snoring, wan-faced members waiting for votes. The food is fairly dismal. People drink too much and the air is fetid. The efficient doctor who held a surgery for the three thousand or so people who worked in the Palace told me he was conducting research into the odd skin diseases suffered by members as a result of the poor air.

Its strength was and is that the British Constitution has made it the focus of national argument. R. A. Butler described the uproar at Prime Minister's Question Time as 'the sound of democracy'. Churchill said that it was because of that small room that we would win the war. The intensity – and sometimes the viciousness – of debate does replace actual violence on the streets, at least to some degree. It is a testing ground: a minister who cannot win some respect from the opposition, and an adequate degree of support from his or her own side, will not make it very far. The capacity to hold a line under pressure, particularly when one is forced to defend a weak argument, is a vital part of maintaining the often half-hearted support of the majority necessary to get business through.

In every generation there are some who have that knack of expressing clearly and concisely, preferably with some wit, ideas that are worth hearing. National reputations can be made on the back of that skill: Enoch Powell's and Tam Dalyell's in the generation above mine; Matthew Parris's and Frank Field's in mine; perhaps Jacob Rees-Mogg's and Rory Stewart's in the Cameron generation. A little eccentricity does no harm. Interestingly, skill with other kinds of audiences, whatever the celebrity it brings, does not always transfer well to the House of Commons: Andrew Faulds, Glenda Jackson, Ken Livingstone and Boris Johnson seemed better suited to other stages.

The power of traditional oratory has perhaps declined a little in recent years, or at least its style has changed, but if a Michael Foot or a Jeremy Thorpe exhibited the same skills they deployed in their heyday, they would soon dominate even today's timetabled House. David Cameron won his leadership with a speech, admittedly delivered at a party conference, where most of the audience usually wants you to succeed. Neil Kinnock failed to destroy Thatcher over Westland with a speech which did not do to her what Geoffrey Howe's resignation speech did later. Not that Howe's speech was really very good, with his implausible metaphor of a cricket bat (not a weapon it was easy to imagine Geoffrey doing much damage with, broken or unbroken). But it articulated the anxieties which by then were widespread. If Powell or Robin Cook had been given the Westland brief, Thatcher would have been in serious trouble. Blair's dominance of Parliament and the press came partly from his easy dominance of the House of Commons; both derived not only from huge majorities but, like Thatcher's, from the communication of his apparently unshakeable self-confidence.

In my view, our constitution is far superior to the American or the French: the subjection of ministers to the intense, continual examination of their peers, with few holds barred, is exchanged in the British model for great power as long as they can maintain a majority. They are tested, occasionally to destruction; but if they pass those tests, they are allowed to act. It is a much more radical form of direct democracy than many understand. That is one reason not to disperse the power of our effectively single-chamber Parliament by electing the House of Lords or giving judges too much power. It is one source of the ineradicable tension between the British and the European Union that European institutions blur the crystal clarity of our government's accountability to the electorate through the Commons. Meanwhile, particularly in times of crisis, the US separation of powers is a recipe for paralysis, as the world saw in the summer of 2011 and again in 2012–13. In our great crises, we know who matters, and where he or she is to be found: standing at the despatch box before the House.

So the House of Commons matters, in spite of the eccentricity of the people assembled there, many of them motivated by the strange dreams and desires I have tried to describe in this book. In my time there I did adequately, but no more. Rising to answer my first ever parliamentary question, I swiftly learned one lesson. Pausing slightly before adding an ad lib decoration to my carefully drafted answer, the redoubtable hard-left Stirlingshire MP Denis Canavan interjected the suggestion, 'Resign!'

Other ad libs went better. One afternoon in the Commons Andrew Faulds, a former actor famous for portraying Carver Doone on television, was ranting at me in my capacity as government spokesman for the arts. He was on his usual hobby horse, the return of the Elgin Marbles to Greece, and finished his peroration with the accusation that I had no idea for what the Marbles stood. 'Athenian imperialism?' I suggested, and won the accolade of a wintry smile from Enoch Powell. On another occasion, I sped through my answers to arts questions, dealing with more than usual. As a backbencher stood to ask his question in the time-honoured way – 'Number six, sir' – I turned over the page in the folder to find nothing at all. The press, of course, ridiculed a minister who could not provide an answer without his brief. That was not the problem: I did not know what the *question* was.

I am not very good at my own publicity. Once, just before Christmas, perhaps in 1980 or 1981, I was buying clothes for Caroline's present in a shop just off Bond Street. I was feeling happy; Christmas spirit was all around; a busker was playing good saxophone outside. Then I noticed a man shoplifting. I was angry: how dare he spoil everything? Anger allowed me to overcome normal English embarrassment about making a scene. I left my bags with the startled shop assistant and pursued the thief, quite a long way, across Bond Street and beyond. I felt foolish shouting, 'Stop, thief!' but what else does one shout? People continued about their business. Eventually, I brought him down, with a not very sporting trip, and took back the mass of clothes he had on specially designed hangers under his coat. When he was on the ground passers-by finally came to help, but perversely I began to feel sorry for him and let him go. I returned the clothes to the shop, the sales assistants came round to our house, gave Caroline a free outfit, and we drank champagne. Home at Chewton a few days later, slightly embarrassed, I told this story to my father. 'Have you not told the press?' he asked. I admitted I had not. He was astonished and did it himself. I was quite famous for a day or two, and was thanked by the Society of Bond Street Traders.

This sort of thing was partly residual shyness – never the best quality in a politician – and partly a sort of fatalism. I still believed if you did things right, you would somehow be rewarded by the great examiners in the sky, as if you had done a good finals paper. Some hope, as I later discovered: the truth does not out by itself, if it outs at all. It is the best story which outs. My father, not for the only time wiser than I, knew that.

Despite the shyness, I'm sure I got my first ministerial job in 1981 as a result of an uncharacteristic display of House of Commons chutz-pah. Peter Shore, Labour's shadow leader of the House and at his best a brilliant speaker, was in full, coruscating flow, winding up a no-confidence debate in February of that year. The government, he said, was like Ulysses, strapped to the mast, wax in his ears to block out the Sirens' song, listening to no one. I intervened: 'The Right Honourable Gentleman might like to complete the story, which was that Ulysses' strategy saved the ship from the rocks.' There was an uproar of laughter, cat-calls and general merriment. Thatcher turned and smiled up at me on my high and distant backbench perch.

Having the ability to make the House laugh is a great gift. I am a good speaker to a friendly audience, and I can make people who want to laugh do so. But I am not so good in front of a hostile audience, and that is the test of a really talented debater. Caroline once came to watch me wind up a par-ticularly difficult debate on the Rate Support Grant when I was a minister in the Department of the Environment, during which all the knights of the Tory shires intervened to complain about the unfairness of that year's grant to the impoverished residents of Surrey or Berkshire, or wherever it was. The clock was ticking down to 10 p.m., at which exact moment you have to sit down if you are winding up a debate or you lose the busi-ness. Nonetheless, I had to give way to as many of the complainers on the benches behind me as possible, in the hope that, having got their names into Hansard and thence into their local newspapers, they would join me in the lobby. There was bedlam and uproar on both sides of the House.

A lady next to Caroline in the gallery said, 'I see you are nervous, my dear.'

'That is my husband down there.'

'Oh, I'm afraid it gets worse, my dear. You see, my husband was prime minister.'

It was Mary Wilson. And she was right.

I was best at dealing with Foreign Office questions, because they did not normally run on strict party lines: a good reply could win nods from the other side. Among my proudest possessions is a note from the old-school Liverpudlian left-winger Eric Heffer, passed across during a debate on the Soviet Union, which was collapsing. He was visibly dying of cancer before our eyes. 'The best speech I've heard from your Front Bench,' it read. It is undeniable that the praise of your opponents is often sweeter than the praise of your supporters. But that is a dangerous and seductive syndrome for a party politician who is elected to support a particular policy ticket. Heath suffered from it in an acute form. It never affected Thatcher in any way.

Parliament can be both the source of a media storm and the means of controlling it. I once created, virtually single-handed, a damaging storm through naivety in my parliamentary performance. I had temporarily forgotten something I had learned from Tam Dalyell, the redoubtable, Old Etonian Labour member for West Lothian and later Linlithgow. He is a man wholly without fear; a nightmare, doubtless for his whips; and of utterly unimpeachable honesty. His lesson to me was: always be careful. I learned it in the Halvergate Marshes in East Anglia; and forgot it in a discussion about truth-telling.

Tam was one of the most effective questioners because he had the discipline to be brief. Keith Joseph was another. He used the same technique as Tam when providing answers, racing through his list of oral questions, sometimes saying 'yes', sometimes 'no', and leaving the ponderous questioner at a loss for his supplementary. Time and again I would be grateful when a questioner foolishly dressed up their enquiry in flowery rhetoric and repetition, because that gave me precious time to think up an equally verbose and safe reply. By contrast, directness and clarity can be dangerous: effectively dangerous in a questioner; but naively dangerous for the answerer. Tam was the master of tempting one into a straight answer that one might later regret by using short, pithy questions from which it was difficult to escape because they allowed no time to think up safe obfuscation. Sometimes, he took this to extremes: a simple 'Why?' was one of his favourite questions.

The Halvergate Marshes were for some weeks an environmental *cause célèbre*: high grain prices were leading East Anglian farmers to drain ecologically valuable wetlands to plant profitable cereals. I thought I had negotiated a deal that would stop the practice. Tam asked me whether there would be any more drainage of the marshes. Unwisely, I answered, 'No, sir.' The farmers broke the deal and continued to drain the wetlands. Next month, Tam asked, 'What did the minister learn from his last answer to me?' Answer: that I should be more circumspect.

But I did not learn the lesson well enough. Some years later, I was appearing, alongside my permanent secretary Richard Mottram, before the select committee that covered civil service matters. As chancellor for the Duchy of Lancaster I was responsible for reform of the service, and the committee was interested in issues of accountability in the more devolved bureaucracy we were constructing. What were the relationships between the new agencies, ministers and Parliament? For which issues were ministers accountable and responsible? What should they say to Parliament? Should there be a Civil Service Act? And so on. Somehow, we then strayed on to dangerous philosophical ground and my Oxford training made me reckless. Should ministers always tell the truth? 'Of course,' I replied without hesitation. But the week before, my old CPRS colleague Robin Butler, by now cabinet secretary and head of the civil service, had written to the Scott Inquiry to defend his predecessor Sir Robert Armstrong's view that sometimes it was not advisable to tell the *whole* truth. Robin had been part of the Treasury team that had organised the devaluation of the pound when James Callaghan was chancellor. Could a chancellor, presiding over a fixed exchange rate, but planning to devalue, say what he planned to do if asked a direct question? Of course not, argued Robin: the devaluation would have occurred there and then if he had said so. I repeated this argument, naming Callaghan.

It did not occur to me that I was criticising Callaghan by saying this. Nor, as far as I am aware, did the select committee think there was anything amiss. But a clever, if erratic, young journalist on the *Evening*

Standard, Peter Oborne, spotted a story. 'Minister says it is right to lie' screamed the headline. Then, in one of those temporary spasms of madness that afflict the press sometimes, the heavens fell in. Philip Stephens, the political editor of the *Financial Times*, explained to me how a media lynch mob works. He had initially made the story a small diary piece, along the lines of 'Waldegrave puts his foot in it again'. But when early editions of *The Times* and the *Daily Telegraph* gave it banner headlines he was asked if he would take personal responsibility for any loss of sales compared to the paper's rivals as a result of his decision to downgrade the story. On to the front page it went in the next edition.

Callaghan saddled up a high horse and declared that he had never told an untruth. (This was quite surprising news for those of us who had followed the devious career of this genial politician.) Uproar broke out on the airwaves. John Humphrys, for once, let me win an argument on the *Today* programme.

'Of course, what you say is right, Minister. But it was pretty stupid to say it.'

'Oh, sorry. You mean I should have told an untruth instead?'

My old teacher John Roberts offered his support. So did an old gentleman who had been serving on a battleship as a young rating in early 1940 when Churchill had come aboard as First Lord of the Admiralty. Put in a group to question the great man, he had nervously asked, 'Is everything you tell us true?' The answer, he alleged, was: 'Young man, I have told many lies for my country and will tell many more.' The Tory backbencher, long thought to be dead, who had tabled a question in the House to Callaghan about whether he intended to devalue immediately before he did so – and had received what one might politely call an equivocal answer – wrote from his old people's home, 'You've got him at last!' Roy Jenkins told me, '*Of course* he lied, but incompetently, so we still lost all the reserves. And that was why we lost the next election.' And so on, and so forth. I eventually appeared with a made-up quotation in a *Dictionary of Quotations* as having asserted that ministers could lie.

I had not intended any of this. I rather liked Jim Callaghan: devious though he was, he was a patriot who had begun the process of 'Thatcherisation' by warning the country and the unions that there would have to be pay and public expenditure restraint before 1979. It seemed obvious to me that he had done the right thing in side-stepping the truth in this rare and extreme case: that gave no general licence to ministers – or anyone else – to lie. I wanted to apologise to him, though I felt no guilt. Robin Butler strongly advised me not to, perhaps rightly.

Garland, the greatest political cartoonist of the day, drew a version of Chicken Little to celebrate the furore: a political farmyard panicked amid cries of 'The sky is falling!' as a leaf with 'Waldegrave's Testimony' fluttered down. I offered to buy the original, but he refused payment on the grounds that he was so irritated by the nonsense and gave it to me. I sent him some champagne and received two more free cartoons – one of Callaghan swooning on a chaise longue and the other of Garland himself surrounded by empty champagne bottles.

I thought I had learned from Isaiah Berlin and others that there was no special political morality, no Machiavellian *raison d'état*. Moral dilemmas faced by a minister before Parliament were just like those faced by anyone else in everyday life. Of course, truth-telling is a moral imperative, but it may clash with some other moral imperative; so, just occasionally, it might be wrong to tell the truth. 'Do not kill,' says the Sixth Commandment. But really it should say, 'Do not kill, except when it is right to kill.' Nonetheless, I was a fool to give the answer I did, and a fool not to retract it immediately. I should have left philosophical argument to the philosophers. A more street-wise minister – a safer pair of hands – would have side-stepped deftly, or left Robin Butler to make his own point, if he had chosen to do so, and then briefed the press that these great mandarins are always a bit naive.

A little earlier, after my return to London from a meeting with Yasser Arafat, I had been able to use Parliament to fight back and win through a more important storm. For a moment, our meeting had put me at the

centre of the world media's attention. He was then based in Tunis; it
was January 1990; and I was a minister of state at the Foreign Office.
Arafat and the Palestine Liberation Organization had taken major steps
towards renouncing terrorism and joining negotiations for a settlement
of the Palestinian–Israeli conflict on a two-state basis. This had followed tortuous negotiations in Geneva and London. In the latter series
of meetings the PLO delegation had been led by Bassam Abu Sharif, a
man whose courage and commitment to peace I came to admire greatly.
Before we could upgrade our contact with the PLO to ministerial level –
as we had always promised to do if they made significant steps towards
negotiation and away from terrorism – we had to have an agreed statement endorsed by both the British government and the PLO. Thatcher,
who had powerful Jewish backers in her constituency and elsewhere, and
understandably hated terrorism, had agreed to this, but she was watching
the wording very closely indeed. So were the Americans, who were keen
to respond to the PLO but were unable to make any supportive move
because of congressional pressure. The Bush administration wanted us
to do the job of sending the necessary signal, but only as long as it was
on the right terms.

Rob Young, subsequently High Commissioner in Delhi and an outstanding official, negotiated all night in London with Bassam and finally
reached agreement on the wording. Every single word counted. Next
day, Bassam and I stood in front of the world's television cameras on
the steps of the Foreign Office and I invited him to read out the agreed
statement. He lowered the hand holding the sheet of paper to his side and
began to recite. My heart sank. Had we been tricked, as Assad in Syria
had tricked Kissinger years before? No such thing. The Israelis had once
sent Bassam a letter bomb and his eyes had never recovered. The bright
television lights were hurting them now, as he knew they would. So he
had committed the paper, word for word, to memory.

After those successful negotiations I went to Tunis to meet Arafat.
We drove to his villa from the beautiful British Embassy, formerly the

headquarters of both Rommel and Alexander at different stages of the desert war. The ambassador, Stephen Day, sat, as protocol demanded, on the left of the car, behind the Union Flag, as the Queen's representative. But as we entered the driveway he realised that he would be exiting the car into the glare of hundreds of television lights, while I would be deposited in an oleander bush on the far side. 'Drive on!' he cried to the driver at the very last moment. So round the circular drive and back out we went, doubtless to the astonishment of the world's media, swapped places, and did it right.

Arafat was, of course, a disappointment, both then and later, when he returned to Palestine. The decorated pistols he wore seemed an affectation. He was not a big enough man to unite the Palestinians and deliver a true negotiating partner for moderate Israelis. Perhaps no one was. In any case, the one Israeli who had the power to deliver on the other side, Yitzhak Rabin, was murdered not long afterwards by Jewish extremists.

When I met Arafat, the hard-line Likud were in power in Israel, led by Yitzhak Shamir, a former leader of the Lehi (or Stern Gang) who had invented many of the techniques of modern terrorism when he had fought the British Mandate in Palestine during and after the war. His group had murdered one of my predecessors as minister for the Middle East, Lord Moyne, blown up the King David Hotel, causing many British deaths, and murdered Count Bernadotte, the United Nations mediator who had secured the release of thousands of inmates of the Nazi concentration camps. Now, I was subjected to virulent attack by the Israeli government, echoed in the Murdoch press, which always took the standard American right-wing line on Arab–Israeli matters, most likely for its own commercial reasons. I was attacked for anti-Semitism, for being a toff and for other crimes in leaders in the *Sun* for three days running. (Kelvin MacKenzie, the editor, told me later that he had a fourth prepared but something better came up.) I had no option but to counter-attack. In a telephone call from Tunis to the *Today* programme, I said, carefully, 'Mr Shamir was once what we British called a terrorist. Now he is a democratically elected leader and of course we have normal relations with him. Mr Arafat says he wants to follow the same path, so should we not give him the benefit of the doubt?' Bedlam ensued. Hard-line Zionists, and the spokesmen of the Israeli government, went for me with redoubled fury.

Isaiah Berlin summoned me to his elegant flat in the Albany when I returned home. 'You made a serious mistake. A serious mistake.' My heart sank. Was Isaiah going to take the Likudnik line, too? Not at all. My mistake had been a philosophical one. 'Of course, what you said about Shamir was quite correct. He is a criminal. But you said, "Israel may be left behind by history." That is vulgar Marxism. Vulgar Marxism. There is no such thing as a process of history.'

Isaiah went on to tell me of his meeting with Avraham Stern, the founder of the Stern Gang, whom the British hanged during the war. Isaiah had been travelling – not luxuriously –between Marseille and Palestine in the 1930s. In the canteen of the ship a youth came and sat next to him. 'A very beautiful youth. I fell to talking to him. It became apparent that he was mad, quite mad. I asked, "What is your name?" "Avraham Stern," he said.'*

My tutorial with Isaiah was followed by a piece of good fortune. I would have had no chance of turning the tide of abuse in the press without the opportunity to defend myself in the Commons. So it was with relief that I heard that Gerald Kaufman, Labour's Jewish – but bravely moderate – foreign affairs spokesman, had put down a private notice question, which meant I was summoned to the House. I do not know whether Kaufman, not normally given to assisting Tories in need, meant to help me or not, but his intervention was crucial. I abandoned the cautious Foreign Office defensive brief, deployed a wonderful letter Victor Rothschild had written to *The Times* in my defence, quoted the Book of

---

* This crossing of paths is matched by another favourite: Lenin, when in exile in London around 1900, once attended a meeting at Toynbee Hall addressed by the former prime minister Lord Salisbury. He apparently asked an excited but incomprehensible question.

Ecclesiastes to the effect that there was a time for peace and a time for war, and managed to save myself. I doubt that anyone on my own side would have had sufficient confidence in me to give me a similar chance to do so.

Indeed, on a far more dangerous occasion, the scene with which I opened this book, they did not. At the end of the Scott Inquiry, there was a final debate during which Nicholas Lyell and I were effectively on trial. The Conservatives had a very shaky overall majority in the House, perhaps as small as two if the Ulster Unionists (with whom the prime minister was in critical negotiations about a settlement in Northern Ireland) voted against us. If that vote had been lost, in spite of contrary advice from Douglas Hurd, I would have resigned. Incidentally, his advice was probably right: in such a case the world interprets resignation as an admission of guilt; and I was innocent. It would have been braver and wiser to stand with those – like Major, Hurd and Heseltine – who were convinced of my innocence than to run away. Nonetheless, I know I would have resigned if we had lost that vote, and my career would have ended in spectacular disgrace.

Robin Cook, Labour's foreign affairs spokesman, made a poor foreign secretary later, but he was an outstanding, forensic House of Commons speaker. He led the attack brilliantly, a fine prosecuting counsel in full flow. It was the kind of speech F. E. Smith or Lloyd George might have made. In my defence, Ian Lang, President of the Board of Trade, did an extraordinarily good job when introducing the debate. I was moved by his comments and by several speeches in the House of Lords, where great lawyers like Richard Wilberforce, Johan Steyn and Tony Lloyd spoke to refute the allegations that were being made against me.

I had been subject to vilification for months, and by now I was in a very strange state. I passed a note to Cook at the end of his speech, thanking him for not making it a personal attack. He passed back a note saying that the real villain, Alan Clark, was not present. (Clark had left the Commons before the 1992 election, thinking it was lost, and had subsequently been lobbying for a peerage.) I wished that I had been allowed to defend myself, but that was out of the question. Lyell, the attorney general, and I were both under siege, with the attack against him possibly even more unfair than that against me. It was impossible for both of us to wind up the debate, so the task was given to Roger Freeman (later one of my successors as chancellor of the Duchy of Lancaster). But it would have been satisfying to face that baying mob and put everything on the line myself, once and for all. I probably would have done less well than Lang or Freeman, but the chance to fight back, to lose it all or win it all oneself, would have been a fine thing. And at least I might have won some applause for my courage.

As it was, I just had to sit there, 'whey-faced' – as one reporter described me – on the front bench, waiting for the tellers to come through with the result, thinking the strange thoughts with which I began this story.

CHAPTER FOURTEEN

Thatcher and Other Explosives

Because of the luck of the political draw, I was a minister continuously for a very long period of time. A few – Ken Clarke and Tony Newton, for example – served from the very beginning to the very end, 1979–97. I managed 1981 to 1997.

Charles Moore's authorised biography of Margaret Thatcher, if its subsequent volumes are as good as the first, will give the definitive, rounded portrait of what she was really like. I was never part of any inner circle, but my perceived 'wetness' never appeared to be a bar to promotion (perhaps because she understood I had greater sympathy for her economic policy than was felt by some of my friends). On one occasion, when yet another autumn reshuffle left me at parliamentary under-secretary level in the Department of the Environment, she apologised for not yet making me a minister of state. And she rescued me from a kangaroo court called by Norman Tebbit after the 'Luxembourg Deal' on car exhausts in 1984.

On another occasion, she easily outmanoeuvred me when I attempted a mild plot on acid rain, an issue much exercising the Germans, who accused us of damaging their forests by failing to eliminate sulphur emissions from the chain of big coal-fired power stations built in Yorkshire and Nottinghamshire in the sixties and seventies. (In fact, if we were damaging any forests, they were in Scandinavia.) I wanted to change government policy – which would be expensive and would make coal even less competitive as a fuel – so I had urged my friend Horst Teltschik, the head of Chancellor Kohl's office, to raise the subject clearly at a bilateral summit in Germany. However, Kohl was liable to quail during confrontations with Thatcher, not being alone in that. It was a hot summer's day, with a hazy smog, when we arrived in our helicopters at a military airport near Bonn. 'Now, Helmut,' Thatcher announced, 'you have a smog problem here, I see. I will explain, as a chemist, what is happening. What you need are proper clean-air laws, like we have in Britain.' That was the end of Kohl's courage on atmospheric pollution, and of my plot. I suspect she knew exactly what I had been up to.

She liked people who had a reputation for intelligence; she didn't mind toffs as long as they did not attempt to patronise her; she was far less demanding with younger colleagues, particularly those who had somewhat more modern views than some of their older colleagues about the equality of the sexes. She liked my patrons, Rothschild and Weinstock, and did not hold my loyalty to Heath against me, as I was clearly not part of any court in exile. (In fact, no such a thing existed, much to Heath's annoyance.)

There was one occasion, quite early on in Thatcher's leadership, before I entered Parliament, when I had to apologise for causing a leak. I was a member of a working group on trade union reform under Jim Prior. Its conclusions were very timid, and I was far too frank with Peter Hennessy, then a very well-informed and persistent political correspondent at *The Times*. An embarrassing story duly appeared saying that the conclusions of the working group were likely to be dovish. I summoned as much courage as I could muster, arranged a meeting with the leader, admitted the source of the story was me, and apologised. She probably liked that. Hennessy was cross with me: it was very unprofessional for his sources to be revealed. This seemed odd to me, as I was the source.

Curiously enough, a few years later I made another appointment to see Thatcher to apologise after making a mess of something or other when I was a junior minister (I forget what it was exactly). I made an appointment to see her to apologise again. On this occasion however, it rapidly became clear that she did not know what I was talking about. Like Mr Attlee she did not waste much time reading the newspapers. Probably, she quite liked her ministers being honest, even if they looked silly.* That was something I had learned from Weinstock: never hide your mistakes from your boss, because if you do, your boss cannot help you if he wants to; and if he finds out you have hidden something, he will not want to help you.

Norman Tebbit's kangaroo court was more alarming. When I was Britain's representative on the European Environment Council in 1984, the EEC was, quite rightly, trying to clean up pollution generated by the car industry. Britain, as usual, created difficulties. We made large touring cars with powerful engines that produced lots of fumes – Rolls-Royces, Jaguars, Aston Martins. We also made Land Rovers which had antique and extremely polluting engines. And we had British Leyland, always teetering on the brink of bankruptcy, which had invested little in clean technologies (or anything else) and was always lobbying that it could afford to do nothing new. So, as usual where Europe was concerned, I had a difficult negotiating brief. It was agreed in a cabinet committee involving all the key departments – Trade and Industry, Transport and the Treasury – and it gave me a very detailed range of figures within which I could negotiate emission limits for nitrogen oxide, sulphur

---

* It was perhaps during this meeting, sitting opposite Thatcher in the Cabinet Room, that I said I was pleased to see a picture of my ancestor, Sir Robert Walpole, hanging behind her chair. She peered round and looked at Sir Robert. '*Direct* ancestor, William?' 'Yes, Prime Minister.' 'Well, he looks much better since he has been cleaned.'

dioxide, particulates, and so on. The Environment Council meeting stretched over several days (and nights) in Luxembourg, with the UK mostly isolated, but still in those days theoretically possessing a veto.

Late one night, Tebbit rang me at the offices of UKREP (the UK Representation to the European Union – our Brussels offices), where I was taking a short break with my officials. There was no speaker phone, so my private secretary could not listen in and take notes of the conversation, which turned out to be a robust, unilateral attempt by Tebbit to bully me into changing my negotiating remit in favour of British Leyland and more pollution. I refused.

Eventually, the Council settled on a deal that was within the remit sanctioned by the cabinet committee. Back home, exhausted, I was summoned to Number Ten – because Tebbit had complained about me to the prime minister. Nicholas Ridley, the secretary of state for transport, Patrick Jenkin, my own secretary of state at Environment, and I sat round the table. David Williamson, now of the Cabinet Office's European staff, was next to the prime minister, providing the briefing notes. Long before, he had been my father's principal private secretary when he had been parliamentary under-secretary at the Ministry of Agriculture in Macmillan's government.

Tebbit opened with a vitriolic personal attack on me. As a toff, I understood nothing of the concerns of working people at British Leyland, I had betrayed Britain, and so on. Ridley, up to that point not much interested, and doubtless inclined to Tebbit's view when it came to regulations emanating from Brussels, woke up sharply. 'No colleague should refer to another colleague in such terms,' he said. The atmosphere became electric. My secretary of state did not intervene. The prime minister began to purr dangerously. 'Now, Norman, I am a chemist. You probably do not understand these matters very clearly. I will explain them to you.' She took him through the negotiating remit numbers that were attached to the cabinet committee minutes which Williamson placed in front of her. 'Now, Norman, you probably don't understand the terms as well as

I do. It says "ppm" – that's parts per million. Norman? Do you see? And this symbol here means a range: greater than five and less than twelve. And here – do you see? – is the report that says William has settled at ten. Now, Norman, ten is between five and twelve. And here is *your name*, Norman! You were at the cabinet committee meeting which agreed it.' And so on until he had no argument left. I said absolutely nothing. I just sat there, terrified, while these great animals fought over me. As we all filed out, she grasped my elbow, quite hard, and said, 'I always look after my young people, William.'

Incidentally, British Leyland subsequently bought an up-to-date engine from the Japanese and made cleanliness and modernity the focus of their next advertising campaign.

It was difficult not to respond to such style, even though we rarely agreed on the touchstone social issues: she was pro-hanging; shared the antediluvian views of older party members about homosexuality; and opposed the imposition of sanctions on South Africa. I never heard her express a racist view of any kind, however, and when she met Nelson Mandela she instantly recognised his quality and courage, and they got on very well. Indeed, she turned her earlier opposition to sanctions to very good effect with F. W. de Klerk, chivvying and harrying him along in the right direction when he finally began to move. In those last months of the old South Africa her influence was formidable and wholly positive, rather to the annoyance of almost every long-standing campaigner against apartheid on the left.

She could certainly be terrifying, and it took courage to stand up to her. Occasionally, I found it – on the Swinnerton-Dyer University Grants Committee appointment, for example, and on Britain's policy towards the reunification of Germany. Life was far more difficult for senior colleagues who were her contemporaries, above all Geoffrey Howe, whose dogged persistence, and inaudibility, during cabinet debates seemed to infuriate her, and could prompt her to treat him abominably in front of colleagues. The best technique for such seniors was to roll with

(*above*) Tenants' lunch for my brother's twenty-first. Miss Moseley still in her cloche hat. Surely nothing could change?

(*left*) The picture of my parents (circa. 1954) that I took to school. My father always had the right clothes.

Eton aged 12. Prizes begin to glitter.

Five years later. No chance of looking like
McCartney. Dylan a better bet.

Still some glitter: between The Queen and Harold Macmillan at the Union. Leslie Crawte, far right gave the wrong answer about my future.

Full circle: back at Eton.

Another royal person makes my daughters laugh.

Victor Rothschild:
glamour and secrets.

Throwing grit
into the Whitehall
machine. Robin
Butler to my left.

Victoria and her
non-semitic nose.

(*above*) The Chairman probably disapproved of my hairstyle as much as Ted Heath did.

(*left*) Ministerial boxes at home. A great ancestor looks down.

"THE SKY IS FALLING ... THE SKY IS FALLING ..." (CHICKEN LICKEN)

Creating a storm about truth …
(© Garland/The Daily Telegraph)

… and giving Callaghan the vapours.
(© Garland/The Daily Telegraph)

Marc thinks I might be back in fashion.
(© the estate of Boxer)

Rose Cecil's picture of the Blue Chips. Chris Patten and I are central, but the painter's brother points to John Major.

Thirty years on, Lord Salisbury seems happy with the outcome …

(*above*) Caroline.

(*left*) The prophet Job did not do so well.

with Caroline ...

the punches and return to the fray with good humour the next day; Carrington and Whitelaw mastered this. Sometimes, though, it was hard to stomach her humiliations of those like John Biffen and Norman St John Stevas, who were willing to be extremely loyal but did not always stick to a script. She also seemed to have a weakness for old-fashioned good looks, with the consequence that she overrated Cecil Parkinson and John Moore (though neither was without ability).

She did not always forgive brave disagreement. I suspect that George Young's sacking in 1986 had more than a little to do with his support for the campaign against smoking and a number of other matters that she regarded as leftist. By getting rid of him, she lost her best housing minister. When George was exiled to the backbenches, the permanent secretary at the Department of the Environment, Terry Heiser, wrote a personal letter to his children, telling them that politics was an unfair business and that they should be proud of their father. That is how a permanent secretary should behave. I suspect that Denis Thatcher regarded George's anti-smoking crusade unfavourably. On social matters, he was unlikely to have been a particularly progressive influence on his wife. He could, however, provide moments of pure comedy. On one occasion, the Finnish prime minister, Taisto Kalevi Sorsa, was the guest of honour at a lunch in Number Ten. I sat on one side of Mrs Sorsa, a primary school teacher. Denis, who was mostly engaged with a rather pretty Finnish diplomat on his other side, was Mrs Sorsa's other neighbour. I was running out of small talk, all translated by kneeling interpreters behind our chairs. Having shown off my fading memory of the *Kalevala*, I was labouring through a compliment to the Finnish people for their courage in the Winter War when Denis swung into the conversation. He demanded to know what we were talking about.

'The Winter War.'

'Oh. Who was that against?'

'The Russians.'

'Oh. What does she think of the Chinese?'

The interpreter reported that Mrs Sorsa had no particular views on the Chinese.

'Well, she'd better, because there's a billion of those little buggers.'

Richard Ingrams and John Wells's 'Dear Bill' letters in *Private Eye* were really not much of a parody.

Thatcher was more pragmatic than she herself pretended to be; and far more so than she appears in the accounts of those who have promoted the mythology of 'Thatcherism'. In reality, there was no such thing as Thatcherism, at least not as a coherent doctrine. She knew that merely to stop public expenditure growing as a percentage of national output you had to maintain immense downward pressure, so she invented a rhetoric that convinced many people that the government was imposing constant, ongoing, savage cuts. In fact, public expenditure did not decrease in real terms during her time in office, and it decreased as a percentage of national output only right at the end as a result of two years of unsustainable, almost unprecedented GDP growth. Overall, though, she managed to keep the percentage fairly steady, which was a considerable achievement, given the immense pressure in any democracy for its growth as a result of the work of myriad powerful and media-supported lobbies. If Blair and Brown had managed that, Britain would have weathered the storm after 2008 in far better shape. But, unlike Thatcher, they bought popularity by the simple expedient of never saying 'no' to a serious pressure group arguing for higher spending.

Hard right-wingers sometimes deride Thatcher for not being tougher on public expenditure, and President Reagan would sometimes tease her about the extent of the welfare state in Britain. Nonetheless, she delivered a reformed supply side through new trade union laws and the privatisation of state-owned industrial monopolies, while doing her best to restrain the growth of spending. It was a sensible and pragmatic combination.

As I learned when she appointed me secretary of state for health in 1990, she was extremely cautious about sweeping change in that most beloved of British institutions – the NHS. She made it perfectly clear that if I decided to strangle Kenneth Clarke's extremely controversial reforms of the Health Service in their cradle, she would not stop me. In fact, I believed in them and went the other way, speeding them up. I had studied the case made by the American health expert who was the theoretician behind Clarke's reforms, Alain Enthoven from Stanford. He was regarded as on the extreme left of health politics in the United States, but as a dangerous right-winger by Britain's health lobbies. His ideas about separating responsibility for commissioning and paying for healthcare from responsibility for managing hospitals (which should be independent and free to compete with each other) made sense to me. I had also consulted one of my constituents, Julian Le Grand, the radical Professor of Social Policy at Bristol University and later Titmuss Professor at the London School Economics – a Labour supporter and subsequently adviser to Prime Minister Blair. He told me not to be wet, in the real sense of the word: reform was vital. With Duncan Nichol, the head of the Health Service, I gave a presentation to Thatcher at Number Ten, just before she went on her politically fatal last visit to Paris, and persuaded her that it was right to continue, though the risks were as high as she recognised. On this matter, I was perhaps more radical, but almost certainly less politically wise, than Thatcher herself.

It was rather difficult not to revel in the fun of the uproar surrounding Thatcher when one knew it was not too serious. On 27 September 1990, a month or so before she appointed me health secretary, as minister of state in the Foreign Office I had to take the place of the absent Douglas Hurd in a bilateral meeting with her about tactics for an upcoming EEC meeting. The Foreign Office brief argued that we had to concede a budget increase that Brussels was demanding in order to forestall something even worse. This was not the sort of argument she liked. I sat across the table from her, feeling as if I was in the exhaust stream of a powerful jet turbine into the other end of which someone was feeding lumps of metal. Jagged, dangerous fragments flew towards me and hurtled past my head. At one point she reached across the table and pointed at my brief. 'The trouble is, William, your man Douglas is a gentleman. These Europeans always cheat him!' I liked the fact that Douglas had become 'my man'! Then Charles Powell came in and handed her a piece of paper. 'And now, William, they are trying to blow you up. You had better have the money.' My next meeting was to have been an address to an assembly of senior counter-terrorism experts from Britain and our principal allies at the Royal Overseas League, just off St James's Street. The IRA had hidden a large Semtex bomb in the lectern from which I was to have spoken. It was discovered by accident. If it had gone off, it certainly would have killed me as well as many others in the audience. This diversion enabled Thatcher to end an unsatisfactory meeting as she knew it would have to end – with a reluctant concession – but without the need to admit that the Foreign Office's arguments were any good. Back at the department, I told the officials we had an agreement. 'Well, Minister,' they said, 'it was a very strong brief.'

When journalists asked, 'What was it like, nearly being blown up?' I could honestly answer that it felt curiously trivial, rather like a near miss on the motorway. With hindsight, perhaps I should have behaved with more bravado and made speeches about how you cannot kill democracy with bombs. Instead, I accepted advice to keep a low profile, to lessen the chance of a further attempt, which might have endangered my family as well as myself. I did, however, have quite a good article drafted in my head about how, if the IRA had succeeded in killing me, though my family would have been shattered, ambitious younger colleagues seeking promotion would simply have remembered Disraeli's remark, 'Where there is death there is hope,' and there would have been two hundred applicants for my safe seat in Bristol. Other than those effects, my death would have had no effect whatsoever. I would also have quoted from another great Conrad book, *The Secret Agent*. There is a passage in which the suicide bomber, The Professor, walking about with his bomb strapped around him and his hand on the detonator (a rubber ball), suddenly feels a pang of doubt:

Lost in the crowd, miserable and undersized, he meditated confidently on his power, keeping his hand in the left pocket of his trousers, grasping lightly the india-rubber ball, the supreme guarantee of his sinister freedom; but after a while he became disagreeably affected by the sight of the roadway thronged with vehicles and of the pavement crowded with men and women. He was in a long, straight street, peopled by a mere fraction of an immense multitude; but all round him, on and on, even to the limits of the horizon hidden by the enormous piles of bricks, he felt the mass of mankind mighty in its numbers. They swarmed numerous like locusts, industrious like ants, thoughtless like a natural force, pushing on blind and orderly and absorbed, impervious to sentiment, to logic, to terror too perhaps.

That was the form of doubt he feared most. Impervious to fear! Often while walking abroad, when he happened also to come out of himself, he had such moments of dreadful and sane mistrust of mankind. What if nothing could move them?

This passage should be read to every would-be jihadi and Real IRA sympathiser. What if it is all pointless? The terrorist's best efforts are trivial compared with a tsunami or an earthquake. They do not matter. The stream soon closes over their memory. But, in the event, I did not test whether Slab Murphy, or whoever organised the bomb, had a sense of humour, or had read Conrad. I did as instructed and kept my head down.

Close protection can be rather fun. Apart from the ice-skating teacher at the Queensway Rink who asked my daughter Katie, 'Oh, was it your daddy who was nearly blown up?' – whom I could happily have strangled – and some neighbours in Palace Gardens Terrace – who objected to us parking our car outside their house in case they were blown up by mistake – most people were wonderfully supportive. To my parents' generation, who had heard German bombers overhead night after night, it cannot have seemed a very big deal. We became firm friends with our

Special Branch protectors, as I believe Salman Rushdie did with his, and with their sniffer dogs.

On one occasion, when I went pheasant shooting, my bodyguard turned up looking like a 1930s fashion plate of a sportsman – in perfectly cut tweed plus fours – to the consternation of my scruffy companions in their ancient Barbours. He had formerly guarded Willie Whitelaw, who used to shoot three days a week, and had bought the suit on expenses. We would drive in convoy down the hard shoulder of the traffic-clogged M4 – me in an unmarked police car, Caroline in our Renault Espace with the four children, then another unmarked police car. Often, by the time we reached a clear section of road, there would be a Thames Valley police car waiting to give us all tickets, and an altercation would take place between the Met and the local force. Sometimes Caroline – 'Sunray Two' – would have to contact me – 'Sunray One' – on the walkie-talkie to tell me we needed to stop to empty the pot. (We had a one-year-old.) We tried to get the police to use their Uzi sub-machine guns to exterminate the grey squirrels that were destroying the beech trees around our cottage in Somerset, but they would never oblige.

Enoch Powell is said to have regretted not dying in the Second World War. I never felt similar regret over not losing my life on that September day at the Royal Overseas League; quite the contrary. But if I had been blown up then, the obituaries would surely have said that I was Hurd's natural successor as foreign secretary; and thereafter, who knew what I might have achieved? There is something to be said, reputationally, for being cut off when still full of promise.

When asked, people normally say of politicians, 'They are just in it for themselves.' But it is worth remembering that a significant number of elected politicians in America, Britain, France, Germany, Italy, Israel, India and Sweden – not to mention countless more in non-democratic countries – have been murdered in modern times. Such assassinations very seldom change anything. Did US policy change much after Kennedy? Did Sweden's after Palme? Only Rabin's murder, of those in my time, seemed decisive. Perhaps even then one is crediting a single brave man with more potential than he actually possessed. If Professor Avi Shlaim in the *Iron Wall* is correct, no one and nothing will ever persuade Israel that real compromise is safe.

But at least I share one thing with the pre-eminent politician of my time, that she and I were both nearly assassinated. Caroline and I were in Brighton that terrible night in 1984, not in the Grand Hotel itself, but next door. We were woken by the long rumble of the explosion and falling masonry, then silence, then a terrified woman's scream. She was an unharmed passer-by, I think. Everyone was evacuated to the front, and wild speculation reigned. Was it a missile fired from the Channel? Who was dead? How many? It was swiftly learned that the prime minister was unharmed. Before long, Blitz spirit broke out: tea was served by Conservative ladies; Keith Joseph, in an elegant but much-frayed silk dressing-gown, sat on a beach chair and went through his red boxes; a colleague with an eye for the ladies appeared to arrive from quite the wrong direction. We panicked about Chris and Lavender Patten until we learned that they had left the Grand the previous evening. Anthony Berry, Eric Taylor, Jeanne Shattock, Muriel Maclean and Roberta Wakeham died that night. The Tebbits survived, but Margaret was terribly injured.

Next day, I was due to address the Friends of the Earth's annual conference in Newcastle. I thought it right, in a spirit of both good manners and sangfroid, to keep the engagement. I was driven the 350-odd miles after no sleep at all. The hall was suitably dowdy and the committee did not seem to think it in any way remarkable, let alone praiseworthy, that I had come. The lack of sleep, and the extreme experience of the previous night, had left me in an odd, fragile state. Before the meeting, we were all asked to rise in memory of a man with a fine old English three-syllable name who had unfortunately been run over by a juggernaut while cycling to the bottle bank. If they read this, I hope his relations will forgive me for saying that – without logic or justification – this tipped me over the edge. It was all

I could do to restrain a mad, grief-stricken noise that the delegates would undoubtedly have taken – not entirely incorrectly – for laughter.

When Thatcher fell, I seemed to see the awfulness and shoddiness of it all more clearly than many of my friends. However, I was not powerful enough, or courageous enough, to do much about it.

Working flat out through the summer and autumn of 1990 on preparations for the war to drive Saddam Hussein out of Kuwait, I had been in and out of Number Ten every day, seeing Thatcher or Charles Powell and attending various planning groups. So I thought nothing of it when another request to visit Number Ten arrived at the start of November. 'I am moving Kenneth to the Home Office,' said the prime minister. 'You must go to Health. Kenneth has stirred them all up and I want you to calm them all down. You look as if you need a large whisky. I will have one too.' So I became secretary of state for health, and Thatcher's final cabinet appointment. It was a department and a subject about which I knew nothing.

I assume she was preparing for the general election, due to take place in a year or two's time. As usual, health would be dangerous for the Tories, and Labour was already opportunistically making hay with the difficult and necessary reforms started by Kenneth Clarke. Their spokesman was Robin Cook, who five years later would wind up so formidably for Labour in the Scott Inquiry debate.

I had missed Geoffrey Howe's famous resignation speech in House; I had my nose so close to the grindstone in the Foreign Office that I was oblivious to the growing panic among our backbenchers.* I also missed the suddenly redoubled activity of the keen-eyed circling wolves as Howe and Lawson outmanoeuvred Thatcher on the European Exchange Rate Mechanism of the European Monetary System and committed the UK to its disastrous attempt to align the pound with the emerging united

---

* Howe's resignation caused the cabinet vacancy that led to my appointment as health secretary.

currencies of what eventually became the Eurozone (crucially without first securing agreement about what would happen if one currency or another came under speculative attack).

The great irony, looking back from the second decade of the twenty-first century, is that Lawson and Howe, not to mention all of my sensible pro-European friends – Hurd, Heseltine, Garel-Jones, Chris Patten, John Gummer – were completely wrong, and Thatcher was completely right, about the attempt to insert the pound into the half-baked currency-alignment system represented by the ERM. The latter was not designed as a prop to British anti-inflationary policy, so attempting to use it in that way was bound to be disastrous. Further, they were completely wrong about their largely unspoken assumption that this would – and should – lead the UK into monetary union. Nonetheless, their mistake was at least partly caused by Thatcher's own tenuous connection to what the world now calls 'Thatcherism': she always seemed to want lower interest rates, whatever was happening in the economy. Attaching the pound to the Deutschmark, or its proxy, was partly a way for the Treasury and the Bank of England to build a barricade behind which to hide from her pressure. Moreover, as later with German unification, by openly opposing Britain's entry into the ERM, she was opposing the announced policy of her own government, which was surely not the best way to proceed.

The true horror of Thatcher's position, incompetently communicated to her by her parliamentary private secretary, Peter Morrison, was that while her natural supporters on the backbenches were panicking about their seats (mostly because of grim opinion polls and the poll tax), her former senior supporters, Howe and Lawson, the joint architects of the successful liberalisation of the economy in her earlier governments, were taking Britain down a path she hated in relation to Europe. Most crucial of all, her most powerful allies – Whitelaw, Tebbit and Young – had all left the Cabinet by 1990, so they were no longer able to provide the ballast that might have steadied the ship. The men who had replaced them were dedicated Europeans (Chris Patten, David Hunt, John Gummer), carried little weight on the backbenches and were anyway muddled about Europe (myself), were more suited to think-tank discussions than cabinet battles (Peter Lilley), or were loyal but somewhat distanced (John Major; who, at the crucial final stage, was absent, having a dental operation). Meanwhile, on the backbenches a very big beast indeed at last provided a real focus for the opposition to Thatcher: Michael Heseltine.

The chief whip, Tim Renton, took his independence from the prime minister very seriously, quite properly regarding it as the primary duty of his office to hold the party together. The press were full of glee as the crisis developed at headlong speed. The atmosphere was febrile and bloodthirsty, like the audience at a boxing match when one fighter sustains a cut. On the crucial night after the first leadership ballot, our old dining group, the Blue Chips (which had hardly met for months), gathered in Garel-Jones's house. Alan Clark came (uninvited). He had been to see Douglas Hurd a few months previously to urge that action must be taken to get rid of Thatcher;* now he was implausibly advancing the non-existent cause of Tom King, the defence secretary. I am grateful to that destructive man for one thing (and one thing only): in the published version of his diaries he records that I was the only person present who said that what was happening was tragic. I still believe that it was.

Earlier that same night, in the House, by error I had stumbled into a white-faced meeting of right-wingers, with Tebbit in attendance. I made my apologies and left. At that moment I recognised not only the tragedy of what was happening to Thatcher herself, but also how irredeemably our party would be split in due course.

Next day came the dreadful one-to-one interviews as the Cabinet lined up to tell her that she should not fight on. Being the most junior, I was at the end of what must have been a wearisome procession for her.

---

* This is not, for some reason, recorded in his diaries.

I am rather ashamed now that I stuck to the formula we had all agreed beforehand: we would vote for her if she chose to go on (and I, at least, would have done so), but she would still lose. 'They are running around out there like headless chickens,' I said, not very helpfully.

Less than twenty-four hours later came the famous cabinet meeting during which her voice choked when reading out her written statement; she was helped to finish it by the Lord Chancellor, James Mackay. Then the subdued departures, with many of us going, surreally, to Westminster Abbey for a memorial service for Libby Douglas-Home, Sir Alec's widow. We sang 'All Things Bright and Beautiful' and no one could plot because we were all in the choir stalls. En route, I had asked Chris Patten whether he would stand. He said 'no'.

At the cabinet meeting she had asked if anyone had voted for Heseltine. It was said that David Hunt had done so, but he was not there. Nor, as I have said, was Major. Later in the day, Heseltine stopped me in the lobby.

'If it's me against Major, who?'

'Major,' I said, without hesitation. Then, I am ashamed to say, I went after him. 'Perhaps we should talk?'

'No. Your instant answer is the truthful one.'

In retrospect, my instant answer may have been the wrong one. At the time, I and many others thought that Heseltine would have split the party, because of the Europeanism that was increasingly separating the true leaders from both the backbenchers in the House and Conservative supporters around the country. That was probably correct, but Heseltine was – and is – a very big man. Perhaps an early showdown, rather than the long, drawn-out civil war which continues to this day, might have provided at least a chance of unity.

But in my heart of hearts I think that it was wrong to depose Thatcher at all. Such a figure should only ever be defeated by the electorate. I say this not for any reason of constitutionality – indeed, what happened was perfectly acceptable in a parliamentary system – but because there was something unfitting, wrong, about a party that owed one person so much disposing of her in such a callous way, romantic, rather than pragmatic, though this view may be.

Despite my instinctive response to Heseltine's question, I did not believe Major was up to the job of leadership. He was not odd enough, ruthless enough, strange enough for it. I supported Hurd, who had the steel for the task, I knew. But perhaps I should have gone the whole hog and crossed the floor to Heseltine – a strange and brilliant loner who is undoubtedly a leader. When Major won, backed by all the Thatcher loyalists and indeed by Mrs Thatcher herself, who misread him as one of her own, I nearly destroyed my career by speaking disrespectfully of him at a dinner hosted by John Sainsbury behind the Royal Box at the Opera House. Too many people were there, and a version of what I said found its way into the press. Some of my comments were justified, I think; but others were undoubtedly motivated by jealousy. I had become used to Chris Patten beating me in our generation, but *John Major*? He would have been quite justified in not reappointing me, and would have saved himself quite a lot of trouble if he had done so. But his kindness, and perhaps the influence of Chris Patten, then and subsequently, kept me in the Cabinet.

Only once – after Britain's disastrous ejection from the European Exchange Rate Mechanism in September 1992 – did I contemplate disloyalty to Major. I asked to see Heseltine and suggested he should stand against the prime minister. At least I thought I'd said that. So opaquely and obscurely did I speak that Heseltine told me years later that he had no idea what I was talking about.

Then came the Scott Inquiry and Major protected me without hesitation, demoting me first to what was supposed to be the safe haven of the Department of Agriculture and then to the behind-the-scenes job of chief secretary, usually the most junior cabinet post.* All this meant there

---

* Agriculture was indeed a sanctuary during my year there. The following year, however, my successor, poor Douglas Hogg, was caught in the BSE maelstrom.

could be not the slightest question but that I should support him right to the doomed end.

I think my feelings about the fall of Thatcher were right. It was a shameful period, and those days and nights when the sharks circled were truly disgusting.

CHAPTER FIFTEEN

The Poll Tax:
All My Own Work

The poll tax is the issue to which most people attribute Thatcher's fall; and I was central to it. Local government finance is, famously, the most boring and complicated subject in all of public life. The threat of a chapter on it is a serious threat indeed. But my triumph was this, it must be remembered: I made this most tedious of subjects so interesting that it became the cause of widespread riots up and down the land and, one cause of the defeat of a great prime minister. This is how I did it.

The old Heathite pledge to abolish the domestic rates finally came back to haunt Thatcher's government. Revaluations were due, first in Scotland, then in England and Wales, with the perceived threat that this would target Conservative households by shifting the relative weight of the rates towards more valuable properties and away from poorer properties (as it was meant to do). The shires' Conservative associations were on the warpath; the already declining Scottish Conservative Party was in a state of acute panic.

In 1984 I was the third-tier minister in the Department of the

Environment, responsible, under the minister of state and ultimately the secretary of state, for the management of the infinitely complex Rate Support Grant system. This distributed central grants to all local authorities with the intention of equalising the tax base of each authority. Theoretically, if every authority then charged the same rate in the pound, they would all be able to provide services at the same level. Thus, if Sunderland had properties worth 30 units while Guildford's were worth 100 units, and the central judgement was that a rate poundage of 50 per cent on 120 units – 60 – was the correct expenditure level nationally, then Sunderland would receive a grant of 90, while Guildford would get 20. Moreover, if Westminster had 140 units, it might get *minus* 20: that is, it would be penalised if it spent up to its 50 per cent.

Intellectually, this was a beautiful system, invented by Keynes when he was an adviser to Churchill during the latter's otherwise disastrous stint as chancellor. In practice, it was a political nightmare, especially for the Conservatives. Why should Tory Guildford get only 20 units in its grant and Labour Sunderland 90? And why should allegedly frugal, efficient Westminster actually be penalised? The economists' answer was that in Guildford any property was worth more than three times the value of an equivalent property in Sunderland. But that was no comfort to people who had always lived in Guildford and wanted to continue to do so.

And how was the redistribution grant to be calculated?

Over the years, infinitely complex formulae had been generated to assess the needs of different places that were to be 'equalised'. These attempted to measure poverty, educational needs, density of population, sparseness of population and hundreds of other factors. To the ratepayer, the whole system was utterly incomprehensible, as indeed was the rate poundage concept itself: a 50 per cent rate on a three-bedroom house in Guildford of course resulted in a much bigger cash bill than a 50 per cent rate on a three-bedroom house in Sunderland. Surely that was unfair! Then there were criticisms relating to the fact that the rates were a capital tax, not an income tax: those four wage-earners living next door to the impoverished widow who received exactly the same rates bill as they did. In response, the economists would say that the widow should sell her house, buy a flat, and boost her pension fund. Then everyone would benefit. Such arguments did not go down well at the Conservative Party Conference.

Two further problems were non-domestic business rates, and social security help with rate bills for the poorest members of society. The Gestetners, who ran a family business in Islington, were great lobbyists on these two, intertwined, issues. Such boroughs received considerable funding from business rates, perhaps as much as two-thirds of the total income of the council. Of the remaining third, which came from domestic households, perhaps half came from people who were poor and whose bills were paid by central government's social security payments or were disguised in subsidised council rents. Thus, it was said that a poor person living in Islington, looking only to the best interests of his household, would be mad not to vote for more local spending, as this would be funded by local businesses and the national social security budget, not by the householder himself. Moreover, if a council was prepared to ignore the effect on local business, there were no costs to its voters in forever increasing expenditure. Consequently, businesses and the few (mostly Conservative) voters who paid full domestic rates out of their own pockets were bound to suffer. And neither could do anything about it: businesses because they had no vote; and Conservatives because they were always a small minority in such places.

Thus, the equalisation scheme, with its infinitely complex grant system, business rates and the social security system made any connection between how you voted locally (or what your council spent locally) and the rates bill you paid so random that there was really no local accountability. A thrifty council might lose out because of some vagary of the grant system; a spendthrift one might be bailed out by business rates and the Welfare State. Local voters could do little to change this and they knew it, as was reflected in a steady decline of turnout in local elections, often down to between 20 and 30 per cent, and the 'nationalisation' of those elections, which were increasingly run on central party platforms and mirrored national voting trends.

Into this heady mix were thrown the upcoming revaluations, Thatcher's eloquent exposition in October 1974 of Heath's pledge to abolish the domestic rates, and my ambition and self-confidence. I could understand the existing system of which I was now in charge (more or less) and thought that there must be a solution to all these problems which I would find. (This was perhaps influenced also by the overlay of Rothschild's scientism – the belief that every problem has a rational solution, which clever enough people can find – over the other lobe of my brain which retained a more pessimistic Conservative belief in the imperfection of things.) The opportunity all this offered to an ambitious young minister was obvious, anxious as I was to lay at the feet of the prime minister a prize that would put to rest doubts about my soundness as well as any residual contempt for my 'wetness'.

So I began agitating to be put in charge of finding the solution. Irwin Bellow, Lord Bellwin, my minister of state, who actually knew about local government, not just the numbers, having been Tory leader of Leeds City Council, was lukewarm. I suspect that Patrick Jenkin, my secretary of state, hoped I might produce a rabbit out of a hat that would advance his ambition to be chancellor. Terry Heiser, the newly appointed permanent secretary, was a results-oriented, can-do sort of person, not given to old-style caution that might be interpreted as feebleness. He and I went to visit the prime minister at Chequers. We drank whisky in front of the fire in one of the downstairs studies. A few days earlier, Tess Rothschild had begged me to find something for her husband to do. He was bored and underemployed and making her life a misery. So I suggested to Thatcher that he should be put in charge of a task force: half insiders, half outsiders, on the model of the CPRS. 'Oh, would Victor help?' she asked with enthusiasm, and so it came about.

The task force included some brilliant Department of the Environment civil servants – Tony Mayer, Robin Young, Chris Brearley and others; an outstanding Treasury representative, Jill Rutter; and several more, equally talented, officials. The outsiders were Rothschild, Professor Tom Wilson, a distinguished academic economist with wide experience, and Lennie Hoffmann, QC, requested by Rothschild on the basis that he had succeeded Stuart Hampshire as the cleverest man in England. I met this formidable team for a crucial meeting on 29 December 1984 before travelling to Chewton House, and between then and New Year 1985 I wrote in long hand, and then typed out on my father's secretary Mrs Wilkes's old upright typewriter a paper that set out the main elements of the decisions we had reached during the meeting. I have it still.

To restore local accountability, a direct link should be reconstituted between voters and the local household tax; so business rates should be removed from the equation and nationalised. Any grants should be extremely simple: preferably distributed on a per capita basis. Total freedom should be given to local authorities to set their tax at whatever level they deemed necessary: all central capping of local tax levels should stop, to restore direct accountability. But what should the tax be? Both Thatcher and the Treasury had already ruled out a local income tax. This was the era when Liverpool City Council was being run by Derek Hatton and his allegedly Trotskyite friends; giving the likes of them access to the income tax system was simply out of the question for a Conservative prime minister. What about a local sales tax? The country was too small: people could easily drive a few miles to a lower-tax area. Moreover, any tax that cycled with the ups and downs of the economy (like a sales tax) would mean cities running out of money during every downturn. Only one option was left. Something like a uniform charge for local services; a big version of the BBC's licence fee; a per capita tariff. A poll tax.

There were rumours in the press, around that Christmas of 1984, that we were contemplating this idea. My father said to me, 'Be careful of a poll tax.' He perhaps remembered that our ancestor, Sir Richard, had been threatened in his Suffolk estates by the Peasants' Revolt against a predecessor poll tax in 1381. But I was too far gone in the logic and pride of what I had invented to listen. I was also well aware that it went with the grain of what some on the hard right, including in the prime minister's policy unit, wanted. They had made no contribution to the generation of the policy, but they had certainly created fertile ground in which my seedling could root.

It was such fun. It is hard to think of another parliamentary under-secretary who was ever given such a free run in Whitehall. Rothschild added to the glamour, as in our CPRS days; not now with regular meetings in the Mirabelle, but in Wiltons and elsewhere. In the middle of it all, in September 1985, a new minister of state who at least equalled my level of ambition was appointed to the department: Kenneth Baker. Early on, he took me out to a splendid lunch. 'My plan,' he said, 'is that by next year you will be the minister of state and I will be the secretary of state.' And so it turned out.

During one policy-making evening in the hideous departmental tower block in Marsham Street (now thankfully gone), I worked late into the night with Young, Mayer and the others while an enormous electrical storm raged around us. Everything was dramatic, fast-moving, exciting – even the weather. Of course, my anxiety had not disappeared entirely, and nor had the objections from senior colleagues, especially Michael Heseltine, secretary for defence at the time but a former environment secretary, and the chancellor, Nigel Lawson. (We agreed from the outset to hide absolutely nothing from him.) When Rothschild produced his characteristically beautifully printed report, there was a dissenting note from Professor Wilson, who had more or less dissociated himself from the whole enterprise by then, and another from Hoffmann, who produced a minority report which argued that it was unnecessary to abolish domestic rates: local accountability would still be restored if they were left in place as long as all our other recommendations were implemented.

I had smart answers to every objection. Would the new tax be regressive? Of course: it was a charge for local services, and such charges were not meant to redistribute income or capital. The central tax system, not local authorities, should handle redistribution of wealth. If dukes were thought to be getting off lightly compared to dustmen, since both would pay the same poll tax, we should put up income tax or central capital taxes. (Admittedly, this was not a very likely scenario under a Thatcher–Lawson government, but it was a sound debating point.) In any case, we would (and we did) add to the payments poor people received through social security the average cost of what they would have to pay. The point was to make it clear that their votes now had consequences. They would actually have to hand over the money, rather than have their rates automatically relieved, as happened under the old system. Yes, nationalising non-domestic rates was a form of centralisation, but it was the only way to escape the far greater centralisation involved in the equalisation system.

The greatest local authority official of his day was Maurice Stonefrost, who had run the Greater London Council and kept it more or less on the rails even during the frivolously left-wing regime of Ken Livingstone. I talked to him. Probably taking from the conversation what I wanted to hear, I felt he endorsed the trade-off between the restoration of local autonomy that would follow the abolition of rate-capping and the provision of a painful local tax. (Rate-capping was the horribly centralising interim measure government had invented to limit councils' power to raise rates.)

I travelled to other countries to see what they were up to. At the time, Italy was talking of reforming its own system by moving to the one I was hoping to abolish, which they regarded as by far the best in the world. Tokyo seemed to be running a per capita element alongside a property tax. All I really learned from these visits, though, was that every country thought that someone, somewhere, must have devised a better system than their own.

I thought that if the poll tax proved too unpopular, we would not go back to a local tax based on property, but end up introducing a graduated personal tax – a local income tax – with the local authorities given limited access to the Inland Revenue's records. This would not do much for accountability – because not many more people pay income tax directly than paid the old domestic rates directly – but at least it would have fulfilled the pledge to abolish domestic rates. In the immediate short term, I certainly thought that no one would be so rash as to move in one leap to the poll tax. Instead, I believed it would run alongside the rates for a time, and could be limited in its weight if there were too many objections. That would also have had the advantage of widening the local authorities' tax base, a vital objective since the weight of modern services for which they were responsible was far too great for the narrow base of the rates alone.

It is one of the mistakes of populist politicians that they always seek to maximise the number of voters who pay no tax at all – by lifting the income tax threshold, for instance, or piling exemptions on to VAT. This is, I believe, very damaging for a democratic state, since it divorces ever more people from understanding the consequences of how they vote and sharpens the division between those who pay tax and those who do not. It inches countries towards a Roman bread-and-circuses polity, where the government is supposed to produce doles for the populace – which, as far as the latter is concerned, have no cost. That part of my plan was sensible, I still believe; but spreading the burden of taxation rather than making yourself popular with specific groups by exempting them is not the sort of thing successful politicians tend to do.

Before the crucial cabinet meeting that would either accept or reject the poll tax, I – still a mere parliamentary under-secretary – was tasked with seeing all cabinet ministers personally to explain the policy. Tebbit said that at last we were doing something for our own people. George Younger, the Scottish secretary – one of my principal supporters in Cabinet – said that he had been waiting all his political life for something like this. Whitelaw said, 'Very good, very good.' Heseltine said it was nonsense; but he was preoccupied. Lawson, who always called the policy 'the Waldegrave Reforms', was dismissive, particularly of the name we had coined – the Community Charge. He said, rightly, that it was a tax, not a charge; but he did not fight. By now on the backbenches, George Young led an eloquent campaign against the policy.

At the cabinet meeting itself, on 6 January 1986, just over a year since I had written my paper, more immediately dramatic events unfolded. It was the climax of the Westland affair. Heseltine walked out of the Cabinet, declaring that he had just resigned to an astonished reporter in Downing Street. For some days thereafter, the prime minister's power teetered. She was saved by Neil Kinnock's poor performance in the House, and by the fact that the country could not really understand what the problem was between Heseltine, Leon Brittan and Thatcher herself. Amid all this, the poll tax quietly became policy; the revaluation in Scotland was stopped; and immense care was taken to explain the new system, first in a Green Paper, then in a White Paper. It was put before the electorate at the 1987 general election and perhaps played a part in the Conservative victory: ratepayers hoped for some sort of respite from escalating bills, and everyone else assumed it could not be as stupid as it looked.

As Ken Baker had predicted, I had finally been promoted to minister of state, but my brief was now housing, not local government finance. Others, first Nicholas Ridley and then Chris Patten, assumed responsibility for the introduction of my policy. Fatally, Ridley won enormous cheers at the 1987 party conference – triumphalist after our third consecutive victory at the polls – by announcing that he had no intention of running domestic rates alongside the Community Charge. As I listened at the back of the hall, my heart sank. But it was no business of mine any more. Perhaps the big beasts knew more than I did. After all, they had been right about everything else – confronting the unions, privatisation, dramatic income-tax cuts. Perhaps they would be proved right again.

Could it have worked? And was it really what brought down Thatcher? If the government had been more cautious, introducing it in a phased way, and if Lawson had surrendered some of his income-tax cuts rather than taking the opportunity to cut local authority grants further (thus increasing the pain of the poll tax), it might have survived in a truncated form, or at least might have been less of a source of grievance. In Wales, where the central government grant was higher than in England, and the local tax lower, the anger was lower, too. But it was fatal to introduce it in one go, especially at a time when income tax was being radically cut. It was impossible to argue against the widespread impression of a huge shift to the better-off, because it was true. Moreover, the fundamental deal that I thought I had brokered was never even given a chance, because the Community Charge itself was capped. Localisation gained nothing. Local elections continued to be blighted by pitiful turnouts.

In the end, however, mine was simply a bad policy. It was a bad policy not because you could not make clever rebuttals of all the points against – you could, and I did – but because, for example, there was no chance in reality that its perceived regressive nature would be corrected elsewhere in the system. It was always bound to contribute to the formation of a political underclass because, although the Community Charge household lists were separate from the Electoral Roll, no one in my constituency ward of St Paul's, for example, believed it. Finally, although the idea that even the poorest members of society should pay at least a bit towards their local services – and receive compensation in the social security cash they are given – makes a certain sense, they soon forgot about the social security compensation and only saw the tax demand. It was not workable, because it was perceived as deliberately unfair. My father was right.

The poll tax was eventually accepted as a failure and withdrawn by John Major's government in favour of a simplified local property tax (though the nationalisation of business rates continued, just as Hoffmann had argued it could). We fought and won the 1992 election – and in so doing helped to turn the Labour Party upside-down – partly on the repeal of the 'Waldegrave Reforms'. My friend Professor Vernon Bogdanor called regularly for my resignation, but there was little real pressure on me: in the public's mind it was *Thatcher*'s poll tax, and she had already gone. It was also relatively easy for me to defend myself: 'What? Do you really think one lowly parliamentary under-secretary in the Department of the Environment could have orchestrated something like that? Ridiculous!'

But the truth is, I do not believe it would have happened without me.

CHAPTER SIXTEEN

Arms to Iraq, Rounded to Zero

To try to defend yourself against a widely held judgement – a judgement on the way to being that judgement of history against which there is no appeal – is a risky business. Disraeli, Gladstone said, advised that you should never complain and never explain. However, a great many people who are judged successful are judged so because they were eloquent propagandists for themselves. At the top of the tree is Churchill: 'History will be kind to me because I intend to write it myself,' he said. Of course, Churchill's greatness would be assured if he had never written a word, but plenty of others, particularly those in the second and third ranks, are there because they took trouble over their posterity. Horace Walpole was perhaps the most thoroughgoing of all. He kept two or three copies of his letters, wrote a detailed description of his house and collection, commissioned numerous portraits of himself, and thought with military precision about mechanisms through which he might transmit himself to posterity, with my family being one of them. The diarists Samuel Pepys, Chips Channon, Harold Nicolson and Alan Clark are other examples.

It is also difficult to defend oneself without recourse to that unsatisfactory false, double-edged form of self-deprecation of which both Horace Walpole and Alan Clark were masters. The former pretends to doubt, as he begins his minutely detailed description of the contents of Strawberry Hill, that his poor collection will be of interest to anyone. And whenever the latter confesses a sin in his diaries, it is always with a little chuckle: 'What a wicked chap I am!' he says. This technique is designed to disarm and charm, and it often succeeds. There is no mention of things he did which were, arguably, genuinely nasty. It is all cheeky-chappy Alan, the left-wing journalist's favourite right-winger. The British will let you get away with almost anything if you make them laugh. Thank goodness Oswald Mosley had no sense of humour. Thank goodness Boris Johnson is no Oswald Mosley.

We also like to sort our history into stories that fit certain age-old archetypes. The heroic rebel Fletcher Christian gets a better press than the dour disciplinarian Bligh, even though the former was the leader of a gang of murderers and rapists, while the latter was a seaman whose skill rivalled that of Cook. And it should not be forgotten that most of HMS *Bounty*'s crew opted to go with Bligh – to what must have seemed like certain death – rather than return to Tahiti with Christian. Yet Marlon Brando played Christian, not Bligh. The truth does not always out; the best story outs.

Challenging the now deeply embedded myth of the 'Arms to Iraq' inquiry, taking on the leading diarist of his day, and trying to reverse the public's understanding of two archetypal stories of the kind we all love to believe are probably well beyond me. But I must try. Throughout this book I have attempted to provide an account, as true as I can make it, of what drove me into politics, how I scrambled some way up the greasy pole, found I could climb no further, and slipped back down again. It would be odd not to attempt to describe the main episode which accelerated, at the very least, my descent; and I must try to describe what it felt like, since the feelings which surrounded that time were the most extreme (outside the grief I felt for the death of my parents and of other people I loved) of all my life.

One of those archetypical stories against which I have to struggle is that Britain (and America) first armed Saddam Hussein's appalling regime in Iraq and then subsequently sent our troops to fight against the weapons we had sold him. That is not true. If you want the truth, you can find it on pages 46–7 of Nick Cohen's book, *What's Left?*[*] This is what he says:

> After the fall of Baghdad in 2003, the Stockholm International Peace Research Institute examined the records of 'actual deliveries of major conventional weapons' to Iraq between 1973 and 2002 and found that 57 per cent of Saddam's weapons came from the Soviet Union, 13 per cent from France, and 12 per cent from China. The United States sold about half of one per cent, while Britain's sales were worth $79 million, or about one-fifth of one per cent, a fraction so small that the Swedes rounded it down to the nearest whole number, which was zero.

The archetypical story is false. Britain did not arm Iraq.

The other satisfying story against which I have to struggle is this. Wicked government ministers tried to send innocent, even heroic, people to jail to cover up our own misdeeds, only to be foiled by a courageous whistle-blower helped by brilliant lawyers. The movie almost casts itself. The supposed victims of this plot were the managers of a machine-tool company called Matrix Churchill, who were prosecuted by HM Customs for allegedly breaching export laws. The story was that we ministers had encouraged them to break the law, so anxious were we to arm Iraq, and then abandoned them to their fate when they were caught. This makes no sense at all when you consider it objectively: why would anyone try to suppress their misdeeds by approving a court case that was sure to

---

[*] I quote Cohen, rather than more boring and academic sources of the facts, because if you read his book you will be in no doubt that he has no interest in defending Tory ex-Ministers.

bring those misdeeds to light? But I fear it will be as difficult to convince people of that as it would be to persuade an Australian that more
Frenchmen than Australians died in the Gallipoli campaign (which also
happens to be true).

So, I approach the story of the Matrix Churchill affair with a certain
amount of fatalism. I know that nothing I write here will stop it featuring
prominently in my obituaries. But I still feel a burning resentment about
it, about Lord Scott, about Alan Clark, and about those who organised
the systematic leaking of the first drafts of Scott's comments about me,
which he subsequently largely retracted. Those leakers surely knew that
my reputation would never truly recover, and they succeeded in shattering what was left of my self-confidence along with any enjoyment I still
felt in my trade of politics.

The story itself is not very complicated. By the time I arrived at the
Foreign Office in 1988, the Iran/Iraq War had reached near stalemate,
after terrible losses on both sides. Iraq had used poison gas, including on
several of its own Kurdish villages, judged to be disloyal to the regime.
Iran had been the victim of aggression, but its own irresponsible government was hardly blameless.* It is often said that US and British policy
favoured Iraq, since Iran had been leading an extreme anti-American
campaign in the Middle East, had taken American Embassy staff hostage
in 1979, and was funding terrorists and extreme Shia groups wherever it
could find them. But certainly during my time at the Foreign Office – that
is, from 1988 onwards – Britain was strictly even handed: apart from the
Americans, we were the only major arms-manufacturing country to have
tough controls on what could be exported to either country, and those
controls favoured neither side over the other. The controls were exer-
cised under legislation left over from the Second World War, and Foreign
Secretary Geoffrey Howe had informed Parliament of the criteria Britain

---

* Iran's early successes resulted in another Harold Macmillan *bon mot*: 'Of course they did
well, dear boy. They had shot all their generals before they started.'

was following. These 'Guidelines', as the criteria were known, were not law; instead, they advised officials on how to proceed when receiving requests from firms seeking export licences. They applied not only to arms themselves, but to goods that might be used in the manufacture of weapons. It should be remembered that these were voluntary, British controls; no UN embargoes were in place. The French, not to mention the Russians and the Chinese, had no such controls and sold whatever they could.

In the autumn of 1988, a ceasefire was brokered on the basis of a UN resolution. British diplomacy had played a considerable part in this, and the Foreign Office was rightly proud of its contribution. Taken literally, this ceasefire meant that the Guidelines which Howe had presented to Parliament were now meaningless because they referred to a conflict that had ceased. Without hesitation, the two departments sponsoring arms manufacture and industrial goods – the Ministry of Defence and the Department of Trade and Industry – began to agitate for the abolition of *all* controls, not only those on industrial goods but those on actual weapons. The Foreign Office countered that this would be a serious mistake: both regimes were still dangerous, not only to their immediate neighbours but further afield; and the ceasefire might prove to be temporary, used simply for rearming. Both also had appalling human rights records. So we deemed it essential to keep a tight lid on the sale of arms, and on both sides' capacity to make their own. (The latter aspiration would be much more difficult to achieve, of course.)

This view was naturally very unpopular with the trade lobbies. I remember one outstanding Foreign Office official, David Gore-Booth, returning steaming with rage from a meeting of COMET – the Committee on Middle East Trade – and exclaiming, 'These people are dead set on undermining government policy!' He and another fine official, Rob Young, undertook negotiations with their counterparts at the MoD and the DTI and comprehensively outmanoeuvred them. They reached a tentative agreement at official level not only that the Guidelines should stay in place, but that the wording should be so little changed to reflect the ceasefire that it gave virtually no room for relaxation of the export controls. The Guidelines would now refer to the possibility of export for 'purely defensive purposes', but in reality any potential exporter would find it so difficult to prove that their goods would never be used offensively that this made little difference. We knew that we could continue to reject every straightforward request for an arms export licence, and that was exactly what we did.

I thought the Foreign Office had scored a signal victory. As far as I was concerned, the Guidelines were, to all intents and purposes, unchanged. The DTI even proposed that there was no need to announce these 'new' Guidelines to Parliament, as they were essentially the same as they had been before. It was here that I made a mistake: I agreed to their request, believing that the DTI was motivated by the desire to avoid embarrassment with its lobbies over its inter-departmental defeat. Nor did I cover my back by consulting my boss, Geoffrey Howe, though I think I assumed that the Permanent Secretary would have discussed what was happening at one of the weekly meetings he held with him.

In retrospect, I think Foreign Office officials might have rung more alarm bells. Anything announced years before to Parliament and then changed, even to a minuscule degree, should always be announced again. I should also have had more sense of self-preservation and made sure that the issue was signed off formally by Howe. But in the event it did not matter, because of what happened next.

On 14 February 1990, the Iranian religious authorities – indistinguishable from their political authorities at that point – issued a *fatwa* against the London-based novelist Salman Rushdie because of his allegedly blasphemous novel, *The Satanic Verses*. The British government's response was uncompromising and instant: Mr Rushdie should be defended, and no compromise would be made with Tehran. However, John le Carré, Roald Dahl and I was astonished to find many of my old colleagues at All Souls thought we were wrong to stand up for Rushdie. I met Rushdie in Harold and Antonia Pinter's house to discuss the situation.* Harold was very fierce indeed, perhaps even fiercer than Rushdie himself. When Václav Havel, playwright and recently elected President of free Czechoslovakia, came to Britain and attended a Number Ten reception he asked to speak to me in private about the matter, without Mrs Thatcher, which caused some consternation. (Charles Powell slipped into the room anyway.) But no compromise was available, although Rushdie said conciliatory things. Real attempts were made by extremists trying to win the reward Teheran offered for his murder. The precedent – a *fatwa* issued in the 1930s against a writer in British India – was not good. There was at that time no possible acceptable approach to be made to Teheran: it took years for their internal power structures to shift a little, and for enough of Iran's leadership to be willing to distance themselves decisively from the *fatwa*.

In *Joseph Anton* Rushdie blames us for not doing more to 'resolve the crisis' in the months after the *fatwa* was issued. I do not believe that is fair: there was no resolution possible then. Over time, power structures in Iran changed a little, for a time at least, and the Foreign Office was able to take advantage of the shift. Robin Cook, by then Foreign Secretary in the incoming Labour Government, and his officials, were able to take advantage of this and did well. But there was nothing to be done in 1989 and 1990 except ensure Rushdie's safety to the best of our ability.

I believe Britain behaved honourably in physically defending Rushdie, while many British Muslim 'leaders' behaved despicably. But the government did not always get the words right: some colleagues muddled our duty to defend Rushdie with their views about the merits of his novel; some sought to establish common ground with moderate Muslim opinion by belittling him. Rushdie's complaint about this in *Joseph Anton* is fair. I hope I was innocent of this. The novel in fact is a fine one: I still have the copy the Foreign Office bought for me to read on that black Valentine's Day.

---

* Oddly, this does not appear in Rushdie's account of these events, *Joseph Anton*, although he generously corrected the omission in his speech of acceptance for the PEN Pinter Prize in 2014.

The *fatwa* made it impossible to undertake anything that might be misinterpreted in Tehran as some sort of deal, including any relaxation of the export guidelines. We could no more horse-trade over Rushdie than we could over the hostages held in Lebanon, mostly by Iranian-sponsored Shia groups. And if relaxation for Tehran was now out of the question, it was out of the question for Baghdad, too. The process of seeking three-way departmental agreement over the revised guidelines stopped overnight, uncompleted. The three ministers never agreed to a change.

In any case, Iraq's behaviour, murdering journalists, including the *Observer's* Fazad Bazoft, and threatening other neighbours, was making as much of a mockery of 'peace' as was Iran's. There was no question of relaxing export controls, even to the minuscule degree the new Guidelines (which were designed to reflect the fact that the shooting war between Iran and Iraq had stopped) might have allowed. The papers of the tri-departmental committee that considered export licences show that it continued to work in a muddle. As far as I was concerned, there had been no change in anything. However the 'new' guideline had been tried by officials, to see whether it made any significant difference to the old (it did not); and then they drifted back to using only the old one. But they faced a problem; they were supposed to be using a guideline which referred to a conflict which had not existed for a year or more. They muddled through, sometimes trying to use the 'revised' version as a gloss on the 'old' version. As far as Scott could see, in only one case did the new gloss make any difference; in the case of a genuinely defensive radar for Iran. By the end of the summer of 1990 – the 'new' version seemed to have been forgotten by the officials in their committee. Most of the applications for export were not for weapons. One of the absurdities of the whole affair was that euphony led to the whole thing being dubbed the 'Arms for Iraq' enquiry. There were almost no applications for the export of arms; the manufacturers and MOD, their sponsor, knew they would be turned down. At one point, MOD and their client, British Aerospace, supported by DTI, were lobbying extremely hard for the export to Iraq of the BAe Hawk aircraft, a trainer, but quite a formidable aircraft, even if of the previous generation. Its rival was the French Alpha-jet, which the French were desperate to sell. I was asked to go over to MOD for a joint lobbying session by officials and the company: if only we could close this deal it would put paid to the Alpha-jet forever! Just this one deal . . . Think of the employment! Think of the future of British Aerospace . . .

I wrote an agonised minute to the foreign secretary recommending that if we were rich enough not to trade with Saddam Hussein's despicable regime, we should not do so. But perhaps, I said, we were not in a strong enough position to be so self-controlled. The case went all the way to the prime minister, who turned down the application. There were no Hawk sales, and Alpha-jet won the day. Incidentally, as Scott himself accepted, if the decision had gone the other way, Parliament would have been informed, because it would have clearly breached Howe's Guidelines – both 'old' and 'new'.

Much more difficult cases concerned so-called 'dual-use' items. These posed extraordinary problems. As I wrote in one minute, not entirely foolishly, a screwdriver could be used in the building of an atomic bomb. So should we ban the export of screwdrivers? There was acute anxiety over Iraq's interest in what became known later as 'weapons of mass destruction'. Exports that fell under that head were banned by international law: though again dual-use items – screwdrivers or their modern counterparts – were extremely difficult. Was a radioactive isotope really for medical purposes, or not?

So along came Matrix Churchill, all that remained, virtually, of the once proud British machine tool industry. They were a medium-sized, Birmingham-based company doing their best to sell where they could. They appeared to be at least partly controlled by shadowy Iraqi interests. Their machines, FCO thought, could be used for arms manufacture, being far beyond the specification their alleged end use required. They denied it. The Foreign Office thought they were lying. They lobbied

DTI. DTI said it was the FCO who were causing the trouble: they had better lobby FCO. They saw Rob Young, who reported to me that he was extremely dubious about them and offered no encouragement. They complained again to DTI and saw Alan Clark, along with their Trade Association, the Machine Tool Manufacturers Association. According to the MTMA minutes of this meeting, Clark said that no one cared about the Guidelines, so Matrix Churchill should fill in whatever they liked on the form.

It subsequently transpired that one of the firm's directors, who travelled to Iraq on a sales mission, was providing information to the Secret Intelligence Service. Of course, no minister or official outside the SIS would have known such an operational fact. Certainly, the man was brave. But did he perhaps also think that his SIS role gave him some kind of immunity from the law?

Matrix Churchill then applied for an export licence, filling it in as they believed they had been advised to do by Clark. HM Customs, which was responsible for enforcing the export controls legislation, prosecuted them on the basis that they were lying about the end use of their machines. Shortly before the case was due to go to court, in an article in the *Sunday Times*, Graham Turner, a journalist of impeccable moral standards, quoted Clark as saying that he cared little for the control of exports to Iraq (or indeed anywhere else). Before bringing their case, HM Customs sought assurances from Clark that he had been misquoted, and he duly signed an affidavit to that effect. The prosecution went ahead.

During the trial, a formidable lawyer, Geoffrey Robertson, cross-examining Clark, produced the MTMA minutes and forced Clark to admit that they were an accurate record of what he had said. However, he instantly tried to spread the guilt among his colleagues: 'None of us cared,' was his line. Not so: Matrix Churchill had gone back to lobby the DTI for a second time because Rob Young, on behalf of the Foreign Office, *did* care and had refused to help them.

* * *

In November 1992 I was at a grand dinner in the Painted Hall, Greenwich, for Boris Yeltsin. His entourage was little short of anarchic: Georgian and Ukrainian officials, still working for Russia despite the collapse of the Soviet Union, were open about their disaffection and their desire to go home. Robin Butler approached me after the dinner: 'You remember that trial of the machine-tool exporters?' I did, but only vaguely: it had really been nothing to do with the Foreign Office. I assumed, on the basis of their lobbying of Rob Young and his report of that meeting, that they must have been found guilty. 'Well, it has collapsed . . . because of Alan Clark. There will have to be an inquiry.'

Butler rang me the next day. I was in my ministerial car, en route to Oxford. 'The PM will announce an inquiry. He thinks the terms of reference should be wide. I think they should be narrow. What do you think?' And then I made another mistake, this time for reasons of pride. 'Make them as wide as possible,' I said, sure that the FCO (and I) would come out as heroes, having fought and fought to limit exports to Iraq and Iran; Clark and MOD and DTI would be in the frame and serve them right. Well, such pride served me right.

I had had nothing to do with the trial, and had not signed a Public Interest Immunity Certificate. These were certificates which Governments had for many years used to prevent the unnecessary release of sensitive government material in Court, if justice could be done without it. Otherwise every such defence would have attempted to ward off prosecution by threatening to release material not truly relevant, but damaging to the public interest. Government might then fear to allow prosecutions of the clearly guilty in case of wider damage. Nicholas Lyell, the extremely careful and cautious attorney general, had authorised the use of these certificates in the Matrix Churchill case, since intelligence matters were bound to come up in court. He took the conventional view that the trial judge would see all the material covered by PIICs and release it to the defence team if he judged it was necessary for a fair trial. By seeking the certificates in the first place, the government indicated that if justice could be achieved without the release of the sensitive material, it was in the best interests of national security to keep it secret. But it acknowledged that the needs of the defence overrode this, if the judge so ordered.

Sensing an opportunity, the defence lawyers in the Matrix Churchill case led a high-profile campaign against PIICs, government secrecy and the British Establishment in general, stirring up a hornets' nest in much the same way as their Australian counterparts had done during the *Spycatcher* trial. Geoffrey Robertson assumed the theatrical anti-establishment role played earlier by Malcolm Turnbull.

The conspiracy theory ran like wildfire. Government ministers were trying to send heroic, SIS-employed exporters to jail in order to cover up the fact that they themselves were selling arms to Iraq. I never understood how this conspiracy was supposed to work. Why, if the government wanted Matrix-Churchill to export, were Customs allowed to prosecute them? In such a conspiracy-rich universe, stopping Customs prosecuting would have been easy: indeed the conspiracists assumed Customs had been *told* to prosecute. But why?

Alan Clark presented the story as something like this: we the Government gave a nod and a wink that it was OK to export, but were too wet to stop the heroes being prosecuted when they were caught. He had then blown the whistle in court. But this was patent nonsense: he had denied on oath in his affidavit doing any such thing, and if you read the transcript of his cross-examination, he blew no whistles, but surrendered under good cross-examination on the basis of the non-government, MTMA minutes of his own meeting.

One of the farcical elements of the evidence which emerged in the inquiry was that it turned out that when the formal Matrix Churchill application came to be considered by the FCO, the official dealing with it had not yet been security cleared, and so could not read the relevant papers, let alone send them up the line, ultimately to me. In one of his rather rare succinct paragraphs, Scott in any case said that he was in no doubt that if I had seen the advice on the Matrix Churchill application, I would have turned the application down under either 'version' of the guidelines. So much for Clark's alleged government-wide policy of nods and winks.

However, brilliant opposition work by Cook, Peter Mandelson and the rest swept away any doubts based on logic and reason. They accused wicked ministers of trying to send innocent men to jail and using PIICs to suppress the information that could have saved them. Bernard Levin, in his most Chestertonian style, accused me of utter depravity for signing one of the PIICs. As I wrote to him to point out, I had done no such thing.

The inquiry dragged on and on, with Scott and his assistant lawyer, Presiley Baxendale, hunting as a pair in interminable cross-examinations. I had three days of it. The Lord Chancellor, James Mackay, advised all of us to waive our right to a lawyer as these were not judicial proceedings, under the Tribunals Act, merely an informal seeking after truth. One junior colleague ignored this advice and took along the warden of All Souls, Patrick Neill, a very distinguished lawyer. He was treated with kid gloves. By contrast, Scott helpfully discussed a line of criticism of me with Alan Clark; together they concluded that one of my arguments was 'Alice in Wonderland'.

I asked James Mackay about questions that clearly assumed a particular answer. He said, 'It's a heuristic device. He is not assuming anything . . . yet.' He was wrong: the inquiry started, and continued, with a certain view and amended its opinion only under powerful challenge. Most journalists loved it. Only the very best remained objective, Matthew Parris, for example, who attended the hearings and wrote that the atmosphere was like a lynch mob.* Simon Jenkins wrote that he longed for the common sense of an Oliver Franks.†

After two years or so of snail-paced progress, the inquiry sent me its

---

* If so, it was partly organised by the Labour Party; Mandelson was a regular attender.
† Franks was best known for heading the inquiry into the Falklands War.

terribly damaging draft conclusions, which stated that I had lied when signing letters to members of the public to the effect that there had been no change to the Guidelines. Within a few days these draft conclusions were leaked, in an operation so efficient and widespread that I have always assumed that Labour's publicity machine was involved – one bit to the BBC, then some to ITV, then some to favoured newspapers. Not the technique of a disgruntled junior civil servant.

I opened the envelope containing the draft conclusions walking along the corridor at Westminster behind the Speaker's Chair. I knew instantly that my world was really over then, as I read what Scott and Baxendale had written. As the leaks came – postponed a few days, I believe, by the BBC so that the bit they had been given should not be published on the day after my father's death – I lived in a terrible private world. When I rang my mother to warn her (she died later in the same year) she said, 'Oh darling, it is only politics'. What my wife and children can have gone through, I do not know; though I know that St Paul's Girls School took special steps to try to help protect my eldest daughter, Katie, then fifteen.

To live in such a maelstrom, day after day, week after week, reading and listening to appalling things being said about yourself that you know are not true, is something strange. Only chemicals allowed sleep. I could not read anything except wholly escapist comfortable words: Wodehouse, mostly. I tried to learn poems off by heart. Anything to blot out the pain. Suicide? I only thought of it melodramatically, never in reality, because suicide of that sort destroys all those you love, and is perhaps also an admission of guilt.

I swiftly learned who my friends were, for the second time in my life. All sorts of people had stopped taking me out to lunch as soon as Ted Heath fell from power. On the intervening upswing, I had made many new friends. During the 1980s, virtually everyone would accept an invitation to dinner: David Bailey and Marie Helvin came; so did Alfred Brendel; and the Prince and Princess of Wales. Hugh Casson asked me to address the Royal Academy's annual dinner, a white-tie affair at which the Prince of Wales was also a speaker.*

But after Scott, things were different. On the downswing, the invitations dry up. For instance, my name was deleted from the invitation list for the Bilderberg Conferences.† On the other hand, there was solidarity far beyond the call of duty. Particularly touching were friends who offered asylum from the ever pursuing press. The great Duke of Wellington had set up a good defensive position at Stratfield Saye House, hidden in its park. Charles and Antonia Douro often protected us there. They also took us, with another beleaguered person, to the Dunhill Cup at St Andrews. I know nothing about golf, but was grateful for the way the huge crowds kept their eyes on the ball and ignored both Camilla Parker Bowles and me. So did the golfing journalists: our handicaps were of no interest.

---

* This dinner, in May 1984, was memorable. The other speaker, apart from the Prince and me, was Laurie Lee, author of *Cider with Rosie*. He had been told, like me, to speak for exactly ten minutes, so that the prince should not be inconvenienced by a late night. Mr Lee, however, had drunk a very great deal, not on this occasion cider. He spoke for twenty minutes, having placed an egg timer in front of him, which went off after ten minutes with no effect on the flow. The late Princess of Wales, who was sitting next to him and to me, made it worse by trying to reset it: you can only turn egg timers the wrong way. I think we had forty minutes. Late in the evening, Lee was found asleep in a corner. The Lord Chancellor, Lord Hailsham, in full fig, white tie, decorations and sashes and all, rescued him, and put him in his ministerial car to take him home. Unfortunately, Lee could not remember where this was. They cruised down the King's Road, and found a man sweeping up outside a pub. He joined the party in the car, recognising a familiar customer, and knowing where he lived. So was Laurie Lee delivered home, by the Lord Chancellor of England and the publican in the ministerial car. That is how things should be.

† Bilderberg is an entirely innocent and admirable talking shop set up by the Dutch royal family after the war. In the 1990s the meetings were still hosted by the Queen of the Netherlands. (She told me that when she had accompanied her father to the conferences as a teenager she had usually been the only female present, and the leaders of the free world had assumed she was the waitress.) American conspiracists claim that the world is ruled by Bilderberg. That is certainly not the case, but the conferences can be rather fun. Bill Gates told us that the difference between his electronic machines and their electro-mechanical predecessors was that his never broke down. He was offended by the incredulous titter from Microsoft users in the audience. Gianni Agnelli, the boss of Fiat, conformed to every stereotype with bodyguards and consiglieri in dark glasses. Rupert Murdoch came alone with no pomp – an attractive trait. On one occasion a protestor made a mockery of all the security by leaving a rude message on all our pillows, a soul brother of Richard Feynman, who made similar mock of General G. G. Groves's security at the Manhattan project.

My private secretary at the Ministry of Agriculture (where I was by then), Andrew Cahn, became a life-long friend as a result of the quiet and utterly stalwart support he provided.

Then, into my office one day walked Lennie Hoffmann, the formidable QC and High Court judge, member of my poll tax task force, and soon to be a member of the House of Lords Judicial Committee, subsequently the Supreme Court. 'Who is your solicitor?' he asked. I said I had a share of a worthy young Treasury lawyer. 'You need a proper lawyer,' he said. I asked whether it was right for him, a judge in the highest court in the land, to be advising someone who was currently facing such an inquiry. 'It is not a trial,' he said. 'It is a kangaroo court invented by your government and I shall help my friends if I want to.' He wrote the name of a solicitor at Allen & Overy, David Mackie, on a piece of paper. 'This is the person you need. And you should get the government to pay. I shall help with advice.'

From that moment, the balance of argument began to shift. There was nearly a year after the leaked, disastrous draft report before Scott finally published. For months I spent painstaking hours at Allen and Overy's offices going through every paper. I remember the day when they made their fundamental point. There was no reply from MOD to the minute agreed by me and by DTI on the revised version of the guideline; 14 February had stopped everything. It took all these Departments to agree. There had been no such agreement; therefore the guidelines had not changed.

Mackie and his team at Allen & Overy showed me how lawyers' minds work.

'Where is the evidence that the Guidelines changed?'

'There isn't any.'

'So you were right, then. They didn't change.'

My further submission to the inquiry set out the case I should have written in the first place.* Hoffmann contributed a beautiful essay on the

---

* In my original account, drafted alone over the course of a summer weekend in Somerset, I had stated that Whitehall is a procedure-driven place. So if procedures have not been completed that, in itself, is evidence that no action has followed. This was the 'sophistic' argument

level of proof needed to destroy someone's reputation: 'high', since what is done is irremediable. When the final, amended version of the report appeared, all the worst criticism had gone. I was acquitted of lying, albeit in typically convoluted sentences: 'Though Mr Waldegrave's letters were designedly misleading he had no intent to deceive.' I was, however, still criticised for being 'sophistic'.

The time around the publication of the final Report was strange. I was exhilarated by my acquittal, however grudgingly expressed, of the charge of lying: Cummings, the powerful cartoonist of the *Daily Express*, showed Scott's canon as having fired a dud shell. Garland, however, was more accurate. There was an oil slick in the Channel killing sea birds at the time. He drew Lyell and myself as doomed, oil-contaminated, sea birds. I accepted television interviews and stuck simply to saying, 'He said I did not lie.' I wrote a foolish, in retrospect, over-confident article in the *Sunday Telegraph*. The exhilaration did not last: the archetypical stories, and the assault on my reputation, were not to be suppressed by words as opaque as Scott's. A comedian called Mark Thomas parked a cardboard Iraqi tank outside our house in London, to the delight of my ten-year-old son (who must have therefore been relatively well protected from it all). Of course, there were no British tanks in Iraq – they were Russian. But a cardboard tank outside the Russian Embassy would not have been nearly so funny. After the initial sense of reprieve, I realised that I was not tough enough to fight my way back, in spite of sometimes unexpected support.

The Lord Chief Justice, Peter Taylor, to whom I had never previously spoken, came across the room to me at a party of Kenneth Rose's. 'For a man to say you wrote designedly misleading letters but had no intent to deceive and then to accuse YOU of sophistry is going it a bit,' he said. I heard those great men – Wilberforce, Steyn, Lloyd – defending me. Such support was intensely moving, but I was under no illusion that I would

---

that Scott – extraordinarily – discussed with Alan Clark before they reached their joint 'Alice in Wonderland' verdict. How grateful Clark must have been!

ever be the same again. In my Constituency at the election I was spat at, 'You wanted to send innocent people to jail'. My Labour opponent made the most of it all. I lost with no greater swing than in other urban seats where tactical voting was well organised; but I was not tough enough ever to enjoy political knock-about again. All my life I had attempted to make a reputation for trying to tell the truth – even about the necessity sometimes to lie – and now it was exactly that central part of my identity that had been destroyed. And, as opposed to the Poll Tax, I was innocent. That is the symmetry with which those sharp and humorous gods work.

From all this I learnt that the Rolls-Royce Whitehall machine I loved could sometimes break down. As Scott agreed, key pieces of evidence were not shown to me; shabby things were done. Muddles were made, though there was indeed 'no conspiracy and no cover up' as he unguard-edly said when presenting his report at a press conference. But the biggest lesson is one that Britain could still, I believe, learn with benefit. It is wrong to commit the state to the support of the arms trade. It is wrong that the Ministry of Defence is a promotional arm of British Aerospace and other arms manufacturers, and that the Department of Trade backs up MoD in a perpetual joint campaign to promote the export of weapons.

The arguments they deploy are that Britain must have an indigenous capacity to manufacture weapons needed by the British armed forces. And since we are too small a market to support serious companies by ourselves, we must export so that unit costs are lower and prices afford-able. And how can we not support the successors to those who built the Dreadnoughts and the Spitfire? What is more (and this is an even worse argument), if we do not sell, the French and Americans will. As Warren Buffett said in a different context, 'The five most dangerous words in business may be, "Everybody else is doing it." '

Those are the arguments. But I believe that the gains are outweighed by the damage. As President Eisenhower warned long ago, the military-industrial complex is too powerful, and the arms trade is inherently corrupting. There are pragmatic considerations, too. Often, the systems produced by our protected companies and supplied to our forces are not very good: we would do better to buy the best from America. And the diversion of limited scientific and engineering talent from other sectors may well have damaged the balance of our industrial base. But it is the deployment of ministers, senior officers of the armed forces (serving or just retired), and civil servants as weapons traders and lobbyists for the weapons manufacturers which does the most damage. At the very least, we should restrict sales to formal NATO allies. We are not alone in damaging our political life in this way: France, the US itself, even high-minded Sweden, do no better, let alone the non-democratic countries who do far worse.

British institutions in my time were very seldom corrupt. The great Victorians had done a remarkable clean-up job; what they did was just as important to Britain's world-wide success as the industrial revolution itself, a lesson which China, Russia, and India have not yet understood. Even the planning system, where huge fortunes depend on discretionary decisions by ministers and civil servants, was astonishingly clean. No country run by John Major and Robin Butler is likely to be in much danger of systemic corruption. There were only two sources of danger against which Britain was not well enough defended in my time – that of weapons exports, and that derived from that other great commercial overlap with politics: the politico-media nexus. The latter is now partially at least on the way to being disinfected, at least for a time, in the aftermath of the fall of Murdoch and of his would-be hereditary empire, though of course he was only the most effective among many players of that game. The former has not yet been tackled.

CHAPTER SEVENTEEN

What Was Happening in the Rest of the World: the Wall, Mandela, Palestine and Hostages

It is strange now for me to look back on those two years, 1988 to 1990. It is the time when the seeds of my personal catastrophe were sown, though I did not know it then. My true memory, not overlaid by hindsight, is of a triumphant upswing, of success in a job I could do well, in a department full of stylish and imaginative people at a most fascinating period of history when Britain played a leading and honourable part in titanic events.

When I arrived at the Foreign Office in 1988, I found that the head of the planning staff, David Gore-Booth, had made an appointment to discuss the Third World War. What could he be going to say? 'It's over, Minister. We won.' He warned of the vacuum that would follow by leaving me a copy of Cavafy's poems, with a bookmark at 'Waiting for the Barbarians':

Some of our men who have just returned from the border say,
There are no barbarians any longer.
Now what's going to happen to us without barbarians?
Those people were a kind of solution.

It was reported to me that a group of backbenchers standing behind the Speaker's chair, watching me in action at the despatch box as minister of state, agreed that, 'He sounds like a real foreign secretary, doesn't he?' After a visit to Moscow, internal briefing documents stolen from the Russians and shown to me read, 'He has been selected for promotion.'

It was a glorious time. I visited Vaclav Havel in the citadel in Prague, and discussed how to make the new state dignified but not militaristic: what uniforms should the Presidential guards wear? Would patent leather boots be all right? Then there was Havel again in London, talking to me about Rushdie. There was an intensely moving visit to Hungary, visiting graves of those who had been executed after the uprising in 1956, including children whom the Communists had kept in jail until they were old enough to be 'legally' executed. I became friends with Miklos Nemeth, prime minister of Hungary, in his modest way one of the key heroes and the immediate cause of the collapse of the Wall, because he opened Hungary's frontier with Austria and let the people go.

I took tea with Lech Walesa in Poland; a tough old Catholic Trades Unionist, and called on the formidable Cardinal Glemp. I visited the martyred Father Popieluszko's grave and recognised the unbreakable strength of the Polish people. At a drunken dinner with dissidents (and doubtless many KGB men) outside Kiev, I proposed a toast to 'An independent Ukraine,' when that was not yet Her Britannic Majesty's policy. Simon Hemans, my FCO minder, was on his feet in an instant to suggest, 'The Minister means the *cultural* independence of the Ukraine.' I staggered to my feet again to repeat my original toast. Simon Hemans later, as HBM's first Ambassador to an independent Ukraine, claimed credit for 'our Minister being the first to endorse it'. I called on the poor Communist official in western Ukraine who was doggedly trying to mediate in quarrels between Uniates, other Catholics, and the Orthodox about whose reopened churches were whose. Stalin's and Kruschev's high-handed rewriting of Ukrainian borders came back to haunt us twenty-five years later.

The Orthodox, however, are always the State church. When Caroline was taken by a handsome young priest to inspect the catacombs beneath Kiev, where the bones of saints lie, she was told that the sacred unguent expressed from the skulls of the holy men was now, in the days of perestroika, flowing freely again. In the days of Stalinism it had stopped.

The range of opinion in the countries freeing themselves, thanks to Gorbachev's restraint, was immense: from Václav Havel, a true European social democrat, to Václav Klaus, in the same city, sharing nothing but a first name with his first free president: Adam Smith on his desk, far more Thatcherite than Thatcher, promising no nonsense about welfare payments. Romantic nationalists and poets around the Kiev table; indestructible Polish patriots: wherever one went as a Minister of Mrs Thatcher's Government, recognised as uncompromising about freedom, but nonetheless influential with Gorbachev as well as the Americans, one was welcomed by the heroes who won back the freedom of central Europe.

Our return hospitality was not always so welcome. One of my duties, when a visiting foreign minister came to London, was to round off his stay with an evening at the theatre. The Communists had always requested to see *Cats*, which we got to know quite well, and made palatable by taking our children, and arranging for the cats to come and purr over them. Left to themselves, the Foreign Office hospitality department were more interested in whether the theatre contained a decent room in which to give a dinner than in the play. This took us regularly to *Les Misérables*. This came to an end when one distinguished ex-dissident asked to be excused from Victor Hugo, on the grounds that at school the

Communists had allowed nothing else, and he had had enough of people struggling into the wind bearing red flags.

In Bulgaria, where the Communists had merely changed labels and continued in power, I made it a test of their born-again commitment to democracy whether or not they would now tell us the truth about the murder by their secret police, helped by the KGB, of Georgi Markov, whose wedding to Annabel Dilke Victoria Rothschild and I had attended many years before. In the gloomy rebadged Politburo offices where my opposite number Gotsev received me, I put this to him. Like the conditioned Pavlov dog he was, he responded instantly in old-speak with, 'Markov was murdered by the British Secret Police to discredit Bulgaria.'

What to do? I stood up and left, finding myself alone in the dirty corridor outside with a black-clad old lady dabbing gloomily at the dust with a broom. There was a pause before our ambassador and my private secretary joined me. What did they say in the short period before they, too, left? The FCO had been strongly against my raising the issue. But I was right and they were wrong; Foreign Ministries always want to deal with regimes which are in place, and are bad at seeing when a regime is so worthless as not to be worth bothering with. All Souls had helped me to see a little further. Leszek Kolakowski, one of the most good-humoured and humane of all the brave dissidents, had found refuge there from persecution in Poland; and when the first free Foreign Minister of that country, Krzysztof Skubiszewski, called on Her Britannic Majesty's Government in London, he wore the tie, decorated with the college symbol of the mallard, which showed him to be a friend of the Codrington, All Souls's great Hawksmoor library. Thanks to Leszek, he had been a visiting Fellow too. He met me in an office I then occupied overlooking Whitehall (my proper office, the old Secretary for India's magnificent office which looked out over St James's park, was being refurbished). It was the day of the Opening of Parliament; there were bands playing, the guards marching, shouted commands, hoof beats and the jangle of harness, the clash of a perfectly executed 'Pree-sent Arms'. The Minister was not listening to me. He wanted to watch. 'The Communists robbed us of our rituals,' he said, as the Queen's carriage went by. Not only foreign ministries failed to predict how swiftly the Soviet empire would fall. In West Berlin when I visited a young man was taken back by the Stasi in a motorboat, dragged by force off our side of the canal border, having swum across to freedom. This was against the rules of the Cold War game: he was free if he had his hands on our side, like the runaway slaves in former times in the gulf states if they got their hands on the flagpole in the British resident's compound. I caused a row, and sent protests. The Mayor of West Berlin, Walter Momper, a cool Social Democrat in a leather jacket, asked me to come and see him, in his man-of-the-people beer garden. 'Don't make a fuss,' he said, 'it is all very well for you to come here and grandstand and go away again. We will have the Wall here for another thirty years, and we have to live with it. We have this lawyer go-between, we'll get the boy out in the end.' He was ost-politik personified, by then parasitic on the status quo. I continued my fuss. The boy was returned. It was the summer of 1989. Doubtless to Mr Momper's surprise, and probably to the annoyance of his go-between lawyer, the Wall was down by November. I am proud of getting it right that it was all up with the USSR and realising that the days of playing games with the successors of Lenin and Stalin were over. In 1989 I was outraged that Mrs Thatcher was trying to collude with Gorbachev to delay or even stop the reunification of Germany, the peaceful achievement of which had been for decades and was still British and NATO policy. I believed that the FCO should stand up to her more vigorously and minuted Douglas Hurd to that effect; a minute now published and of which I am proud. It was nonsense that a reunified Germany would leave NATO; nonsense that it was all a plot by Kohl to force Britain into a German-dominated Europe with social security at a level designed to make Britain's industry uncompetitive with German industry (all of which Mrs Thatcher believed); it was nonsense when the frivolous and irresponsible President Mitterrand came to see her, talking about it being 'Autumn 1913', stirred her to fury, and then scuttled back to Kohl to tell him how impossible 'Margaret' was.

Of course the Russians needed careful and tactful handling, and the Americans at this time were doing that very well; of course Kohl went faster than strict diplomacy would have liked – it was the crowning year of his, and every German Conservative's life. None of this justified Thatcher joining with pacifist Lutherans and Trotskyites in the East and, with Herman Hesse, to try and stop what was the greatest of all triumphs of Western policy. And to try, futilely, to collude with the Russians against her own Government's policy was worse than absurd.

For six crucial months Britain was marginalised; the French laughed at the success of this latest, easy success of their perennial policy of trying to keep Britain well divided from Germany; the Americans were dismayed. The FCO rowed us back on course in the end, but it was a sad waste of Thatcher's stalwart support for freedom which had made her a hero of dissidents from the Baltic states to Romania.

On my minute to Douglas Hurd I found when it was published that the Permanent Secretary had written, 'Discussed with the Foreign Secretary. No further action.' But I tried. I was the first British Minister to return to Aden, whence we had scuttled in 1965, disgracefully betraying our friends, giving rise to a local Arab saying: 'It is better to be an enemy of the British than their friend. If you are their enemy, there is the chance of being bought. If you are their friend, there is the certainty of being sold.'

By now, the Russians had, overnight, cut off all aid to the People's Democratic Republic of South Yemen, the title of the territory under the empire which succeeded ours. The Adenis suddenly discovered they were keen to rejoin the West. Before I went, Lord Goodman came to see me and asked me to seek payment of debts owed to the estate of Anton Besse, once a trader in those parts, the founder of St Antony's College, Oxford, whose lawyer he had been. (Besse was long dead.) Some hope: there was nothing left in Aden except one rusty hulk in the harbour and a few old GPO letterboxes for some reason painted green.

*   *   *

Before his country disappeared altogether, as it did, the Foreign Minister of the People's Democratic Republic of South Yemen told me a joke about Gorbachev. Gorbachev decides to go to a remote village to discover the truth about living conditions. He puts on a wig to cover the famous birth-mark on his forehead. He asks the villagers, 'How are things? Do you have television here?' 'Television, comrade?' they say, 'Of course we do! Full colour!' Pleased, he persists. 'What about washing machines?' 'Washing machines! Comrade! Of course! We all have washing machines!' 'Have you heard of these latest things, microwave ovens?' 'Heard of them, Comrade? Where have you been? We all have them!'

He takes off his wig, displaying the famous birth-mark. 'Come on now! Tell me the truth. You can see who I am. I think you are exaggerating.' 'Comrade, there is no need to take off your disguise. We know you are a CIA agent. No one but a CIA agent would be so stupid as to come to a village where there is no electricity and ask whether we had televisions.'

Then we drove to Sana'a, and saw ancient wind-tower houses, some say the oldest continuously inhabited houses in the world, and the remains of immemorial terraced agriculture, predating the Romans.

I was the Minister in attendance on her Majesty the Queen during a state visit: not a top-rank visit, it must be said, but to Iceland. We stayed on the Royal Yacht *Britannia*, one of that beautiful ship's last appearances. My sister Susan was the lady-in-waiting, instantly able to rescue me when, after some Ministry of Defence mix-up, the combat uniform of a Royal Marine, on his way to Canada for training but sharing our RAF baggage aircraft, was unpacked and laid out on the bunk in my cabin for me by the valet before a black tie dinner. Did the Marine have to wear my dinner jacket while practising arctic warfare, I wonder? The Icelanders, though bellicose members of NATO, had no armed forces, so we were greeted by the band of the Salvation Army. They were very proud of being mentioned in Shakespeare (Henry V, Act 2, Scene 1:

Nym: Pish!
Pistol: Pish for thee, Iceland dog! Thou prick ear'd cur of Iceland!

The country appeared to be run exclusively by very beautiful blonde women. Then there were my South African duties. I met, in our Embassy or the old, thatched Consulate in Capetown, all the dissidents ranging from the Azania black power party to the Broderbund, thanks to Ambassador Robin Renwick's brilliant diplomacy. Like everyone I fell under Mandela's spell. Later, I greeted him and Winnie at Heathrow on his first official visit to Britain. In relation to South Africa Thatcher had moved from her and her husband's out-of-date position far more quickly than had some of her worshippers; she was no supporter of apartheid. Britain had, I had come to believe, been wrong about trade sanctions: America's tougher policy, particularly in relation to banking sanctions, told de Klerk and his predecessor that the game was up. But at the crucial end-game Britain was fully involved, unlike over German reunification, and had nothing to be ashamed of. The prime minister knew that Mandela was the real thing, and knew that de Klerk had realised it too. She saw that de Klerk, like Gorbachev, was serious about real change: it was crucial to support him, but also to chivvy him. She used the credit she had built with him by resisting the clamour for sanctions to the maximum, well advised on tactics by an efficient embassy: at crucial moments she hustled de Klerk on, and played a real part in the process of Mandela's release. Indeed, observing Gorbachev and de Klerk quite closely at that time, I believed that the latter, though a less sympathetic figure, had a far more realistic plan than the former, who hoped that a miraculously democratic Soviet Empire would somehow emerge and then maintain imperial borders won by force of arms by the Tsars, by Lenin, and by Stalin. De Klerk knew the wagons had to be moved or overwhelmed.

Gorbachev did not tell us the truth about, for example, the USSR's immense biological warfare programme, which he was maintaining. An

impressive defector came to tell us about it. When I asked him why he
had come to us rather than the Americans, he replied, 'Because we are
all Europeans; we must sort out our own problems.' And I was sharply
rebuked when I asked Gorbachev when the Kirov Ballet would be
allowed to return to its proper name, shedding that of one of his thugs
Stalin had given it (after having the man murdered). 'Kirov was a hero of
the Soviet Union,' snapped Gorbachev. Nonetheless, by stopping above
all the East German regime from responding to the huge protest move-
ments with force, he saved many lives and helped to steer the world safely
through a very dangerous time.

Then there was the agonising and time-consuming issue of British
hostages in the Lebanon. The chaos of that disintegrating country provided free space for bands of hostage takers who preyed on Westerners.
Some gangs were simply criminal. The most dangerous were Shia clans
within Hizbollah, answering ultimately to Iran, though with sponsors
also in Syria. Some could be influenced, perhaps, or perhaps not, by Iraq.
Good intelligence was extremely sparse; rumours and misinformation
abounded.

Some of the hostages were themselves annoying. 'Please do not go to
Lebanon. If you do, do not travel in this area,' the Foreign Office would
advise. The advice not taken, thousands of man and woman days and
scarce political capital in the region had to be expended trying to free
the brave traveller from his predictable captivity. This did not, of course,
mean that the hostages did not suffer: they did, and some died. Terry
Waite, not a man given to taking advice, suffered terribly for attempting to conduct a sort of one-man foreign policy not entirely separately
from the dangerous people involved in the illegal Iran-Contra deals run
by mavericks in the US government. Others were more touching and
innocent, quiet people, like Jackie Mann and his wife, just caught in the
wrong place at the wrong time.

* * *

I spent huge effort, with my patient officials, on the issue. We tried to explain that campaigns in the British press simply raised the price demanded by the hostage takers, and that the British government, unlike the French, would in any case not pay ransom or do deals, for obvious reasons. I spent hours in negotiation with the Iranian foreign minister, Velayati, believing nothing of what he said. We talked to disgusting Iraqi officials, who pretended to have influence. We listened, sceptically, to self-appointed experts and middlemen who offered their services, usually for money. Meanwhile, brave people made dangerous contacts. In this process I met one of the finest people I have ever had to deal with, Patrick McCarthy, the father of the journalist hostage John McCarthy. He was brave, honest, almost saintly in his understanding of the pressures we were under. He rang me (by then I was health secretary) at our home in Somerset, one August day in 1991, from Lyneham RAF base, thanked me for my part (a small one among the hundreds who had helped), and put his released son on the line. Few people I met in politics ever thanked you and my part had been limited, but his doing so gave me one of the best moments of my life. 'Why did you go into politics?' One answer could be, for moments like that.

Putting aside the final idiocy about German reunification, it was wonderful to be a Minister in the British Foreign Office in those years, equipped with roughly the right perception in relation to the Soviet Union's imminent collapse, one of the better predictions of my little 1978 book. Thatcher had been foursquare beside the Americans in refusing to compromise with the terrible Brezhnev regime; and above all, thanks to the crucial briefings of Oleg Gordievsky, had led the way in recognising that Gorbachev was something different. Gordievsky had run the KGB station in London, while working for us; summoned back to Moscow as the result of information given by the American traitor Aldrich Ames and about to be arrested, the SIS in a stunning operation, conducted by friends of mine, managed to rescue him and smuggle him to freedom. It was an extraordinary achievement; far more thrilling than anything in a James Bond book.

Gordievsky became a friend of mine and of my family; he came to Chewton, and showed touching Russian respect for my mother, the matriarch. Walking in the woods at Stock Hill he had told me, 'If I had been a poet, I would have written poetry against them, if I had been a craftsman, I would have made things to fight them; I was a spy, so I spied against them.' His Russian patriotism was profound: there was none of the sneering vanity of Philby or Blunt. Gordievsky and his kind stood shoulder to shoulder with a million of their fellow citizens in the gulag. They wanted, of course, to be free of the vicious and incompetent regime which had ruled them since 1917, but they did not intend that communism should be replaced by new externally imposed ideologies, imposed by foreign arms or economic power; they wanted self-determination for Russians, and for Russia's conquered peoples.

I was determined that the Soviet authorities who had been systematically bullying Gordievsky's wife in Moscow should let her go, and argued for raising the pressure on them. They, after all, had flaunted and fêted the infinitely less morally defensible Cambridge spies, servants of the same Stalin whom they themselves had now denounced. In the end they did let her go, though the story did not end happily when she was reunited with her husband.

And there was Israel, Palestine, Jordan, Egypt, Saudi Arabia, the Gulf, Sudan, Ethiopia, Tunis, Morocco and Algeria to visit: all the seductive, insoluble problems left behind by the fallen empires of the Middle East, given new edge by the rising tide of Islamism, not uncorrelated with the fastest-growing populations anywhere in the world, and many hundreds of thousands of young men and women with little work, a deep sense of grievance, and ruled by incompetent and corrupt authoritarian governments.

In Israel, I was not welcome after my spat with Mr Shamir over the airwaves. Caroline and I spent a week or so in the uncongenial company of the clever but facile Bibi Netanyahu, then deputy foreign minister, subsequently several times prime minister. I thought him empty of ideas, but brilliant in debate. Even Teddy Kollek, formerly famous as a liberal mayor of Jerusalem, let me down: a relatively friendly talk was followed by a press notice which bore no relation to what he had said face to face; but he was fighting an election. David Gore-Booth and my press officer somehow rescued me from one terrible blunder. Taken to see Masada, the fortress where in AD 73 most of the last few survivors of the first Jewish revolt against the Romans killed themselves rather than surrender to the 10th Legion, I heard myself mutter something about another failed strategy. My officials were as horrified as I was when I realised what I had said; somehow they prevented it being reported. I remember them physically upending cameras. But there was a grain of truth in my reaction. I have come to believe, like Conor Cruise O'Brien in his book *The Siege* or Avi Shlaim, in *The Iron Wall*, that there is no solution to the Arab-Israel conflict. On the one hand, with the Shoah dominating their minds, as how could it not, no Israeli will ever make any compromise which puts Israeli security at any risk (and any compromise can easily be presented as doing just that) but would rather die like those at Masada. On the other, no young Palestinian will ever give up the dream that Israel is just a new crusader state, which will survive perhaps for a century or so, but be driven out in the end. All our well-intentioned peace broking is likely to be futile if, as Shlaim argues, Israeli thinkers have right from the beginning judged that the injustice to the Palestinians perpetrated by the establishment of their state can never in truth be rectified for those who were displaced: and that there is no alternative, therefore, to the iron hand behind the iron wall, and the attempt to last as long as possible – perhaps as long as the kingdom of the Biblical kings. If this depressing view is correct, all we in the outside world can try to do is mitigate the effects of the conflict on ourselves; and there is not much we can do even about that. There is no law of nature, sadly, which says that all problems have a solution.

One conversation sticks in my mind. When I went to Gaza, an old man said to me, standing dignified in front of his hovel: 'I do not understand. Because you Europeans murdered your Jews you have taken my land.'

I dealt with many leaders in the Middle East, most regularly with Hosni Mubarak, who fell in the ridiculously misnamed 'Arab Spring'. It was never likely that revolts against ruthless regimes in Egypt and the Maghreb would release the social democracy which would, without Soviet intervention, have returned to Czechoslovakia in the original 'Prague Spring' of 1968. Always more predictable was that the chaotic regimes which would follow, open to pressure from Islamists and less amenable to American pressure to moderate opposition to Israel, would heighten tensions in the region, provide bases for anti-Western terror, and, most likely in the end return to authoritarian rule as people begged for order again. Mubarak's methods of dealing with his opponents were those of eighteenth-century England, not twenty-first century England, no doubt, but we will have to wait before we can be sure that what follows is better. I met his ruthless Chief of Police, General Zaki Badr. In the course of the meeting, he asked his aides in Arabic, pointing to my private secretary, 'Who is that man?' When told, he gave his view that I should not trust him: 'He looks like a fox.' The private secretary, who spoke perfectly good Arabic himself, and who at the time of writing is the permanent secretary at the FCO, reported all this to me afterwards. The general sent, much against the Embassy's will, two truck-loads of not very secret policemen to escort the Embassy car on our trip to Upper Egypt. The first truck burst a tyre; our armoured Range Rover crashed into it and largely demolished it; the one behind crashed into us. We extricated ourselves unharmed and drove on. In the Valley of the Kings, the police, having caught up, drove the patiently waiting queues of tourists back with rifle butts to let me pass. All I need now, I thought, is to meet a constituent. And there was one! But she was the constituent from heaven, calling as she was shoved back against a wall at machine-gun point, 'I am so glad they are looking after you!' I was sent to see the governor of the Egyptian Central Bank to give him impertinent advice about the management of his currency. He was far too fly. Having discovered that I liked the poetry of Cavafy, we never descended to the tedious matters in my brief at all.

The destruction of the last ancient Christian communities in the Middle East, in Syria, Iraq, southern Turkey, and Egypt itself marks the end of an old pluralistic tradition inherited from the Romans and the Byzantines by the Umayyads and the Abbasids and passed on to the Ottomans and thence to the British and French. It is not yet obvious that what will follow two millennia of intermingled faiths, races and cultures will be better, as the world-wide Muslim civil war between Sunni and Shia cleanses each territory for whichever faction is on top. But I am glad to have seen the old Middle East, with all its gross imperfections, just in time.

In the Gulf, I arrived at the end of the old, too. I would not recognise modern Abu Dhabi or Dubai; though there were modern buildings, in 1988 the little states were still rooted in a traditional past. The Emir, Sheikh Zayed bin Sultan al Nahyan, President of the United Arab Emirates, whom the British had placed in power long before, met me first at a desert palace, under awnings on the roof, a falconer with a hawk on his arm standing in the background. After elaborate greetings, discussion of mutual friends such as Sir Alec Douglas Home, and contemplation of the unsatisfactory nature of the Americans ('a mongrel people'), I had to deploy my list of requests – principally I remember to do with a young expat couple who had been thrown into some frightful dungeon for having sex in a public place. One of the parents of the foolish pair, for some unfathomable reason, had complained to the police about the behaviour of the boy, who had done her daughter wrong, she said. The other parent took the opposite view. The result was an offer to have the girl stoned or the boy castrated, or some such, and the dungeon had ensued for both in the meantime while the parents made their choice. I begged for mercy. The Emir turned to his Wazir, enraged. 'You have put my friend's friend in prison! You will suffer for this!' I congratulated myself on a mission accomplished as we drove back to the embassy. 'I shouldn't count on it, Minister,' said the ambassador, 'He has said the same thing to your three predecessors.'

One day Sir Patrick Wright, the head of the Diplomatic Service, came into my office. 'I have a somewhat embarrassing personal matter to discuss, minister of state.' My heart sank. What on earth had the spies discovered about me? 'I am sorry to have to tell you that His Holiness the Pope has awarded you the order of St Gregory the Great, First Class. Luckily, we classify his Holiness as a temporal power, so under Queen Elizabeth's rules we were able to refuse this embarrassment for you.' Queen Elizabeth I had said, 'My dogs will wear no collars but mine own,' after she learned that one of her diplomats had accepted a foreign decoration. I was furious. I am, therefore, at least a Papal Knight, refused.

A kindly watching Olympian (there are such) gave me another treat. Canvassing one day, in I think the euro elections of 1989, in a respectable suburb of London, the Tory lady in charge with her clipboard sent me down a short residential street. 'There's no one worth calling on down there,' she said, 'Except perhaps the funny old German in the house on the left.' I rang the doorbell. There was a nurse, in starched white, and behind her, Karl Popper. Even more surprising was my brief period as Harold Pinter's political adviser. Antonia Fraser had always been someone I admired at a distance; her mother Elizabeth had been a friend of my mother's. After Victoria Rothschild married Pinter's friend and sparring partner, Simon Gray, Caroline and I developed a friendship with Harold and Antonia. It was sometimes explosive: I learnt better than to place next to Harold at dinner a very beautiful woman who had failed to note that he had had a new play opening the day before to great acclaim. 'What have I been doing? Oh, writing plays. You wouldn't know. Plays. In places called theatres . . .' and so on; tears; me sending flowers next day. I got into trouble myself for asking him to get me tickets for *The Blue Room*, a play in which Nicole Kidman took all her clothes off, thereby making tickets impossible to obtain. I had failed to go to Harold's last play; I did not get to see Nicole Kidman naked. But the warmth and generosity of his friendship matched the heat of the explosions. We used to play bridge with them: Antonia an accomplished player; Harold, as you might expect, fiercely intelligent but not much bound by conventions.

One day he asked me alone to lunch at the Ritz. He paid. He wanted tutorials on political philosophy. It was a failure. I would introduce the subject of, say, John Stuart Mill. 'When are we getting on to the electrodes? The ones they attach to their genitals to torture them?' We only had two tutorials, as I remember.

His reading at Simon Gray's funeral, Pinter himself dying, was beyond words touching. Simon loved teasing him – most famously in relation to the poem about Hutton. Harold used to send his friends, including me, poems for comment. A comment was required. One poem went:

I saw Len Hutton in his prime.
Another time, another time.

When Simon had not commented, an inquiring call came from Harold. 'I haven't finished it yet,' said Simon.

Harold championed Simon's work, however, which in the latter part of his life never received the public respect it deserved: as soon as he died, *Butley* and the rest began to be performed again, which would have confirmed Gray's blackly humorous view of the world. He is in fact one of Britain's greatest twentieth-century playwrights and diarists. He introduced me to Stefan Zweig's despairing but brilliant novel, *Beware Pity*, the argument of which is that even the kindliest of acts – the young officer seeking to apologise for his gaucherie in asking the crippled girl to dance – may end in catastrophe. So how are we to act? How can we trace the consequences of what we do?

As I look back over the best period of my political life, with one part of my memory I remember Iraq as a name which recalls pride. I remember myself given the huge privilege of presiding over the Whitehall machine at its best in the run-up to the expulsion of Saddam from Kuwait, often chairing the transition to war committee of all the great men and women of the state. It was a just war, the war I helped to prepare, with clear United Nations' legal sanction, and every conceivable ally from Syria to Japan on-side; and a war rightly ended when its purpose was accomplished. I had testing times throughout that run-up, including a huge press conference on the matter of the British hostages held in Iraq where, having virtually run from the other end of the FCO building to the room where the press had assembled, I suddenly found I physically could not speak: aphasia, I believe it is called. Once again I thought this pathetic performance had put paid to my career, and indeed this was suggested as a good outcome by some newspapers. Mrs Thatcher did not appear to notice such things.

I remember greeting the hostages returned from Iraq, those whom Saddam Hussein had taken in Iraq and Kuwait and threatened to use as human shields. There were many who claimed the credit, dubiously, for their release, including Heath (who had not much to do with it) and the Reverend Jesse Jackson (who had less). The latter turned up 'uninvited' at Gatwick Airport with his public relations team to grandstand in front of the cameras when they returned. I watched in astonishment his camera-hogging technique as I tried to help organise a smooth re-entry into their lives for these harassed and exhausted people.

Like many others in Whitehall I was working round the clock, sleeping in the office (breakfast provided from the Metropolitan Police canteen), having gone to and fro from a mostly missed holiday in James Guinness's beautiful villa at Gassin near St Tropez. One Sunday I was rescued for lunch by Paul and Ingrid Channon at their perfect house, Kelvedon, in Essex. Van den Broek, the Dutch Foreign Minister, rang me on a telephone which somehow (pre-mobiles) worked on a lilo in the swimming pool.

But the counterpoint overlaid on this music in retrospect all relates now to what was then a second or third order matter – stopping MOD and DTI, both at different times represented by Alan Clark, from loosening to any significant degree exports to Iraq and Iran – an issue over which if you had asked me about it at the time, I would have said I had done rather well.

It is as if the fates had said of me: give him a good run for a year or two. Let him do well, let him hear people say he will one day get the one job other than the premiership which would have fulfilled all those childhood dreams – and then let us use those self-same years to pull his wings off. What fun!

Probably, I did not do as well as I believed when I thought I was doing well; but I know I did not do so badly as the Scott lynch mob claimed, either. Oh, for the pen of a novelist: it could be a neat double story, perhaps in reality a short story – by Somerset Maugham, perhaps, or Patrick O'Brian.

Would I like revenge? For some miraculous paper to be found saying it was all a mistake? For the invitation to *Desert Island Discs* to be renewed? The Foreign Secretaryship restored by some miracle of coalition, with its CH or its KG? Of course I would. In reality, I had only one revenge. In 1994, the still-ubiquitous Robin Butler came to me and said that the Lord Chancellor, the equally omnipresent James Mackay, wanted to make Scott Vice-Chancellor, head of the civil courts. Would I object? I could, if I wanted. For a moment I had power over Sir Richard. But what was the point? It gave me some satisfaction *not* to object; it made me feel magnanimous.

Much later, when life had gone on and scar tissue grew over the wound, I found myself becoming a guru on the matter of the shattering of reputations, and of spectacular falls from grace. Friends who were well-regarded chairmen found their banks suddenly bankrupted after 2008, and themselves converted overnight from pillars of society to pariahs. Like others who fell one way or another while media mobs cheered, quite a number came to me for advice. I had none, except that things would never be quite the same. It was like losing a limb, I would say: you got used to it, but it never grows back. This was not much help, I fear. Time does pass. Other scandals come and go. People forget. You do not, but the scar tissue does its job.

CHAPTER EIGHTEEN

Over a Precipice

When one is a child, at least a loved and happy child as I was, there is no gap between reality and the perception of reality. The experience may be – in the eyes of adults or one's later self – imagined, as my epiphany of the ancient Greek gods was imaginary. Or it may be real, as my child-hood relationship with the colour red was real. Things are what they are. But then the shades of the prison house begin to close in. If you are like me, self-consciousness, anxiety, fear of ridicule, division and artificiality replace authenticity. I take it that those who have mastered the craft of how to live remain undivided.

> Between the idea and the reality
> Between the motion
> And the Act
> Falls the Shadow.

The people I envy seem to avoid Eliot's Shadow. They remain in the state of Philip Pullman's Will, when he was able to cut through to another world with the subtle knife because his mind was undivided.

I was never a great politician, or man of action, because of the very
intermittent nature of my self-authenticity. I have had those moments
when I feel wholly united with the world and its history; when the reality
of things glows and reverberates, and everything seems possible.

Points have we all of us within our souls
Where we all stand single,

says Wordsworth. On the high Acro Corinth as a teenager, with a few
marble blocks, the dusty ground, the sky and heat: this is real, as it
was and always will be, the past becoming part of me for the future.
At our wedding when an old familiar hymn began, sung with a will by
a big congregation, it is real, for us. They mean it, it is not an act. At
Kelvedon once, sitting on the sunny grass, Antonia Douro and Paul
Channon rode into the garden: those are real horses, horses now and
from Bucephalus's day the same. Up on Eaker Hill on Mendip, above
the Roman Road: this is my place, and the Roman soldier seventeen
hundred years ago here was as real as the hare zigzagging away in front
of me. The surging love that hits you as you watch your child or wife
smile. These are real and undivided. Rather few of those moments ever
came to me in my chosen life of the pursuit of prizes and the capture of
that inner castle keep where finally I would have arrived. There were
too many shadows.

Even when I thought I came close, it was self-conscious. I remember
spending an afternoon and night at the SIS training base, talking with new
entrants and dining with senior officers; then flying back in the morning
in a special forces helicopter to the old Chelsea Barracks so that I could
attend a meeting at Buckingham Palace with Sir Michael Peat about the
Queen's finances; then on to EDX, the central public spending cabinet
committee, where power really resided in John Major's government.* I

---

* EDX could be an exciting committee. It met in Cabinet Committee Room A, which contains a throne on which George III presided over a cabinet, the last monarch to do so. At one

remember thinking, 'Have I not made it?' The natural craftspeople of politics do not think this way; they just are what they are.

Maybe there is little difference between those natural craftspeople of public action and other craftspeople who produce pictures, music, poetry or novels, who run perfect races or perfectly propel a racing shell. There is nothing easy about it: it involves infinite hard work; but infinite hard work that is not self-referential and artificial; it goes with the grain. I had this for a time when I was on the upswing. When I did as well as I could that was good enough for other people. Later, the harder I tried, the less safe my pair of hands looked to others – and, worse, to me. So perhaps Caravaggio, Velázquez and Cézanne, Austen, Tolstoy and Conrad, Bach and Mozart, Eliot and Shakespeare are cut from the same cloth as Churchill, de Gaulle and Thatcher. And perhaps all of them have more in common with the true craftsman making furniture at his bench, or ploughing straight on his tractor, or sitting in the stroke seat of an Olympic rowing eight than we sometimes recognise. These are the people who do not have thoughts that interpose themselves before the action and prevent authenticity.

Sir Alec Douglas-Home, that shrewd and underestimated conqueror of the clever fellows of his day, from Cyril Connolly to Quintin Hogg, sent me a card after I had won some prize or other. 'Your progress is like Halle's Comet,' he wrote, not diminishing the slight warning inherent in likening me to an object that disappears for seventy-five years at a time by spelling the astronomer like the orchestra. He turned out to be right.

Finally, along came the precipice of the 1997 general election. Of course,

---

meeting in my time, the chairman, always the chancellor of the Exchequer, became so irritated by the lack of respect shown him by Kenneth Clarke and Michael Heseltine that he stormed out, slamming the huge oak door, the lintel of which shook. We looked at one another with a wild surmise. I proceeded to my constituency on a train, having rung the prime minister's political adviser, Sarah Hogg, to suggest that this was not the best way of conducting business. She was in Birmingham for a Euro summit with her boss. At Swindon, I was taken off the train by the police and told to return to London. EDX had resumed its discussions.

almost all of us knew we would lose. Only Michael Heseltine – indomitable campaigner that he was – seemed optimistic, on the grounds that real personal disposable income in Britain had been rising and incumbents always won under those circumstances.

I hated it all as Labour ensured that I was pursued by Scott wherever I went. Conservative Central Office, in their wisdom, sent me to campaign alongside Tony Marlow – an extreme right-winger and not exactly a soul brother. But at least my visit to his constituency produced a moment of comic relief. Canvassing some houses inhabited by extremely robust individuals he claimed as supporters – some of them (not only the men) wearing string vests and sporting tattoos – I once again saw the delight of democracy in action. 'You're a useless bastard,' they shouted at Marlow. 'You said you was going to hang all the immigrants and you haven't hanged a single one. We're voting Liberal, we are.'

Though I was flown from Dudwell Field Farm, our Somerset home, around the country in a helicopter, I was not exactly central to the campaign. Apart from visiting Marlow in Northampton, I posed with amiable elephants at Whipsnade Zoo and looked in vain for Tory votes in central Newcastle. I left the traditional note for my successor as chief secretary to the Treasury, Alistair Darling, when I cleared my last ministerial desk for what I knew would be the last time; I advised him to look after science and the intelligence services. They are both long-term assets for the nation, and cannot be stopped and started.

I did not think I would actually manage to lose Bristol West until the final week, when I met a constituent in the street whom I knew had supported me in the past and asked if I could count on his vote again.

'No, I am voting Labour this time.'

'May I ask why? The economy? Sleaze? What?'

'No, nothing like that. You and I, Mr Waldegrave, have often talked about how Britain would be better off if we had two moderate centrist parties competing to manage a mixed economy, rather than violent swings to left or right. Well, this Blair, from what he says, is really a moderate sort of Tory, like his dad, and his views seem to be not much different to yours. So, as a Conservative, I would be mad not to vote for him, wouldn't I?'

I had no answer to that.

In fact, the country had long since made up its mind. When, on 16 September 1992, Britain was ejected from the ERM into which Howe and Lawson had led us, and handled the ejection badly, the Conservatives lost their reputation for skill in economic management and did not regain it, in spite of the excellent performance of the economy in John Major's subsequent years. The Conservative share in the polls plummeted to the 30 per cent mark and remained there for the next five years.* Internecine warfare over the Maastricht Treaty, and doubtless Scott and a variety of transient scandals must have helped, but Labour's success was little to do with Alastair Campbell's and Peter Mandelson's media skills, and the supposed brilliance of their campaigning. We Conservatives created their, and Blair's, reputations for electoral genius; and we bequeathed them an economy that let them ride the boom years in populist style. Blair simply had to look like a renewed and more attractive version of us. He was able to do it – if his book is to be believed (and on this subject it should be) – because that was precisely what he was.

Sadly for the country, however, his and Gordon Brown's economic competence was no greater than ours had been at the time of Black Wednesday and the ERM debacle. By letting public and private debt increase, keeping interest rates too low, focusing only on inflation, and allowing public expenditure to increase faster than the growth of the economy year after year, they left us in far worse shape than we should have been when the crisis arrived in 2008. Luckily, though, Blair was too frightened of his chancellor to insist on what would have been the

---

* Gallup, 7 September 1992: Conservative 43; Labour 41; Liberal Democrats 12. Gallup, 19 October 1992: Conservative 29; Labour 51; Liberal Democrats 14. In January 1993 one rogue poll gave us a two-point lead, but a few days later Labour was back to being 12 per cent ahead, and they maintained a double-digit lead from then on.

biggest policy mistake of all: joining the euro. So let us thank Gordon Brown's obduracy for maintaining what John Major had won for us in that respect, at least.

Losing a formerly safe seat is humiliating. I felt, in a small way, what Heath must have experienced on a far larger scale. My eldest daughter and Caroline came along to the count, where no one except myself and my agent thought I was going to lose. Of course, people delighted in my humiliation; not as much as they delighted in Michael Portillo's, but not far short.

It cannot be pleasant to be the family of a politician in the public eye. Assassination attempts, scandal and invasion of privacy must make a strange background for childhood. One day, high on Mendip, badgers dug up the body of a poor murdered girl, killed by her Japanese lover. We were at home on holiday at the time. Caroline turned round in the kitchen to find a reporter from the *Daily Express* eating the carrots she had just peeled and announcing that he just wanted a pic of the minister with the body.

In 1992, when I was health secretary, Alastair Campbell, then a sort of journalist on the *Daily Mirror*, put a photograph of me taking my son to school on the front page. This was justified on the grounds that one of Jamie's socks, in *Just William* style, had fallen down: another Waldegrave shambles said the headline. But what a self-righteous uproar there was from Campbell when newspapers photographed Blair's children! My daughter Liza, now (in 2014) a paediatrician, had to withstand the backwash of the onslaught on her father, the secretary of state for health – the man whom the health lobbies had accused of destroying her beloved NHS. And so forth.

During one of those explosions of sentiment to which the British are prone – this time over the export of calves to France and Holland, where a short, miserable life in veal crates awaited them – the *Independent on Sunday* sent a reporter to interview my farm manager at Chewton.

'Where did your calves go?'

'To market,' said the manager, puzzled.

'Minister of Agriculture Sells His Calves to Dutch Veal Crates,' blared the newspaper in its next edition, even though neither they nor we knew whether they went for export or to a farm just down the road. Bombs were sent in the post; police protection started all over again. White veal consumption in Britain did not decline, in spite of the hysteria. And it was useless to point out to the *Independent on Sunday*, or anybody else, that there was absolutely nothing I could do to stop the unpleasant trade since the export of calves was governed by European law. The *Daily Telegraph* went one further and put Caroline on the front page, because Leiths had said in one of their cookery books that Dutch veal was generally considered the best. In the days that followed the charming people who claim to protect animals phoned her and explained the tortures they intended to inflict on her and our children.

Subsequently, once the brief frenzy was over and the newspapers were looking for other ways to boost their circulations, and when the British people had forgotten all about veal crates, the editor of the *Independent on Sunday* at the time, Ian Jack, apologised to me. The editor of the *Daily Telegraph*, Sir Max Hastings, apologised to Caroline. That is the way the world goes.

In the end, it just gets wearying: the relentless hypocrisy of the high moral tone maintained by journalists utilising the methods the Leveson Inquiry has now made familiar, for proprietors who normally base themselves in tax havens, if they pay any tax at all, and rarely follow the moral advice doled out by the leader writers they employ. For some reason, their own behaviour is very seldom reported.

When you are on the upswing, it is all a game. You have the energy and the anger and the good humour to put up with it. When you start to swing downwards, it is a pleasure and a relief to leave it behind. Enoch Powell said that a politician complaining about the media is like a sailor complaining about the sea. But perhaps it is allowable even for sailors to get seasick from time to time. To put it another way, do we really want politicians so tough that they never feel the pain? If they are that tough, will they ever feel anything at all?

In a democratic society, as Rab Butler once said, the noise represented by the continual cacophony of free political argument – among politicians themselves and between politicians and the media – is partly the noise of freedom. But before entering the maelstrom one needs to understand that, in addition to the noisy, necessary turmoil of political argument, something else is going on. There is a ritual purpose to the hatred heaped on politicians and others in the public eye. In modern democracies politicians play the role of the ancient scapegoat, tethered in the desert to die, carrying the sins of the people. The psyche of the internet troll, bullying some poor soul just for the fun of the sadism involved, is not as divorced from the psyche of the mob harrying the public enemy of the week as we might like to think. Film stars, sportspeople, politicians and anyone whose trade demands publicity can find themselves chosen to be the kings and queens who must die, like the priest at Nemi in James George Frazer's *Golden Bough*.

Even then, though, there can be moments of pleasure. The *Mirror* camped outside our family home for weeks after Scott. Following the IRA's assassination attempt, Charlie, our postman, had been told to report any suspicious people to the police. Knowing exactly what he was doing, he did just that, and the heroic representatives of Fleet Street were escorted away for questioning. That cheered us up.

CHAPTER NINETEEN

Epilogue

This book is an attempt to explain how things felt, to describe the weather of a life, not to be a manual of history or political philosophy. But what would I answer finally to Isaiah Berlin's question, put long ago in the garden at Corpus Christi: 'What did you learn? What did you learn?' What would I mutter, inadequately now as then, in reply to his question?

First, I have learned that Isaiah's own doctrine – that there is no such thing as a process of history – is correct. Nothing is inevitable; people can and do make a difference. When Victor Rothschild delivered his speech in the autumn of 1973, predicting that Britain would be half as rich as France or Germany, per capita, by the year 2000, it was not an implausible forecast. Yet, at the turn of the millennium, we were actually a little richer than France and not far behind Germany. So what had happened over the intervening twenty-seven years? Margaret Thatcher had happened. Rothschild's forecast would not have been confounded if James Callaghan had been returned as prime minister in 1979; nor if Willie Whitelaw, or Keith Joseph, or anyone else had led the Tory Party to that election victory. She made the difference. The force of will she deployed to achieve that turnaround damaged much that need not have been damaged; but without it, Britain's restoration would not have happened, at least not in that relatively short timescale. I was part of those governments, and I am proud of that. All that pain was not in vain.

Second, I have learned that the occasions when such a decisive swerve can be imparted to history by a leader are quite rare. Churchill in the May days of 1940 did shift the direction of history. So did Thatcher in the key years between 1981 and about 1984. But most politics is not like that: it is normally an unending struggle to make things a little better, or to stop them becoming a little worse. There are almost never grand solutions to grand problems; it is usually better to have honest and decent people in power, rather than heroes. And it is important that they use rhetoric that reflects the routine nature of most of what they do. Overpromising, raising the stakes artificially high, pretending to be able to control the myriad things that are far beyond the control of government, using the language of war when there is no war; failing to moderate the bitterness of conflicts that are often trivial: these are all things that threaten civilised government more than most of the threats that they are allegedly deployed to repel. Democracy – not just head-counting in order to avoid rational discourse, but real, complex democracy – faces as much danger from the ridiculous mutual savagery of those who compete for its prizes as it does from external hazards. Intelligent people helped to wreck the financial system of half the world by forgetting the bounds of normal moral behaviour towards each other and the outside world. Politicians have the capacity to do the same.

Therefore Isaiah's other doctrine is right, too: there is no special morality for politics, no realpolitik. Politics is just ordinary life, writ slightly larger. So ordinary morality must apply, and ordinary decencies of behaviour should be respected.

Finally, there is the simplest lesson of all: if you wake up one day and think, 'There is no significant life beyond politics,' then that is the time to quit. You are an addict, in the grip of an addiction that threatens both yourself and others. The electorate rescued me from this danger; and, in the end, I was grudgingly grateful.

Walking along the street in 1998, a young man stopped me. 'You were one of those Tory cabinet ministers, weren't you?' he asked, with a tone of wonderment. I admitted that I had been. 'How strange! I thought you had all just sort of disappeared. Not that I had anything against you personally. But that — [he named a more prominent colleague] really gave me the creeps!' As soon as you are out of it, you stop being a scapegoat and become a person again.

One of the more amiable aspects of re-entry into the world after being for twenty-six years in the bubble where I felt those peculiar feelings I tried to describe at the beginning of this book was that, on the whole, one received a friendly welcome back from the inhabitants of Planet Earth, in particular from immigrant citizens, who always seemed to know who one had been more accurately than longer-established Britons. Do new citizens pay closer attention to politics than others? It would make sense.

For the first few years, taxi drivers would vaguely recognise me. 'You were on the telly, weren't you? I had that Portillo in the back of my cab the other day . . .' Slowly, though, I returned to blessed full anonymity.

No more ministerial cars to make me feel special; now it was the Central Line.

I became chairman of the Science Museum and its sister museums in Bradford and York – the Media Museum and the Railway Museum – thanks to Tessa Blackstone, minister for the arts in the Labour government. A barely perceptible green shoot of self-confidence began to return: to my astonishment, I began to understand that not everyone was as obsessed with Scott as I was. The Railway Museum let me drive a magnificent steam engine, *Green Arrow*. For a moment, I was back at Bath Spa station, aged seven, looking up at 5057 *The Earl Waldegrave*'s heroic engine driver, and begging for permission, which was sometimes granted, to stand on the footplate.

I became chairman of the Rhodes Trust in its centenary year. We decided to mark the occasion by putting £10 million back into South Africa, the new South Africa, to help develop the leadership it so badly needed. We approached Mandela's people – in the shape of Jakes Gerwel, his wise adviser and former cabinet secretary – to see if we could, in some way, win the great man's endorsement. We won much more than that: Mandela would associate his name with ours. The new organisation would be known as the Mandela Rhodes Foundation. He knew exactly whom he was offending – on the right and the left – by doing this, and he rejoiced in it. There is a photograph of him standing beneath a glowering portrait of Rhodes in the MRF headquarters in Cape Town (formerly Rhodes's own HQ, donated by Nicholas Oppenheimer). He is wagging a finger at the picture, and was saying, 'Cecil, you and I are going to work together!' When I met him at Groote Schurr, Rhodes's old home in Cape Town, we talked about money, good and bad. I told him that the Emperor Vespasian was mocked for taxing urinals to help raise money for rebuilding Rome after the civil war of AD 69. He sent for a bag of the resulting coins and declared, *'Pecunia non olet'* – the money doesn't smell. Mandela liked that story. Our new foundation thrived under the leadership of Shaun Johnson, formerly a brave campaigning journalist at the end of the apartheid years.

Mandela managed, in a way unique in my experience, to combine humour, toughness and generosity. He seldom spoke about the end of apartheid without paying tribute to F. W. de Klerk, the man who had surrendered power to him. He could make you laugh. You were never quite sure he was joking when he said he would rather have been light-heavyweight boxing champion of the world than president of his country. When my daughters were introduced to him in London, his opening line was, 'What is it like, having a famous father?' The camera shutter clicked to record them doubled up with merriment at the moment they met the most famous man in the world. Mandela was morally comparable to Gandhi in his commitment to reconciliation, but he was also a great flirt. I had appointed Rosalind Hedley Miller, living proof that not all investment bankers are wicked, to the Rhodes Trust. She was at the top of her profession, personally formidable and the embodiment of moral rectitude. 'When did they let you out of school?' asked Mandela. He was not the greatest flirt with a Rhodes connection, however. When Caroline and I lunched with loyal Rhodes Scholar William Jefferson Clinton at Rhodes House, my wife almost needed a cold shower afterwards. 'But he's talking to that woman just like he talked to me!' she cried, later the same day, pointing in disbelief at the former President's betrayal. Clinton, Blair, Mandela and I spoke to an immense gathering in Westminster Hall to celebrate the centenary of Rhodes and the launch of the MRF. Later, at Buckingham Palace, we witnessed the easy affection between two natural-born monarchs: Elizabeth of Windsor and Mandela, by then, of the world.

I was offered, and with considerable trepidation accepted, work in the City, a place where I had never set foot after those two contrasting job interviews long ago. People were very kind to me: old hands twenty years my junior showed me the ropes. I did exams (for the first time since the All Souls' prize fellowship exam in 1971) surrounded by twenty-four-year-olds. These were the boom years. I was, by political standards, very well paid indeed. This confirmed my belief in my father's paradox – that there is roughly an inverse relationship between what people earn and the usefulness of what they do. Would anyone notice if there was one less wildly overpaid bond trader? Probably not. Would we notice if the person who cleans the lavatories at the Leigh Delamere service station on the M4 didn't show up for work? Yes, we would.

It is easy now to vilify everyone who worked in the City during those years. But the boom and the bust were not created solely by Wall Street and the City of London; underneath it all was a very long period of sloppy economic management and lax monetary control. Bubbles have to be inflated by something. Some of the people I worked with were as good as any I had met in the civil service, but there was also a very unpleasant new culture sapping the older values that an increasingly beleaguered honourable minority attempted to maintain. The new ethos was totally fee driven, ruthlessly selfish, disloyal to employers. It was a sort of travesty of ancient heroic culture: there was no guilt, but no shame either. If you won a new client, you had to get it sold, or drive its board to undertake transactions that paid your bonus. If you succeeded, you then turned on your colleagues to try and keep their fingers out of your bonus pot. Huge sums were spent on consultants and advertisers to convince the public and potential employees of the care we all felt for our clients and the loyalty we all showed to our employers . . . until we could find a way of selling the one and abandoning the other for the promise of a bigger bonus. It was a little like the British Raj in Warren Hastings' day: by the standards of the time, it was not all wicked, but some of it certainly was. And by doing things they would never have countenanced at home, as it were, some people made themselves very rich indeed.

In 1998, just after I started in the City, I encountered Margaret Thatcher at the memorial service for Ronnie Millar, the playwright who had provided the jokes for Thatcher herself and for Edward Heath. He had come up with the famous 'the lady's not for turning' and had fought hard to stop her changing a dig at James Callaghan, who had unwisely likened himself to Moses, leading the people to the edge of the Promised Land but no further. Millar had written, 'All I can say to Moses is: keep taking the tablets!'

'Couldn't we say "pills"?' suggested Thatcher.

Now, in the sunshine outside St Bride's, she asked me what I was doing. When I replied that I was working in a bank she said, 'Ah, that's a proper job. Which bank?' My courage failed me: I took refuge in the old English name of Kleinwort, missing out Dresdner, the German bank that had just bought it. She looked at me suspiciously. Then, apropos of nothing at all, she announced, 'The trouble with the Germans, William, is that they never had Magna Carta.' It was typical of her: a remark that was rather mad but nonetheless had something in it. And it showed it was still no use trying to slip anything past her.

Nor was it possible to escape her, anywhere in the world. In Texas with my friend Senator Phil Gramm, a powerful and subtle politician of the right, I noticed that Mrs Thatcher had a very prominent place in the picture gallery he had created of his career.* During dinner with Phil's neighbours we learned that some southerners still harboured suspicions about Ronald Reagan: he was, after all, a Californian; and his daughter had appeared naked in *Playboy* and written a novel about lesbians! Of Mrs Thatcher nothing bad was known. When I noticed Caroline struggling to control her temper after yet another right-wing sally by one of the neighbours, I was able to defuse the situation with: 'I was Mrs Thatcher's last appointment to the Cabinet, you know.' A reverential hush descended, and Caroline's explosion was averted.

The City paid for our holidays. We walked with the great tracker John Stephens in Zimbabwe, hearing the rumble all around us as, just out of sight in the long grass, a huge herd of buffalo rose to its feet. We rode horses of astounding good manners in Idaho above the Salmon River, and talked over camp fires to charming young wranglers who earnestly explained that the federal government was an enemy against whom it might be legitimate to take up arms. We dived along the edge of the immeasurable depths of the Blue Hole in Belize, and, with hammerhead sharks above us and mad, amphibious iguanas below, in the Galapagos. We trekked in Tibet, and bore witness to the steady destruction of an ancient culture as China attempted to emulate Cromwell's policy in Ireland – but this time with more than a billion people from whom to draw the settlers. Over the border in Nepal, we flew out just before the weather closed in aboard a battered, windowless Russian helicopter as Maoist rebels blocked the roads and rolled boulders down on to the town. Nepalese soldiers armed with ancient .303 Lee-Enfields stood guard.

---

* However, the room was dominated by a quotation from one of Phil's own speeches: 'It may be that the lion will lie down with the lamb. But I say let's be the lion anyway'.

We saw incomparable antiquities in Syria, revelled in the friendliness of the people, and saw that Assad's ruthless regime had offered a haven to ancient Christian sects, driven out of Turkey, Iraq, Iran and Egypt. We heard wailing Shia mingle with Sunni and Christians in worship around the burial place of John the Baptist's head in the great Umayyad mosque of Damascus. Perhaps we witnessed the last, dying days of the old Levant. Now, however, travelling was at last an end in itself: no more prince's education. Perhaps a little late in life, I was finally doing things simply because they were worth doing.

In 2009, back at Eton, full circle, as provost, two courteous boys came to talk to me about possible dates and speakers for the Political Society. 'We have discovered, sir,' they said, in the manner of archaeologists showing off a recently unearthed artefact, 'that you were in politics once yourself.'

There are no sunlit uplands, especially on the Mendips. But perhaps time, and forgetfulness, can bring peace. When I was young, I was of the party of Prometheus – in love with heroic endeavour, even if it meant agonising failure to reach the stars. But perhaps Job's story is a better one in the end: reconcile yourself to what you have and remember how little you know; and shout for joy whenever you can.

> Where wast thou when I laid the foundations of the earth?
> When the morning stars sang together and all the sons of God
>   shouted for joy?

It is true that the Lord blessed my latter end more than my beginning, as he did Job's, because although my beginning was undoubtedly blessed, I have even more now – not, admittedly, fourteen thousand sheep and six thousand camels, having had merely half those numbers originally; but it is true, as it was true of Job, that in all the land there are no women found so fair as my daughters (and my wife and son too, for that matter). But compared to the prophet's, my intervening trials have been trivial.

Throughout, I have had a family I love and who love me, from Chewton House at the beginning to Dudwell Field Farm at the end. And when that family gathers together on Christmas mornings, just as we did sixty years ago, it is just as good now, if not better, than it was then.

Index

Page numbers followed by (fn) refer
to footnotes

Abu Sharif, Bassam 195
Aden 253
Aitken, Jonathan 72, 175fn
al Nahyan, Zayed bin Sultan 261–2
Ali, Tariq 70, 118
Allen, Tim 5
Allington, Cyril 43
Allington, Elizabeth 'Libby' later
    Lady Home 43
Ames, Aldrich 257
Angleton, James 127
Anglo-American relations 76, 111,
    124
Annan, Lord 98
anti-Semitism 38, 82, 95
Apostles 103
Arab Spring 260
Arab-Israeli conflict 195–7, 259–60
Arafat, Yasser 194–6

'Arms to Iraq' affair 230–4, 236–46,
    265
Armstrong of Ilminster, Lord 103,
    115, 119, 125, 170, 192
Armstrong of Sanderstead, Lord
    119, 126–7, 128
Asquith, Hon Sir Dominic 170
assassinations, political 210–11
Attlee, Earl 33, 125fn, 202
Austin, J.L. 72, 74
Ayer, Sir Freddie 72

Badr, Zaki 260
Baker of Dorking, Lord 141, 142,
    175fn, 223, 226
Bannister, Sir Roger 27
Baring, Sir Evelyn (Lord Howick)
    42
Baxendale, Presiley 241, 242
Bazoft, Fazad 236
Beauvoir, Simone de 60fn
Beer, Samuel H. 81, 143

Bell, Daniel 91

Benn, Tony 151, 162, 168, 172

Bennett, Jane 84, 86, 87

Berlin, Sir Isaiah 42, 52, 73–4, 75,
    76, 79, 98, 101, 103, 194, 197,
    275

Bernstein, Lord 97

Bessborough, Lord 93

Besse, Sir Anton 253

Bevan, Aneurin 33

Biggs, Murray 58

Bilderberg Conferences 243

Birley, Sir Robert 34, 51, 53

Bishop, Miss 48

Blacker, Colonel Stewart 21

Blackstone, Lady 107, 277

Blair, Tony 122, 172, 176, 187–8,
    206, 270–2

Bligh, Captain 230

Bloody Sunday 85

Blue Chips, The (dining group) 164,
    214

Blundell, Michael 89

Blunt, Anthony 103

Bogdanor, Vernon 277

Boles, Lady Anne (WW's sister) 1

Bonham-Carter, Lady Violet 31–2

Bond, Kenneth 153

Bonington, Sir Chris 109

Boyle of Handsworth, Lord 44

Boyson, Sir Rhodes 165

Braithwaite, Richard 74

Brearley, Sir Chris 222

Brenner, Sidney 98, 101

Brenton, Howard 43

Brighton hotel bombing 211

Bristol West 48, 155, 158–62, 175,
    246, 270–1, 272

Britten, Benjamin 27

British Leyland 202, 203, 204

Brown, Gordon 206, 271, 272

Buckley, William F. 76

Buffett, Warren 246

Burke, Edmund 76, 103

Butler of Saffron Walden, Lord 45,
    69, 90, 98, 149, 179, 180, 186,
    274

Butler of Brockwell, Lord 107, 108,
    109, 110, 128, 158, 172, 192,
    194, 239, 247, 265

Butler, Rohan 99

Cahn, Sir Andrew 170, 244

Callaghan of Cardiff, Lord 137, 140,
    144, 163, 192, 193, 194, 275,
    280

Cadbury, Jocelyn 164

Cambridge spies 95, 102, 103

Cameron, David 76, 187

Campbell, Alastair 271, 272

Campbell Preston, Dame Frances
    33

Campbell Preston, Patrick 33

Campbell Preston, Robert 5

Carey, Sir Peter 107

Carlingford, Lord 27

Carlisle, Kitty 97

Carrington, Lord 42, 117, 118, 137,
    154–5, 165, 171, 205

Carson, Rachel 36

Carwardias, Mary 24

Casey, PC 4

Casson, Sir Hugh 242

Cavafy, Constantine 248, 261

Ceaușescu, Nicolae 153

Cecil, Lady Rose 164

Champéry 18–19

Changing Gear pamphlet 165

Channon, Lord and Lady 264

Charles, Prince of Wales 40–1

Chevenix Trench, Anthony 53–4

Chewton Mendip 3–4

Chewton Priory 27, 28–9, 30, 159

China 132–5

Chomsky, Noam 75

Christian, Fletcher 230

Christian socialism 28

Christmas 1–3, 30, 283

Churchill, Lord Randolph 16, 67–8

Curchill, Hon Randolph 16, 67, 86

Churchill, Sir Winston 23, 27, 31,
    100–1, 110, 186, 193, 219, 229,
    276

Citizens' Charter 14, 185

City of London 149–50, 279–80

civil service 45, 107–12, 114, 128,
    169–73, 192

Clare, John 58

Clare, Karen 68, 70, 71, 72, 73

Clark, Alan 136, 158, 185, 198–9,
    214, 229, 230, 232, 238, 239,
    240, 241, 265

Clarke, Kenneth 166, 180, 184, 200,
    207, 212, 269fn

class conflict 33, 113

class consciousness 31, 37, 39–40,
    68, 70, 82–3

Clinton, William Jefferson 79fn,
    122, 279

Clostermann, Pierre 26

Cobb, John 27

Cocks of Hartcliffe, Lord 162, 167

Cohen, Nick 231

Collins, Peter 8

Colonsay 6, 7

Communism 23, 75, 77, 114, 145–6,
    249, 251, 252

Concorde 109, 161

Connolly, Cyril 55, 269

Conrad, Joseph 208–9

conspiracy theorists 95–6, 105–6,
    127–8, 240, 243fn

constituency surgeries 160

Cook, Robin 187, 198, 212, 235, 241

Cooke, Alistair 97

Corner, Beryl 12

Costley-White, Anthony 50

Cousins, Frank 52

Crawte, Leslie 71

cricket 8, 15, 49–50

Crosland, Anthony 127, 144

Crossman, Richard 52, 80, 82

cultural schizophrenia 61

Curwen, Sir Christopher 42, 104

Dalyell, Sir Tam 187, 191, 192

Darling, Alistair 270

Darroch, Sir Kim 170

Davies of Stamford, Lord xiii

Day, Sir Stephen 196

de Klerk, F.W. 204, 255, 278

Deng Xiaoping 132, 134

Deutsch, Karl 81–2

Dewar, Lady Elizabeth (Lady Forteviot) (WW's sister) 17, 52, 95

Dirac, Paul 102fn, 107

Disraeli, Benjamin 15, 42, 68, 119–20, 208, 229

Dodds, E.R. *The Greeks and the Irrational* 54

Dorrien-Smith, Alexandra 66–7, 70

Douglas-Home, Sir Alec 43, 52, 121, 141, 261, 269

Douro, Marquess and Marchioness 243

Dresdner Kleinwort Benson 49, 280

du Cann, Sir Edward 138, 139, 141

Duchy of Lancaster 185, 192

Duke, Neville 27

Dutch elm disease 58, 59

Dylan, Bob 65, 68, 70

The Eagle 33, 34

Ecclesiastes, Book of 198

economic liberalism 129–30, 140, 143, 163, 164–5, 184

Eden, Sir Anthony (Lord Avon) 19, 176

education cuts 144, 166–7, 182

EDX committee 268n

Eilean Shona 6

Eisler, Robert, *Man into Wolf* 54

Eisenhower, President 246

Eliot, T.S. 27, 267

Elizabeth II, HM Queen 29, 71, 279

Elliot, Sir Claude Aurelius 52

Emmett, Mrs 1, 5, 11, 40

empiricism 73, 75, 77–8

Englishness 46, 59, 100

Enthoven, Alain 207

environmental policy 36, 37, 184, 192, 201, 202–4

Eton 5, 41, 48, 50–6, 57–8, 61, 63, 121, 143, 177, 282

European Economic Community 91, 112, 115fn, 116, 121, 130, 131, 207–8

European Exchange Rate Mechanism (ERM) 212–13, 216, 271

European Union 106, 188

Europeanism 120, 124, 130–1, 215

Euroscepticism 118, 122, 143, 144, 145

Eyles, Aubrey 5

Fairlie, Henry 69

Falge-Wahl, Valerie 29–30

Falklands conflict 124, 154, 174–6, 181

falls from grace 181, 230–1, 248, 265–6, 273

families, politicians' 272, 273

Fangio, Juan Manuel 27, 65

Farage, Nigel 163fn

farming 35–6, 37, 192, 272–3

Faulds, Andrew 187, 188

Faulkner of Downpatrick, Lord 118

Fergusson, Sir Bernard (Lord
    Ballantrae) 87
Feynman, Richard 80
Field, Frank 187
Finney, Sir Tom 27
Fleming, Sir Alexander 27
Foot, Michael 176, 187
Foot, Paul 70
Ford, E.B. 98
Ford, Charlie and Judy 5, 69
Ford, Melvin 5
Forster, E. M. 103
Fox, James 51
Foxell, Nigel 51–2
Franks, Lord 42, 241
Fraser, Lady Antonia 262, 263
Fraser, Sir Simon 170
free market politics 113, 129–30, 131
Freyberg, General Lord 21
Friedrich, Carl 81

Gaitskell, Hugh 127
Galbraith, J. K. 82
Garel-Jones, Lord 164, 213, 214
Garland, Nicholas 194, 245
GEC (General Electric Company)
    49, 150–6, 173, 184
general elections 86–7, 91, 117–18,
    131, 136–8, 140, 226, 227,
    269–71
German reunification 204, 252–3,
    257
Ghosh, Dame Helen 170
Gilmour of Craigmillar, Lord 130,
    136, 163, 165

Glicksman, Brian 169
global recession (2008) 184, 206,
    271–2, 276
Goldsmith, Sir James 100
Gombrich, E. H. 65
Gorbachev, Mikhail 250, 252, 254,
    255, 256, 257
Gordievsky, Oleg 96, 257–8
Gore-Booth, David 233, 248, 259
Goodman, Lord 253
Gorgas, Angela 146
Gow, Sir Ian 136
Gramm, Phil 281
grammar schools 69
Gray, Simon 93, 262, 263
Greece 22–6, 56–7
Greenhill, Sir James 170
Grenfell, Arthur Morton (WW's
    grandfather) 15
Grenfell, Harry (WW's uncle) 20
Grenfell, Julian 15
Grey, Sir Edward (Viscount Grey)
    15
Griffiths, Miss 159
Grimond, Lord118, 130
Gulf War 212, 264
Gummer, John (Lord Deben) 213,
    214
Gunn, Sir James 41

Haig, Alexander 176
Hailsham, Lord 118–19, 135, 165,
    243fn
Hare, R. M. 74
Harford, John 50

Harris, Sir Arthur 'Bomber' 72
Harris, Ralph 113
Harvard 68, 79–82
Hatton, Derek 222
Havel, Václav 235, 249, 250
Hawthorn, Mike 27
Hawthornden Prize 49
Heal, Seward 1, 25
Healey, Lord 128
Heath, Sir Edward 44, 52, 68, 70,
        86, 90, 91, 100, 101, 112,
        113–14, 115, 116–17, 118, 119,
        120–5, 127, 128, 129, 130, 132,
        133, 134, 136, 137–8, 139, 140,
        141–3, 144, 153, 158, 191, 201,
        264
Heffer, Eric 191
Hegel, G.W.F. 73, 75, 81
Heiser, Sir Terry 205, 221
Hemans, Sir Simon 249–50
Henderson, Sir Nicholas 24, 163
Hennessy, Lord 107, 201, 202
Herbert, Sir A.P. 8
Heseltine, Lord 151, 198, 213, 214,
        215, 216, 223, 225, 226, 269fn,
        270
Hill, Christopher 104
Hillary, Sir Edmund 27
Hitchens, Christopher 70
Hodgkin, Sir Alan 98, 101
Hoffmann, Lord 101, 222, 223,
        244–5
holidays 5–7, 18–19, 56–7, 97
honours system 141–2
Horace 22, 46, 48, 57

Hornblower, Simon 99
hostage-taking 236, 256–7, 264
House of Commons 186–8
Howard, Hon Euan (Lord
        Strathcona) 6, 7, 25
Howard de Walden, Margot 6
Howard, Lady Jinny (WW's sister)
        31
Howarth, Martin 3
Howe of Aberavon, Lord 164, 176,
        187, 204, 212, 213, 232, 234
Howell, Lord 91
Huddleston, Trevor 38
Hughes, Dr 4
hunting 36–7
Hurd, (Anthony) Lord 35
Hurd of Westwell, (Douglas) Lord
        60–1, 114, 115, 120, 132, 133,
        180, 198, 208, 213, 216, 252,
        253
Hussein, Saddam 212, 231, 264
Hussey, Lord 20, 60
Hussey, Lady Susan (WW's sister)
        14, 108, 122, 254
Hutton, Sir Len 27, 263
Huxley, Elspeth 32

imperialism 32, 46
India 88–9
inflation 128–9
Institute for Economic Affairs 113,
        129, 145
intelligence services 42, 99, 102,
        104–5, 111, 112, 127, 128, 238,
        257

IRA 84–5, 128, 138fn, 208, 211, 274
Iran/Iraq War 232–4
Islamism 128, 258

Jackson, Glenda 187
Jackson, Revd Jesse 264
Jackson, Robert 71
James II, King 40
James, M. R. 60
James, William 63
Jay, Peter 144
Jellicoe, Lord 21–2, 23–4, 42, 92,
      107
Jenkin, Lord 203, 221
Jenkins of Hillhead, Lord 121, 130,
      193
Jenkins, Sir Simon 62, 91, 241
Johnson, Boris 137, 187, 230
Jones, Jack 127
Jones, Tom 28
Joseph, Lord 129, 130, 135, 138, 141,
      158–9, 165, 166, 167, 174, 180,
      191, 211, 275

Kant, Immanuel 73, 75
Kaufman, Sir Gerald 197
Keen, Joe and Mary 5
Kemp, Sir Peter 172
Kennedy, John F. 71, 83
Kennedy, Robert F. 71
Keynes, Lord 27, 43, 103, 219
KGB 96, 103, 127, 249, 251, 257
Kidd, Colin 145
King, Cecil 127
King, Lord (Tom) 214

Kinnock, Lord 187, 226
Kipling, Rudyard 9, 32, 58
Kirk, Russell 76
Kissinger, Henry 136, 195
Kitson, Sir Tim 132, 141, 142
Kitzinger, Ernst and Susan 81
Kohl, Helmut 201, 252, 253
Kollek, Teddy 96, 259
Kothavala, Rustam 80
Kundera, Milan 146

Lambton, Lord 52–3
Lang of Monkton, Lord 198
Laslett, Peter 31
Lassen, Andy 24
Latter, Rev Kenneth 2, 41, 62
Lauterpacht, Sir Elihu 98, 101
Lawson of Blaby, Lord 156, 212,
      213, 223, 225–6, 227
Lawson, Vanessa 156–7
Lebanon 256
Lee Kuan Yew 87
Lee, Laurie 243fn
Le Grand, Julian 207
Leigh Fermor, Sir Patrick 22, 23,
      24
Leith, Prue 163
Lenin, Vladimir 78, 104, 197fn
Leopard, The 46
Leveson Inquiry 273
Levin, Bernard 241
Lewis, Cecil 181
Lewis, David 153
Lewis, Wilmarth Sheldon 82–3, 94
liberal pluralism 55

Livingstone, Ken 187, 224
lobbying 182–3
Logie Baird, John 27
Lovelock, James 102
Lubetkin, Berthold 160–1
Lyell of Markyate, Lord 198, 199,
    239, 245
Lyttelton, Hilda (WW's
    grandmother) 15

McCarthy, John 257
McCarthy, Patrick 257
McCartney, Paul 65
McColl, Sir Colin 104
McGahey, Mick 127
Mackay of Clashfern, Lord 215, 241,
    265
Mackie, David 244
Macleod, Iain 121
Macmillan, Harold (Lord Stockton)
    42, 43–5, 50, 52, 71, 72, 86, 90,
    112, 113, 179, 232fn
McNamara, Robert 91
Mailer, Norman 80
Major, Sir John 164, 172, 185, 198,
    214, 215, 216, 247, 271, 272
Makins, Roger (Lord Sherfield) 42,
    99
male primogeniture 41
Mandela, Nelson 38, 53, 204, 255,
    278–9
Mandela Rhodes Foundation 53,
    278, 279
Mandelson, Peter 241, 271
Manningham-Buller, Lady 104

Mansfield, Harvey, Jr 81
Mao Zedong 134
Markov, Georgi 251
Marlowe, Christopher, Tamburlaine
    the Great 56
Marsden, John 51, 53, 63
Marshall, Artie 98
Marshall, Sir Walter 168
Martineau, Richard 57, 58, 61
Marx, Karl 73, 75, 81, 134
Masterman, Margaret 74
Matthews, Sir Stanley 27
Matrix Churchill 231–2, 237–8,
    239–41
Mayer, Tony 222, 223
Mayne, John 108
Medawar, Sir Peter 54, 62
media lynch mobs 193
meritocracy 69–70, 120
Middle, Reg 1
Miles, John 161
military-industrial complex 246–7
Millar, Sir Ronnie 280
miners' strikes 115, 181
Mitokhin, Vasili 96
Mitsotakis, Konstantinos 23
Mitterrand, François 252–3
monetarism 163
Moon, Sir Edward Penderel 99
Moore, Charles 179, 200
Moore, Henry 27
Monk, Thelonious 94, 101
Monckton, Biddy Lady 159
moral dilemmas 75, 85, 194
Morrell, Frances 151

Morrison, Peter 213
Moss, Sir Stirling 38, 65, 76fn
Mottram, Sir Richard 172, 192
Mountbatten, Lord 127
Mubarak, Hosni 260
Muggeridge, Malcolm 65–6
Murdoch, Rupert 124, 196, 243fn
Murray, Sir Gilbert 61
music 17, 18
Mynors, Sir Roger 42
myths, wartime 26–7

National Economic Development
     Council 113
Ne Win 87
Neal, Ernest 36
Needham, Richard (Earl of
     Kilmorey) 159, 164
Neill of Bladen, Lord 241
Nemeth, Miklos 249
Netanyahu, Bibi 259
New Elizabethans 27, 29, 32–4, 79
New Labour 122
Newton, Ivor 6
NHS (National Health Service) 32,
     184–5, 206–7, 272
Nichol, Sir Duncan 207
Nicholson, Max 36, 42
Night of the Long Knives 43, 72
Nixon, Richard 134, 135
noblesse oblige 16, 43
Northern Ireland 111–12, 116,
     117–18, 122, 128
Norton, Martin 101
nuclear waste 168

Oborne, Peter 193
O'Brian, Patrick 59–61
O'Brien, Conor Cruise 259
O'Hagan, Lord 66, 164
oil embargo 115, 126
oratory 55–6, 187, 188–9, 190–1
Oronsay 6–7
Orwell, George 103, 156, 178
Oxford 48, 67–8, 69, 70–7, 80, 104,
     177

Pahlavi, Mohammed Reza, Shah of
     Iran 126
Palestine Liberation Organisation
     (PLO) 195
Pao, Y. K. 153
papal knighthood 262
Parker Bowles, Camilla (Duchess of
     Cornwall) 243
Parris, Matthew 164, 187, 241
Patten of Barnes, Lord 129, 130,
     132, 136, 162, 164, 165, 180,
     211, 213, 214, 215, 216, 226
Patten, Lord 164, 165
Perutz, Max 34
Petri, David 140–1
Petty, Alan (aka Judd, Alan) 59
pheasant shooting 37, 210
Philby, Kim 99, 104
philosophy 72–3, 74–7
Pincher, Harry Chapman 101–2
Pinewood 17, 19, 38, 47–8, 49–50
Pinter, Harold 235, 262–3
planning laws 182–4
Plato 73, 75, 80

Plowden, Hon William 107–8
poetry 17–18, 47, 55
police 70, 84, 86, 112, 114, 170
political philosophy 80, 81, 263
politico-media nexus 247
poll tax 141, 213, 218–28
Popham curse 62–3
Popper, Sir Karl 73, 103, 262
post-war consensus 112–13, 125
postmodernist relativism 58
postwar Britain 32–6
Poujade, Pierre 163fn
Powell, Anthony 31
Powell, J. Enoch 63, 73, 116, 117, 129–30, 135, 144, 176, 187, 188, 210, 273
Powell, Lord (Charles) 208, 212, 235
Powell, Jonathan 172
prices and incomes policies 112, 113, 115, 119, 194
Pridgeon, Walter 87–8
Prior, Lord 136, 154, 163, 201
Private Eye 100, 110, 206
Pullman, Philip 177–8, 267
Purnell, Mr 5
Pym, Lord 163
Pynchon, Thomas 48

Rabin, Yitzhak 196, 210
racism 37–8, 39, 129, 204
Radzinowicz, Sir Leon 98, 101
Rand, Ayn 76
rates, business 220
rates, domestic 139–40, 190, 218–20
    see also poll tax

Rawls, John 77, 80
Reagan, Ronald 124, 206, 281
Rees-Mogg, Jacob 187
Rees-Mogg, Lord (William) 120
Reilly, Sir Patrick 99
Renwick, Lord 255
Rhodes Trust 53, 278, 279
Rhodesia 77, 121
Richardson, Lord 98
Ridley, Sir Adam 108, 129
Ridley, Nicholas 130, 203, 226
Roberts, John 54–5, 61, 193
Robertson, Geoffrey 238, 240
Robinson, Richard, *An Atheist's Values* 54
Rockefeller, Nancy 83
Roll, Sir Eric 92
Rose, Kenneth 26, 93, 95, 103
Rosebery, Lord 93, 96
Ross, Sir Dick 108
Ross, Val 3, 4, 41
Rothschild, Cecile de 97
Rothschild, Victor, 3rd Baron 60, 85, 92–7, 98, 99–102, 103, 106, 108–9, 110, 111–12, 115, 126–7, 132, 135, 149, 170, 180, 197, 201, 221, 222, 223, 275
Rothschild Gray, Victoria 92, 93, 95, 97, 99–100, 131, 133, 135, 137, 146–7, 152, 251, 262
Routledge, Norman 94
Rowse, A. L. 98
Rushdie, Salman 210, 234–6
Russell, Lord 27, 63
Rutherford, Lord 27

Rutter, Jill 222
Rylands, Dadie 98
Ryle, Gilbert 55, 72, 74

Sainsbury of Preston Candover,
    Lord 182, 216
St John of Fawsley, Lord 165, 205
Salisbury, Lord 68–9
Salter, Lord 99
Salvidge, Edgar 5
Sargent, Sir Malcolm 8
SAS 85
scapegoating 274, 277
Scargill, Arthur 127
scientism 21, 101
Scott Inquiry 17, 61, 192, 198–9, 216,
    232, 237, 239, 240–6, 265
Second World War 9, 20–1, 23–7,
    38–9, 51
secret world 103–6, 111, 112, 127–8
Seldon, Arthur 113
Sellafield 168
Selwyn-Lloyd, Lord 71–2, 113

Sen, Amartya 77
Shakespeare, *Troilus and Cressida*
    111
Shamir, Yitzhak 96, 196–7, 258–9
Shawcross, Lord 101
Shore of Stepney, Lord 190
the sixties 61, 65–6, 67–8, 84
Skubiszweski, Krzysztof 251–2
Slade, Sir Humphrey 89
Slater, Jim 109
Slim, Field Marshal Lord 21

Smith, F.E. (Lord Birkenhead) 16,
    42, 149–50, 198
Smith, Ian 77, 121
Snow, Sir C.P. 8, 34, 35, 65
Soames, Lord 163, 165
Soames, Emma 123–4
Soames, Sir Nicholas 100, 123–4
social conservatism 16, 33, 130
social contract 2–3, 31, 39, 80, 81,
    143
social hierarchy 4–5, 39
'sofa government' 172–3
Somerville, Admiral Sir James 21
Sorsa, Taisto Kalevi 205–6
South Africa 38, 53, 204, 255, 278
Soviet Union/Russia 96, 103, 121,
    127–8, 145–6, 191, 239, 249,
    251, 252, 253, 255–6, 257–8
Sparrow, John 99
Special Branch protection 209–10
Speed, Bessie 1, 39
Stalin, Joseph 23, 33, 104
Stein, Sir Cyril 182, 183
Stephens, John 281
Stephens, Philip 193
Stern, Avraham 197
Sterne, Laurence 11
Stewart, Rory 187
Stewart, Zeph 80
Stonefrost, Sir Maurice 224
Straus, Don and Beth 83
Straw, Jack 180, 184
Strawson, Sir Peter 73
student radicalism 83–4
Suez 19, 122, 176

Sunningdale Agreement 116, 117–18
Sutherland, Graham 27
Sweeney, Rifleman 98, 170
Swinnerton-Dyer, Sir Peter 166

Tatum, Art 94, 101
Taylor, Claude 58
Tebbit, Lord 200, 202, 203–4, 211,
    213, 214, 225
Teilhard de Chardin, Pierre 54, 62
Teltschik, Horst 201
Thatcher, Sir Denis 182, 205–6
Thatcher, Lady 36, 48–9, 90, 123,
    124, 125, 130, 135, 139, 140,
    142, 143, 144, 158, 165, 166,
    174–5, 176, 179, 181, 184, 187,
    190, 191, 195, 200–2, 203–5,
    206–8, 212–16, 217, 221, 226,
    252–3, 255, 257, 275–6,
    280–1
Thatcherism xix, 162–3, 184, 194,
    206, 213
Think Tank (CPRS) 92, 107–12, 114,
    170
Thomas, Eva 5
Thomas, Mark 245
Thompson, Tommy 2, 5
Thorpe, D. R. 43
Thorpe, Jeremy 117, 118, 187
three-day week 116, 117
Thucydides 13, 57
Tolkein, J.R.R. 61
Tolstoy, Leo 147, 178
Topham, Mirabel 3
totalitarianism 66, 80, 114, 169

trades unions 112, 114, 116, 117, 127,
    132, 146, 162–3, 170, 184, 201
Tree, Sir Ronald 97
Trend, Sir Burke 96, 101, 108, 111,
    112, 170
Trilling, Lionel 82, 179
truth-telling 192–4
Turner, Graham 238
Tuve, Rosemond 13
Twiss, Peter 27
Tyson, Alan 138

UKIP 106
Urmson, Jim 74, 78, 80
Utley, Peter 145

Vallon, Harry 47, 49
Van Oss, Tom 28
Vietnam War 65, 77, 83, 91
Vincent, John 161–2

Wade-Gery, Sir Robert 107, 111, 112
Waite, Terry 256
Waldegrave of North Hill, Lady,
    (Caroline, WW's wife) ix, xiii,
    23, 24, 44, 147–9, 159, 178, 181,
    190, 211, 250, 259, 272, 273,
    279, 281
Waldegrave, Geoffrey, 12th Earl
    (WW's father) 2, 10, 11–12,
    17, 27–8, 30, 31, 35, 36, 37, 38,
    39–41, 42–3, 50, 72, 73, 83, 92,
    93, 189, 222–3
Waldegrave, James, 2nd Earl
Waldegrave, James, 13th Earl

(WW's brother) 3, 4, 6, 11, 17, 34, 37, 41, 50, 51, 66, 97

Waldegrave, Mary Countess (WW's mother) 4, 9, 10–12, 15–16, 18–19, 27–8, 30, 31–2, 37, 38, 39–40, 48, 49, 62, 83fn, 143, 148, 159, 242, 258

Waldegrave, William (Lord Waldegrave of North Hill)
All Souls fellow 49, 98, 148, 167
The Binding of Leviathan 145, 146
Bristol West MP 48, 155, 158–62, 175, 246, 270–1, 272
childhood 1–22, 25, 29, 30–3, 36–42, 46–7
classicist 13–14, 48, 56–7
despondent Waldegrave gene 10, 12, 147
Duchy of Lancaster chancellor 185, 192
education 4
    see also Eton; Harvard; Oxford; Pinewood
family history 15–16, 27–8, 222–3
at GEC 150–6
Heath's political secretary 114–15, 116–19, 120–2, 132–6, 141–3
and IRA bomb plot 208–9, 210
'Jonah effect' 48–9, 57
loyalist 143, 201
marriage and children 14, 147–9, 178–9, 181
ministerial career 85, 164–72,

174–5, 180, 181–5, 188–9, 189–90, 190–201, 202–46, 248–62, 263–5, 268–9
Oxford Union presidency 70–1
philonikia 56
political ambition 15, 43, 45, 56, 67, 68, 177, 179–81
political schizophrenia 16, 63–4, 113
post-political life 277–83
reading 9–10, 12, 13, 54–5, 61–2
reasons for entering politics 76, 78, 257
self-doubt 146, 177, 179, 180–1
Think Tank (CPRS) member 92, 107–12, 114, 170
'wetness' 163–5, 200, 207, 221

Walensa, Lech 249
Walker of Worcester, Lord 72, 115, 135, 150
Walpole, Horace (Lord Orford) 229, 230
Walpole, Sir Robert (Lord Orford) 52, 202fn
Weathermen 83, 84
Weinstock, Lord 101, 150–6, 175fn, 201, 202
Wells, John 148
Westland affair 187, 226
'the wets' 163–5, 200, 207, 221
White, Sir Dick 44, 96, 98, 104, 127
White, Lady (Eirene) 28
Whitelaw, Lord 135, 136, 137, 144, 165, 183fn, 205, 210, 213, 225, 275

Whitfield, Win 5
Whittle, Sir Frank 27
Wilenski, R. H. *Modern French Painters* 52
Wilkinson, D. C. 61
Williams, Charles 61
Williams, Lady (Shirley)120, 144
Williams of Barnburgh, Lord(Tom) 36
Williamson of Horton, Lord (David) 203
Wilson of Rievaulx, Lord 35, 65, 69–70, 87, 91, 112, 116, 117, 118, 119, 125, 127, 128, 136, 142, 156
Wilson, Lady 190
Wilson, Tom 222
Winter of Discontent 162–3
Wolff, Michael fn115, 132

Wootton, Lady 98
Wraxall, Ursula Lady 159
Wright, Ernie (WW's brother-in-law) 39
Wright of Richmond, Lord 262
Wright, Peter 102–3
Wright, Lady Sarah (WW's sister) 14, 39

Yeltsin, Boris 239
Yom Kippur War 115, 136
Young, Sir George 205, 213, 226
Young, Sir Rob 195, 233, 238, 23
Young, Sir Robin 9
Younger, Caroline 72, 177
Younger, Lord 225

Zaehner, R.C. 98–9
Zhou Enlai 132